9162

# THE BUCHWALD
# STOPS HERE

# THE
# BUCHWALD
# STOPS HERE

## ART BUCHWALD

G.P. PUTNAM'S SONS

NEW YORK

SBN: 399-12168-4

**Library of Congress Cataloging Publication Data**

Buchwald, Art.
  The Buchwald stops here.

  I. Title.
PS3503.U1828B8     818′.5′407     78-18919

**PRINTED IN THE UNITED STATES OF AMERICA**

CONTENTS:

# Introduction

Everyone these days seems to ask me the same question, "How well do you know Jimmy Carter?" I'd be stretching the truth if I said I knew him real well. It's true our family lived a few miles down the road from Jimmy in Plains, Georgia, and we both went to the same grammar and high schools. But he sat a couple of rows away from me and I never saw much of him except after school when we used to go fishing together.

One day I said to Jimmy, "What do you want to do when you grow up?" and he said, "I want to go to Annapolis and become a naval officer." I said, "What a coincidence, so do I!" So we both applied. I got the appointment, but I told them I wouldn't accept it unless they took Jimmy as well. Since they wanted me for the football team they relented and allowed as Jimmy could go too.

Jimmy and I were roommates at the naval academy and one day I introduced him to a lovely girl named Rosalynn Smith. They fell in love and were later to marry, which pleased me no end.

After leaving the academy Jimmy and I went our separate ways until we both found ourselves in the nuclear submarine program. Jimmy was given command of a sub, and I was his executive officer. One stormy night he was on the bridge and a big wave came along and washed him overboard. I jumped over the side, without a life jacket, and grabbed him. "Hold on, Jimmy," I told him. "Have faith and we will be saved." I held his chin with one hand and swam back to the sub with the other.

After we were back in the wardroom Jimmy said to me, "I don't know how to thank you. You saved my life."

I remember replying, "Forget it. You would have done the same for me. Besides, us Georgia boys have to stick together."

Jimmy decided to leave the Navy about the same time I did. He wanted to go back to his peanut farm and build it up from scratch. I had a little money I had saved in the Navy and I lent it to him interest-free. "Someday you can pay me back," I told him.

Then after making a success of the peanut business he had the urge to go into politics. One day after Sunday school he told me he wanted to run for governor of Georgia. Jimmy was bitter about Georgia's backward stand on race, and he had no use for the political machine that had been running things down there for centuries.

I got together a group of far sighted Southern businessmen and labor leaders and persuaded them that Carter could turn Georgia and the South around. We worked hard but we got Jimmy into the governor's mansion—something none of us ever regretted.

I lost touch for a few years, but one day I ran into Jimmy in a supermarket in New Hampshire. "Whatcha doing up here?" I asked him.

"Running for President of the United States. Nobody believes I can do it," Jimmy said. "I'm thinking of giving up."

"I believe you can do it," I told him. I talked to several friends of mine, and we raised enough money to back Jimmy in the primaries in Florida and Ohio. I always stayed in the background but every night, no matter how late, Jimmy called and asked me what he should say the next day.

I helped him with the debates and I talked to him about campaign strategy, but I can't say I won the election for him. Jimmy did that himself, and I'd be the first one to admit it.

It came as no surprise to me that we elected Jimmy Earl Carter as our President. I saw it years ago when as kids we were whitewashing a fence and he had that strange look in his eye as if to say, "I'm not going to be doing this for the rest of my life."

So when people ask me if I know Jimmy Carter I have to say, "I've met him once or twice. He seems like a nice person." If Jimmy wants to admit we know each other better than that, I think it's up to him to say so, not me.

# I. Walking With Carter

## WALKING WITH CARTER

Everyone in Washington is still talking about President and Mrs. Carter's walk from the Capitol to the White House, and Carter watchers are still asking, "Why did he do it?" The obvious answer is, "Because it was there."

The President made the walk in 35 minutes and 10 seconds—a new world record for a head of state. He would have probably even broken that if Amy hadn't had to stop and tie her bootlaces along the way.

This, incidentally, was not the first attempt by someone to walk from the Capitol to the White House. In 1957, Mr. and Mrs. Henry Gerard of Tampa, Florida, started out from the door of the Senate building and were making excellent time until they were mugged at 7th St. and Pennsylvania Avenue.

In 1961, Ezra Beatleman of Racine, Wisconsin, decided to see if he could make it. Following almost exactly the route the Carters took along Pennsylvania Avenue in the middle of the street, Beatleman was almost halfway there when he was hit by a Washington express bus and thrown through a window of the Post Office Building. He spent three months at George Washington Hospital and upon his release was given 30 days in jail for jaywalking.

This discouraged people for a little while from walking along Pennsylvania Avenue until 1967 when four Vietnam protesters decided to try it. They were making good time until they passed the FBI Building. J. Edgar Hoover happened to be looking out his window. He flew into a rage and 200 FBI men surrounded the protesters and charged them with walking by the FBI Building without a permit.

In 1970, Gerald Timmons of Chevy Chase, Maryland, had a few drinks and when he couldn't find a taxi he decided to walk the famous route taken by the Carters. Unfortunately, he chose to do it during rush hour and it took an hour to get across 14th St. and Pennsylvania. This discouraged him and, though he was within a few blocks of his goal, he said the hell with it and stopped into Bassin's Bar where he spent the rest of the evening.

Five Cubans hired by the Committee to Re-elect the President were the next people to try the walk. They made it to the White House without incident where they received orders to continue walking on to the Watergate Headquarters of the Democratic Party where they were captured.

Had they not stopped at the White House to rest, their walk would never have been traced to President Nixon's staff and Nixon might have been the man last Thursday to turn over the keys of 1600 Pennsylvania Avenue to the Carters.

The most interesting attempt to walk from the Capitol was made by Congressman Wilbur Mills and his party who decided to do it in October 1974. Mills got off to a good start, but he took a wrong turn at 8th St. and wound up at the Tidal Basin instead. Since it was two o'clock in the morning and a dark night, he mistakenly thought he was at the White House.

He suggested to one of his party that she take a swim in the White House swimming pool. Much to his chagrin he discovered they weren't at the White House, and everyone knows what this simple mistake cost the Arkansas congressman.

When President Carter decided to take the walk, his aides and the Secret Service tried to talk him out of it. But he was adamant and told them, "I have to show the country I can walk and chew gum at the same time."

## A SAD POST-WATERGATE STORY

In the film classic, "On the Waterfront," there is a very poignant scene in the back of a taxi between Marlon Brando and Rod Steiger, who plays his brother. Brando, a longshoreman, was a boxer, and he blames Steiger, who is mixed up with the mob, for ruining his chances to be a contender by making him throw a fight.

I was reminded of this scene the other day when I was sharing a taxi with two gentlemen I didn't know. They were in the back seat and I was in the front, and they didn't think I was listening to what they were saying. I was.

Apparently, one of the men had worked for Nixon in the White House, though now he looked quite scruffy. His leather jacket was torn, he wore no tie and there were holes in his shoes.

The other man, who I found out later was his brother, was well dressed and wore a camel's-hair coat and an expensive hat. His name was Charley.

"What's bugging you, kid?" Charley said.

"You know damn well what's bugging me. You kept me out of the Watergate scandal and now I don't have a nickel to my name."

"I did it for your own good, Terry," Charley said. "I didn't want you to lose your moral compass."

"I could have had a million dollars by now. I knew there was something fishy going on in the White House with Nixon and his crowd, but when I told you about it you said 'Stay away from it, kid. They're up to their necks in trouble and they're going to pay for it.'

"I remember that's what you said and like a dummy I listened to you. I turned my back on Watergate and look at me now."

"But kid," said Charley, "I was just trying to keep you from going to jail."

"I could have done a year at Allenwood standing on my head if I knew what was waiting for me when I got out. If you'd have just let me be part of the coverup, Charley, I'd be a big man today. I could have erased the tapes or deep-sixed the stuff from Hunt's safe or been the bag man for the guys who were blackmailing the White House. Paperback houses would be fighting over me now, I'd be on talk shows and the lecture circuit. I might even have my own radio show. There was a goldmine in Watergate and you wouldn't let me get involved."

"Okay, so I made a mistake," Charley said. "But I only had your best interests at heart. I was trying to keep you from the agony of going in front of a grand jury and then through a trial. I didn't realize how much money the people involved in Watergate would make or how famous they would become. But at the time I thought the best thing for you to do was walk away from it."

"You were my brother, Charley. You should have known how big the payoff would be for a Watergate conspirator. If it hadn't been for you I would now be at prayer breakfasts and in the Bob Hope Golf Classic. I'd be a celebrity and I'd get the best table in a restaurant. They'd have done my novel as a mini-series on television. I would be SOMEBODY."

Charley put his arm on his brother's shoulder. "Maybe it's not too late. Why don't you go to the Special Prosecutor's Office and tell them you want to come clean on Watergate? Tell them the break-in was all your idea and that you and Nixon worked out the coverup before Haldeman and Ehrlichman even got in the picture."

"It's too late. The Watergate Special Prosecutor's Office has been shut down," Terry said. "They aren't interested in anybody else confessing. Besides, everyone in town knows I had nothing to do with Watergate. That's why no one will give me a job."

"I'm your older brother," Charley said. "Are you going to hold it against me for the rest of your life because I made you keep your nose clean?"

"You ruined my life. I'll always be a nobody, the guy who blew the 'Book of the Month Club' because his stupid brother wouldn't let him get involved in the greatest political scandal of all time."

## "I'M WALKING BEHIND YOU"

The Los Angeles Chapter of the National Organization for Women (NOW) has criticized Rosalynn Carter for following the Saudi Arabian custom of walking several feet behind her husband during his trip to the Middle Eastern nation.

The LA persons complained that Mrs. Carter should not have gone if she could not walk beside the President, instead of bringing up the rear.

While NOW may have a point, there is another school of thought that says the custom of walking behind one's husband is not demeaning and has many advantages. This school, which meets at McNulty's Bar and Grill around the corner from my office, was in session late in the afternoon the day the LA protest story appeared in the newspapers.

I believe it was Nolan who brought it up. "I don't think we should be too critical of Arab customs, even though they're socking it to us on the oil."

Novak agreed. "There are many advantages to a wife walking behind her husband and the American woman should examine them before she criticizes Mrs. Carter."

"What are they?" McNulty wanted to know.

"Well, for one thing," Novak said, "if the wife walks behind the husband she can tell if anyone is following him."

"I'll drink to that," Doyle said.

"For another, she can warn her husband if a camel is going to knock him down," Novak continued.

"But camels don't knock down husbands in America," Siegel protested.

"They don't now," Novak replied. "But they might at some future time."

"I'll drink to that," Doyle said again.

"Suppose it's a slushy day and cars are splashing people on the sidewalk. A wife, if she's walking behind her husband, could caution him in time and he could jump out of the way," Stevens said.

"She could also keep her eyes open when her husband walks under a scaffolding, and throw her body in the way in case someone accidentally dropped a brick," Novak added.

"That's true," Evans agreed. "If she was walking next to him they both might be killed. Walking behind your husband is no different than flying in different airplanes to protect the children."

Doyle raised his glass. "I'll even drink to that."

"If the husband is up in front, and the wife is behind, she can keep an eye on him in case he starts ogling pretty girls walking the other way," Hackett said.

Someone said, "And let's not forget muggers. It's much safer for a couple to walk in tandem. Then one or the other can scream for help."

"I don't see why the NOW people are so uptight about Rosalynn walking behind her husband," Novak said. "It gave a lot of dignity to the President's trip to Saudi Arabia, and provided the press with its most newsworthy story."

Someone at the end of the bar chimed in. "You're right. The trip could have been a bust if the Carters walked together, especially since they had done it already at their Inauguration. What's wrong with the First Lady following in her husband's footsteps?"

I guess it was Nolan who summed it up when he said, "American women could learn a lot from the customs of Saudi Arabia. Everyone knows the only reason it's the richest country in the world is because their women walk behind their men."

Doyle was delighted with this last thought and without even making an announcement drank to it.

## WANTED—POLISH TRANSLATOR

Although President Carter has pledged himself to cutting down on government, he made an exception and authorized the State Department to hire a full-time Polish translator.

It isn't that the President wasn't pleased with the translator the Department provided him with in Warsaw (he even told Mr. Vance he would pray for him), it was just that Mr. Carter feels the United States is not getting its message over in Poland with the part-time help it has on its present payroll.

For those of you who were skiing or scuba diving during the holidays, this is what happened. President Carter arrived in Poland on his first stop abroad and gave a very stirring speech about American-Polish friendship. The American translator had trouble with the President's Georgia accent and told the Polish people that Mr. Carter was abandoning Washington and was lusting after Poland, or something to that effect.

In any case the Polish people, who are sick to death of American-Polish jokes, had their first laugh at our expense in years.

Fortunately no serious damage was done. It could have been much worse for both countries if the translator had remained on duty during the conference.

President: It is a great honor for me to be here in Poland to reaffirm and to strengthen the historic and strong ties of friendship and mutual respect which exist between our two countries.

Translator: I am very happy to be here in a country where someone has stolen the pen of my aunt.

Secretary Gierek: Tell him that Polish people do not steal the pens of people's aunts. Ask him if he looked on the dresser next to the door.

Translator: The Secretary says he does not know where the pen of your aunt is, but says he will be very happy to put another quilt on your bed.

President Carter: I do not need another quilt. I wish to have fruitful discussions with the First Secretary concerning bilateral questions which involve the SALT talks.

Translator: The President says his soup spoon is dirty and he would like to have another one. He also wishes to thank you for the salt you put on his fruit.

Secretary Gierek: Tell the President the Polish people do not put salt on their fruit, and also that the reduction of armed forces in the Warsaw Pact is based on the reduction of forces in NATO.

Translator: The Secretary wishes to inform you the train will be leaving late. He also does not change travelers' checks, but will take your personal check providing you do not overtip the boatman.

President: Please inform the First Secretary I never overtip, and that my main concern on this trip is to press for human rights, which is still the cornerstone of my foreign policy.

Translator: President Carter says that he is only human and asks if you know of an honest merchant who will sell him a foreign policy he can put in a stone on a corner.

Secretary Gierek: It is essential that our countries work together to stop the Arms Race. Inform the President that Poland is willing to do its part to reduce tensions in the world.

Translator: The Secretary says he would like to take off your arms and relieve your tension concerning the loss of the pen of your aunt. He wants to know if you looked under the kitchen table.

President: And in conclusion I wish to say on behalf of Rosalynn and myself I wish to thank you and Mrs. Gierek for your wonderful hospitality shown us, and I desire to visit you and your wife very soon.

Translator: The President says he lusts after your wife and has carnal desires to visit Poland again as soon as he gets the hall porter to bring up his luggage.

## A CONTRACT ON HAM

I've tried to avoid it, but I don't seem to have much choice. I'm going to do a think-piece on Hamilton Jordan. Last week the White House ordered its mimeograph machines put on a war footing and issued a 33-page White Paper concerning a subject of urgent national interest: "Whether Ham Jordan, while eating a steak at a singles' bar called Sarsfield's, did or did not spit a part of his Amaretto topped with whipped cream at a lady sitting next to him at the bar."

The unidentified woman said he did. The White House, after interviewing the bartenders and witnesses, concluded he didn't.

I am inclined to believe Ham Jordan and will continue to until the *Washington Post* gossip columnist who printed the item produces the smoking pistol, which in this case would be the lady's Amaretto-stained blouse.

But the question isn't whether Ham did or did not spit his drink as much as what is behind it? The fact of the matter is that there is now a "press contract" out on Hamilton Jordan, and he is a marked man in Washington.

Somewhere out there at this moment is a woman, lady or girl who is prepared to show Ham Jordan he isn't any better than she is, and "he may be the second most important person in the Administration, but by gosh he's just another guy trying to pick her up in a bar etc. etc. etc."

Ham may be sowing his wild oats in Washington, but he isn't any different from most guys of his age who sow oats—with one exception. He now has a REPUTATION and someone is out to cut him down to size. He's now in a class with Muhammad Ali, Joe Namath, Marlon Brando and many other personalities who can no longer go into a bar for a steak without some girl challenging him to spit an Amaretto on her blouse.

If there is anyone to blame for Ham's position it's President Carter. By refusing to let his people drink liquor and whipped cream in the White House the President is driving them out into the streets, where they are forced to take abuse and whatever else they dish out at a singles' hangout on Friday night.

Do you think Ham *wants* to go to Sarsfield's to relax and unwind? Do you think it's fun for him to fight through the women to get to a bar stool for a shot? Do you believe, for one second, that if Ham could get a decent drink in the White House from a friendly bartender he would put up with all the gaff that goes with trying to get a bite in a joint reeking with spilled Amaretto drinks? The answer is obviously "no."

If Ham Jordan was a cheating kind of person, he could tie a liquor bottle on a string outside his White House window as Ray Milland did in "The Lost Weekend," and pull it up every time he wanted a slug. But as Ham told Jody Powell, "I could do it but it would be wrong."

So what have you got? An assistant to the President of the United States who has been fingered by the gossip columnists. Since he has been recently separated from his wife, he is a marked man by every woman who goes to a singles' bar looking how to get even with a guy who won't pick her up. Bring on the photographers and you've got the greatest no-win situation since Norman Mailer took a poke at Gore Vidal.

The real problem is that the aide who sits next to the Oval Office is supposed to be taken seriously. If the aide calls up a union official and says, "I'm speaking for the President. He wants you to start mining coal right away," and the person on the other end says, "Yeh, tell it to the boys at Sarsfield's," this country is in a lot of trouble.

My only solution for Ham is that he stay in the White House day and night. Some day, maybe a year from now, people will forget about the pyramids of Egypt and the Amaretto with the whipped cream on the blouse and he will be a free man again. Right now, he's a sitting duck.

It isn't your fault, Ham, but when Jody has to start putting out White Papers on how you spend your nights, you have no choice but to dig a foxhole in the Rose Garden, cover yourself with a poncho and wait until your long nightmare is over.

## SEPARATE CHECKS

President Carter was asked many questions at his publicized call-in. The one that fascinated me the most was when a young man asked why the President's son Chip and Chip's wife and their son were living in the White House on the taxpayers' money.

The President responded by saying, in part, "Well, I think you ought to know that all personal expenses of our family are paid out of my pocket or the pocket of my children. Our food is kept separate; we pay for all of it. All our clothes and so forth are paid for out of our own pocket . . . ."

Had I been the questioner I would have followed up with "Mr. President, how do you keep track of what each person eats?" Since I couldn't, I'm going to speculate on what might take place at a Carter family dinner.

They've just finished eating and the President takes out a yellow pad and pencil. "All right, now, let's see what everyone ate. Chip, what did you have?"

"I had tomato soup, fried chicken, mashed potatoes, cole slaw and cherry pie."

"Didn't I see you drink a glass of milk?" the President asks.

"I forgot about the milk," Chip says.

"I'll bet," Amy says mischievously.

"Pa, she's picking on me again," Chip says.

"Hush, Amy," Rosalynn Carter says. "Your Daddy's trying to figure out the check."

The President says, "Did Caron have the same?"

"I had a hot roll," Caron replies.

The President says, "The hot roll comes with the meal. Now, Ma, what did you have?"

Miss Lillian says, "I thought I was invited here for dinner."

"I'm sorry, Ma, everybody has to pay for their own food at the White House."

"Well, you know I don't like chicken, so I had some broiled trout."

The President looks up the price of trout on the engraved White House menu and writes it down.

"Grandma had cottage cheese, *too*," Amy says.

"But I didn't have soup," Miss Lillian says. "You're not going to charge me for the soup *and* the cottage cheese."

"No, you can have one or the other."

"In most restaurants the cottage cheese is free," Miss Lillian says.

"She's right, Jimmy," Rosalynn says. "I was at the Women's Democratic Club yesterday and the cottage cheese came with the meal."

"All right," the President says, crossing out the cottage cheese. "Rosalynn, you had the chicken, didn't you?"

"Yes, Jimmy, and a salad."

"What kind of dressing?" the President asks.

"Does it make any difference?"

"I suppose not, but if we get audited by the GSA I want the records straight. All right, Billy, what did you have for dinner?"

"Two beers," Billy says.

"He did not," Amy says. "He had four beers. One, two, three, four!"

"I brought two of them with me," Billy says. "Besides, I didn't eat anything. I don't see why I should be charged for dinner when I just drunk beer."

"The food was prepared for you," the President says. "We have to pay for it whether you ate it or not."

"If I had known I would have to pay for dinner," says Billy, "I would have gone to a bar."

"How much do I owe?" Amy asks.

"We'll pay for you," the President says. "Well, let's see—it seems to add up just right. Wait a minute. I seem to be short 20 cents."

Amy says, "You forgot the baby's warm milk."

"That's it. I forgot the baby!" the President says. "Does anyone want more coffee?"

Miss Lillian says, "No, thanks. On my Social Security I can't afford it."

## THE SANS SOUCI AT HIGH NOON

As if we didn't have enough to worry about in Washington, it is now rumored that the Sans Souci Restaurant is no longer the "in" restaurant since the Carter crowd arrived in town. The nation's two leading newspapers, *Women's Wear Daily* and *The National Enquirer,* have both reported that the Sans Souci is out and a Carter appointee wouldn't be found dead there.

This came as a terrible blow to the elite clientele who eat lunch there every day. Those of us who have been dining through five Administrations have always considered the Sans Souci the power center of the country.

We believed that no important decision was made in the government without it first being discussed at our restaurant over rognons de veau and Dover sole, served with either a respectable Mouton Rothschild or a chilled bottle of Pouilly Fuissé.

High-priced Washington lawyers and higher-priced Washington lobbyists did their business under the watchful eyes of high-priced columnists and television commentators.

The Sans Souci became synonymous with big government and power politics. KGB agents used it to plant stories on unsuspecting newspapermen. World Bank officials met with ministers of finance to negotiate multimillion-dollar loans. Heads of conglomerates used it to plot strategy against SEC regulations. Contractors worked over Army and Navy procurement officials to land contracts. New tax shelters were designed on the white tablecloths.

There was no doubt in anybody's mind that if you wanted to make a deal you had to come to the Sans Souci.

The publicity that the Sans Souci was not the "in" restaurant any more hurt us all. Every day we sat at our tables waiting, hoping, praying that someone from the Carter Administration would walk through the door.

The real problem for all of us was that no one knew what a person from the Carter White House looked like, and even if he did come there we wouldn't be aware of his presence.

Just the other day someone came in the restaurant in a leisure suit and sneakers. We all became excited because he was talking to Paul, the maître d'hôtel, with a Southern accent and he didn't seem to have a reservation.

"It could be one of them," a lobbyist at the next table said to me excitedly. "He seems to be shuffling."

"Carter people don't shuffle," I said. "They have style. Didn't you read Pat Caddell's memo?"

"I hope Paul gives him a table. Wouldn't it be terrible if the first Carter person ever to come to Sans Souci couldn't get in?" he said.

"Poor Paul," I said. "He's in a quandary. He has no way of knowing if the guy's a cotton farmer from South Carolina or Carter's National Security Adviser for Southeast Asia."

"I'd take a gamble," a lawyer from the Hogan & Hartson law firm said, "and let him in. We can't just sit here and wait forever."

"If we don't get someone from the Carter Administration soon," a defense contractor moaned, "our lunches will not be considered deductible."

Paul finally decided to give the man a table.

"Who is he?" we asked the maitre d' excitedly.

"He's a Carter intern working in the mail room," Paul said.

"The White House is back!" a columnist cried. "We can be considered an 'in' restaurant again."

"I knew they couldn't stay away," the lobbyist chortled. "No matter what Carter vowed, he needs the Sans Souci more than we need him."

I asked Paul for a telephone. When he brought it to the table I immediately dialed *Women's Wear Daily* and said to the editor, "Hold the presses!"


## WHO IS IN CHARGE?

Americans were shocked to read last week that a recent survey of teen-agers showed they were completely ignorant of how the American government operated as well as who was in charge.

Some of the findings: Fewer than half could name one of their senators or their representative in the House. About a third did not know a senator was elected. More than a third did not believe a newspaper should be allowed to publish criticism of elected officials. A fourth didn't know that the Senate is part of Congress. A third did not know that the Constitution outlines their civil rights.

While this is very revealing as to where teen-agers' heads are these days, another survey taken at the same time came up with some even more frightening data. In interviews with 150,000 people *over* 35 years of age, the study disclosed a startling ignorance on the part of Americans in the middle and older age groups when it came to the really important issues of the country.

For example, while 70 percent of those questioned knew Guy Lombardo had died, only 25 percent were aware that, although Elvis Presley had passed away, he still lives in the hearts of his fans through a multimillion-dollar souvenir business. Although for all intents and purposes he is gone, Elvis will still outsell President Carter on a magazine cover.

Only 15 percent of those questioned knew the difference between "Laverne and Shirley."

Less than a third of the senior citizens over 65 had any knowledge that Burt Reynolds was now dating actress Sally Field, who is only 31 years old.

Harvey Rothmere, a teen-ager who had taken the survey, said the ignorance of grown-ups when it comes to rock music was appalling.

"Less than 2 percent knew that one of the Sex Pistols had OD'ed on a plane from L.A. to New York."

"What's a Sex Pistol?" I asked.

"There you have it," Harvey said. "That's one of the reasons grown-ups have no idea what's going on. You media people are not doing your job. The Sex Pistols are a punk rock group from England."

"What's a punk rock group?" I asked.

"It's a group of people who play punk rock and do sickening things on the stage that make you want to retch."

"Beautiful," I said, "but what does punk rock have to do with our generation?"

"What does the Senate have to do with ours?" Harvey retorted. "If you don't know Johnny Rotten, why should we know the name of our congressman?"

"Well, you should at least know something about the Constitution," I said.

"We don't have time. We have to keep up with Cher's divorce from Greg Allman. You grown-ups think we're stupid just because we don't know the name of the Vice President of the United States. But can anyone over 35 name the last six women Mick Jagger has taken to a disco club?"

"You owe it to your country to know something about how your government is run," I protested.

Harvey was really hostile. "Suppose we did know the name of our senator. What good would it do us?"

"Well, you could write to him about how you feel on the issues of the day."

"And then what?"

"He could write you back thanking you for your letter."

"I'd rather get an autographed photo of Lee Majors."

"Who's Lee Majors?" I wanted to know.

"I don't believe it. He's Farrah Fawcett's husband. No wonder your generation can't make it on Social Security."

## THE CIA APOLOGIZES

A federal judge has recently ruled that the CIA must write a letter of apology to people whose mail they opened in the United States. The Department of Justice has suggested the text of the letter, which turns out to be a formal apology in typical governmental gobbledygook, which in my opinion would not get the CIA off the hook.

I think if the CIA really wants to show it's sorry for reading the mail of Americans they should make each letter a personal one, which would show that the Central Intelligence Agency has a heart.

Here are a few suggestions of the types of letters of apology Admiral Stansfield Turner, the head of the CIA, would send out to people whose privacy had been violated.

Dear Mr. Mac Comber,

You can't imagine how sorry all of us in the CIA are for reading your mail during the past fourteen years. It was an oversight which I assure you won't happen again.

I regret your Aunt Tilly in Dublin still has pains in her back. Our medical team suggests she use a hot water bottle at night to relieve the agony. Also, I think your son is out of line when he says he wants to stay in Paris to continue his education. Our agents in Paris report that he is not going to school but is spending all of his time at cafes.

The letter you received from the Carlsons in Venice telling you what a wonderful time they were having was slightly exaggerated. Carlson came down with dysentery and Mrs. Carlson's photographs of St. Mark's Square were all overexposed.

We'll be happy to send you information on any other letters we read, if you want us to. I hope it will make up in a small way for what we now consider an illegal undercover program.

Sincerely Yours
ADMIRAL STANSFIELD TURNER

Dear Ms. Halifax,

As you know the CIA was involved in a mail-reading program, and for reasons which no one here can explain all your letters from abroad were opened and scrutinized. You can't imagine how upset we are about this. Some overzealous employee, who will have to remain nameless for security reasons, was responsible. After going through his report on your mail, all I can say is that you have beautiful handwriting and I wish my children could write as well.

Your love letters to Mr. Cesar Randini in Rome were masterpieces and should be published in a book. The CIA would do it, but we recently went out of the book publishing business.

We're sorry that Mr. Randini broke off the relationship by marrying Signora Carmelita Verdi of 14 Via Condotti, but you must take my word for it that Mr. Randini is not a one-woman man. All the time he was calling "his little artichoke" he was spending his evenings at Signora Verdi's apartment, sometimes leaving as late as four in the morning. You are well rid of him.

Sincerely,
ADMIRAL STANSFIELD TURNER

Dear Mrs. Starbuckle,

I am obligated by the federal courts to inform you that we have been reading your mail and that of your husband, whose trips to London, Brussels and Antwerp on business have taken him out of the country six times a year.

I know you are suspicious that some of these trips are not all concerned with business. I can assure you that as far as Brussels and Antwerp are concerned your husband has been conducting commerce for his company.

We are unable to find out exactly what business he has in London, unless his meetings with Lady Mathilda MacIntosh of 1234 Cadogan Square have to do with steel exporting. Our records show Lady MacIntosh has never been in the steel business, nor was the late Sir Harold MacIntosh, who was 30 years his wife's senior.

Unfortunately, the bug we planted in the Cadogan Square flat has always been drowned out by Frank Sinatra music whenever your husband has been there. Since we can no longer, by law, follow this case, I might suggest you inquire about a London private detective who could investigate what Mr. Starbuckle really does in London.

In putting forth this suggestion, it is our sincere hope that you will forgive the CIA for reading your mail. And if anything good comes of our intelligence about Mr. Starbuckle's stopovers in London, we hope you will think kindly of the CIA in the future.

Sincerely,
ADMIRAL STANSFIELD TURNER


## A GREAT HEW SECRETARY

I don't know about President-elect Carter's other Cabinet appointments, but I can speak with authority when I say he couldn't have selected a better Secretary of Health, Education and Welfare than Joseph Califano. You see, Joe Califano has been our football car pool driver to the Redskin games for the past eight years. He learned all his driving skills from his ex-boss, Lyndon Johnson, at the L.B.J. ranch, and if Joe can run a government department as well as he can maneuver his beat-up station wagon on Massachusetts Avenue, this country's health, education and welfare will be in safe hands.

I'll have to admit that the seven of us who ride with Joe to the Redskin games never thought of him as Cabinet material. But then again no football car pool chauffeur is a hero to the people he drives to the stadium.

When the FBI men came to see me to do a check on Joe, I thought they were kidding when they said he was being considered for Secretary of HEW. But I discovered the FBI never jokes.

"What kind of man would you say Mr. Califano is?" one of them asked me.

"He's a gutsy Evel Knievel," I said. "Evel Knievel has jumped over fourteen chartered Greyhound buses on a motorcycle, but Califano is the only man I know who has ever tried to drive straight *through* them. Ask anyone in the car pool," I said.

"Would you say he's unstable?" the other FBI man asked.

"I should say not. He's as stable as they come. Have you ever seen a man drive on the sidewalk for three blocks just to avoid being tied up in stadium traffic?"

The FBI man was taking notes.

"Does he have any deep-seated prejudices that you know of?"

"He hates red lights. I've seen him cuss and scream at a red light for two minutes. He also has contempt for STOP signs. Every time he sees one he goes livid."

"I mean for people. Does he have any prejudice against certain kinds of people?"

"Only pedestrians. Joe thinks pedestrians should stay off the streets during football games regardless of race, creed or color."

"How does he feel about busing?"

"He's for busing people to football games only as a last resort. But if the Supreme Court says you have to bus spectators to the stadium he will follow the law of the land."

"Would you say he's imaginative?" one of the FBI agents asked.

"Yup. No matter how many times he's driven us to the game he always goes a different way. One time he took the wrong turn and we wound up in Richmond, Virginia. The thing that endears Joe to the car pool is that you never know what he's going to do next."

"What would you say are his best traits?"

"He'll always look you in the eye—when he's driving—even

when you're sitting in the back seat. And he's one of the most patriotic men I know. I've seen him sideswipe an ambulance rather than miss the Redskin band playing the 'Star-Spangled Banner.' "

"Then you think very highly of him."

"All of us in the car pool do. He's saved our lives many times."

"How is that?"

"Well, there's this large fountain by Union Station and in eight years of driving Joe has never crashed into it."

"Then you think he'll make a good secretary of HEW?"

"The greatest. Our loss is the country's gain. We hate to see him go, but we would never stand in the way of Joe getting his own chauffeur-driven limousine. Only Jimmy Carter would pluck his HEW secretary out of somebody's car pool."

## FBI OUT ON THE STREETS

I was shocked to turn on the television set a short while ago and see FBI agents taking advantage of the First Amendment to protest the indictments of three of their own for allegedly violating the First Amendment rights of others.

Demonstrating in the streets is not what the FBI does best. Under J. Edgar Hoover and his successors, the role of the FBI was to monitor those people who were organizing and financing protests, to infiltrate those groups that were marching and to report on the "troublemakers" who were using the sidewalks and boulevards to call attention to their grievances.

Old habits die hard for some of the agents, and the FBI demonstration was no exception.

As the FBI agents and former agents were fiercely protesting in front of the U.S. District Court building, a man was taking photographs of them.

"O'Toole," shouted one of the protesters, "what the hell are you doing?"

"I'm taking pictures of the ringleaders of this demonstration for the agency. I got some really good ones."

"Are you out of your mind? We're all FBI agents demonstrating."

O'Toole seemed disappointed. "You mean you don't want photos for your files?"

"No, we don't want photos of us demonstrating. What we're doing is perfectly legal. It's covered by the Constitution."

"I gotcha. I'll tell you what I'll do. I'll infiltrate the crowd with a tape recorder and check to see if anyone is talking about overthrowing the government."

"O'Toole, you don't have to do that. We're all good Americans and what we're doing is calling an injustice to the attention of the American people."

"Yeah, I've heard that one before. But someone's behind this demonstration and I think we better find out who.

"I hear the money's pouring in for a defense fund for the people who were indicted. It could be coming from the Soviet Union or Cuba."

"Dammit, O'Toole, the money for the defense fund is coming from former and present FBI agents. There is no foreign money involved."

"Why can't you understand we've got a legitimate grievance, and we want to see that the people who were indicted are not used as scapegoats just because the Justice Dept. wants blood?"

"I think we should tap the lines of the guys who were indicted. That could lead us to the source of the money, and also to where the orders are coming from."

"O'Toole, do you know who I am?"

"Sure, you're Turnbull from Identification."

"I'm one of the ringleaders."

"You could have fooled me. I never had you down for a radical nut."

"I'm not a radical nut. None of us is a radical nut. We're law-abiding citizens."

"Yeah, but in the Sixties we were told that anyone who demonstrated in the streets was a radical nut. Either that or a misguided pawn in the commie struggle to destroy our way of life."

"That was in the Sixties. Now everyone's in the streets. The farmers, the doctors, the hard hats.

"When you get desperate you have to let everyone know about it. What are you doing with that notebook?"

"I'm taking down names. We'll cross-check them with the Socialist Workers Party. I can't believe all these people are FBI agents."

"O'Toole, this is a nonviolent demonstration."

"J. Edgar Hoover always said those are the worst kind."

## NOBODY VOTED FOR PLOTKIN

Everybody thinks that the Democratic and Republican conventions and the November election decide who is going to run the country.

I hate to be the one to throw cold water on this idea, but neither the President of the United States nor Congress can really do much to change anything.

The guy who runs this country is Plotkin. He is neither elected by the American people nor does he have to answer to them.

Plotkin, and the thousands like him, are civil servants averaging somewhere around $20,000 a year. They are stashed away in large brick and glass buildings all over Washington, Maryland and Virginia, and no matter what Congress or the President decide, they are the people in charge.

Let us say that the President wants a pothole reform bill. He sends it up to Congress where, after two years, it is passed. The President signs it and everyone in the United States believes it is the law of the land.

Except Plotkin.

Plotkin gets the bill and examines it. The wording, after the lobbyists get through with it, is, of course, vague. What kind of potholes does the law cover? How much money should be spent to fill each pothole? Should the work be contracted to private industry or to the Army Corps of Engineers? Was it Congress' intent to deal with all potholes or just those on federal property? And, finally, what constitutes a pothole in the first place?

Plotkin, who has been a civil servant for twenty years, knows if he takes any action on his own, he could be criticized and he could blot his copy book.

So he calls a meeting of all his department heads and asks them to write him memoranda on the best way to administer the pothole bill. He tells them it is a matter of urgency and he wants to hear from everybody in six months.

Six months later the people under Plotkin all submit memoranda. A majority of them suggest that a study be made of potholes by a commission made up of engineering experts from companies, universities and government that will report back to the bureau in a year.

Plotkin likes the idea and approves it. But to play it safe he also hires his own experts to check out the report of the commission. This means larger office space and Plotkin decides to move the bureau to a new building. The move requires tremendous logistics, but also causes fierce competition among all of Plotkin's subordinates as to where their offices will be located, as well as carpeting, furniture and the location of the water cooler.

There is so much controversy over the new quarters that Plotkin hasn't had too much time to worry about the potholes.

Finally the move is made, new people are hired and everyone settles down to the task of administering the pothole bill. The outside commission has submitted its report which is circulated throughout the bureau for comments.

The comments are all negative and it is decided to scrap the commission's report. The fear of most of the people in Plotkin's office is that, if they accept the recommendations of the commission, they would have to put them into action. If they turn them down, they'll have to come up with their own which would mean expanding the bureau, thus guaranteeing everyone a promotion to the next civil service grade.

By this time Congress and the President have forgotten they even passed a pothole bill. But one day the President is driving on U.S. Highway 95 and he hits a pothole. His head bumps the ceiling of the limousine and an AP photographer gets a picture of it. This makes the President very mad and he says to his aide, "Whatever happened to the pothole bill I signed?"

That night Plotkin gets a call from the White House and the aide says, "The President wants a progress report on what you're doing about the potholes in this country."

"We're working on a report right now," Plotkin assures him. "But just because the President signs a bill doesn't mean he can expect results overnight."

## THE LAST TAX LOOPHOLE

Every city, county and state government is trying to think up new ways of raising tax dollars. All the obvious things have already been taxed such as income, cigarettes, gasoline, parking, liquor, everything you buy in a store etc., etc., and it's almost impossible to come up with something new that doesn't already have a tax on it.

I was therefore very impressed with a new revenue-raising idea proposed by Merriweather Sample, who found something to tax that nobody else had thought of. In America today, this is the equivalent of discovering a new constellation in the sky or a virus without a name or a non-carcinogenic spray that will kill fire ants.

Sample revealed his plan at a secret meeting of the board of supervisors of Bleeding County.

"Gentlemen, I think I have it. I propose we put a tax on jogging."

There was a look of surprise from everyone in the room.

"Jogging?" someone said.

Sample continued, "There are thousands of joggers running all around our country right now and it isn't costing them one cent. I say they've been getting a free ride for too long."

One nervous supervisor said, "But how can we tax men and women for just running around?"

"It's simple. They're using county roads and sidewalks to jog. Do you realize the damage they're doing every time they clomp on the asphalt or the pavement?" Sample said.

"I didn't know runners do damage," another supervisor said.

"Take a walk around and see for yourself. There are cracks everywhere, and they were made by pounding feet. There is just so much abuse a pavement can take from a 200-pound man and a 110-pound woman. If they just ran in their bare feet it would be one thing, but most of them wear sneakers and running shoes. We're not just talking about one or two people. There are thousands of joggers out there destroying our streets and sidewalks and someone has to pay for it."

A lady supervisor said, "If we start taxing people for jogging there will be a terrible uproar. Many people consider it the only free thing they're permitted to do."

Sample scoffed at the comment. "Joggers get pleasure out of

running, just as other people get pleasure from drinking beer and smoking cigarettes. No one tells them they HAVE to jog. But if they're going to do it, and if they feel it gives them a lift, let them pay for it."

"What kind of tax did you have in mind?"

"I think at the beginning we could require them to buy a license for $5 a year. It would be printed on cardboard so they could wear it on the back of their running suits. Then we could add a surcharge of one cent for each mile they run."

"Suppose they downplay how many miles they've run?"

Sample grinned, "That's the beauty of it. Most joggers love to lie about how far they've run. I never met one yet who didn't exaggerate the number of miles he completed in a day. Every jogger will gladly pay extra money just to impress another runner."

"It might work," a supervisor said.

Sample hit the table, "Running for free is the last big tax loophole in America, and it's our job to close it."

One supervisor asked, "What do we tell our jogging friends when they say it's unfair that they have to pay to exercise?"

"Just tell them 'Life is unfair.'"

# II. It's All in the Head

## ANOTHER MEMOIR

The little old lady came into my office clutching a yellow manuscript.

"I was wondering," she said in a tiny voice, "if these are worth anything?"

"What are they?"

"My memoirs. I was the mistress of Abraham Lincoln."

"Fantastic," I said. "Nobody knows Lincoln had a mistress."

"It's been my secret for 101 years," she said.

"Why are you revealing it now?"

"Everybody else seems to be talking about their affairs with the President, and I figured I might as well get into the act. President Lincoln and I were more than good friends."

"How good?"

"It's all in the book. We used to meet in the Lincoln Room any time Mary Todd was out of town."

"How did you meet him?"

"Through Frank Sinatra. We were introduced at a party in Chicago."

"Frank Sinatra the singer?" I asked in amazement.

"Not that Frank Sinatra, silly. Frank Sinatra was a colonel in the Illinois Regulars. I met him through Sam Giancana."

"Giancana, the Mafia boss?"

"No, stupid," she said. "Sam Giancana was in the War Department. I used to date him when I worked up on the Hill for Congressman Hays."

"Wayne Hays?"

"No, Rutherford B. Hayes. I couldn't type, but it didn't seem to matter because we didn't have typewriters then."

"Let's get back to Lincoln. You say you had an affair with him?"

"That's correct. He may have been in a wheelchair, but he was strong as an ox."

"Now wait a minute. Lincoln wasn't in a wheelchair. That was Franklin Delano Roosevelt."

"Are you sure?" she asked.

"I'm certain of it."

"Well, maybe it was Roosevelt then. He had a moustache and kept talking about San Juan Hill."

"That was Teddy Roosevelt, not Franklin Roosevelt. Lincoln was the one with the stovepipe hat and a beard."

"It's been so long ago it's hard for me to remember. I know he never wore a stovepipe hat when we had our affair. He told me once that he wouldn't be able to see me for a while because he was going to be impeached."

"The only Presidents who were going to be impeached were Andrew Johnson and Richard Nixon. It wasn't Richard Nixon, was it?"

"I should say not. I would never have had an affair with *that* man. He lied to the American people."

"Then it must have been Andrew Johnson."

"That's funny, I thought it was Lincoln. Do you think Frank Sinatra lied to me?"

"I wouldn't know."

"Well, whoever it was used to take me for long walks by the Tidal Basin."

"The Tidal Basin? Are you sure you didn't make all this up?"

"Cross my heart and hope to die," she said. "I was somebody's mistress and if it wasn't Lincoln, it was the fellow that came a few years later."

"General Grant? Did he drink a lot?"

"Yup. It's all in my memoirs. We used to drink and then we'd go up to the Lincoln Room. Maybe that's why I thought it was Lincoln—because of the name on the room. I remember he said his greatest dream was to return to his ranch on the Pedernales."

"Wow, you do have a story to tell."

"So you think someone might buy my memoirs?"

"Are you kidding? I know seven paperback houses that will give you $100,000 for them, without reading a chapter."

The little old lady said, "I'm not just doing it for the money. I'm doing it because I believe people should know what Abraham Lincoln really was like."

## NO ATHEISTS AT CON ED

There are no atheists at Consolidated Edison. Ever since the New York blackout Con Ed lawyers have been working day and night to prove that what happened was an "Act of God." If they can't prove that the Lord did it, they will be spending their next 20 years in court fighting lawsuits from the Bronx to the tip of Staten Island.

I stopped by to see how Con Edison's lawyers were doing.

"God bless you," the receptionist said as she looked up from her Bible.

"I just wanted to speak to one of Con Edison's lawyers," I told her.

"Thou comest at the wrong time," she replied. "Mr. Flaherty is at Mass, Mr. Bradley is at a prayer breakfast meeting and Mr. Seligman is with his rabbi."

"My, this sounds like a religious office."

"Con Edison would never hire a lawyer who didn't believe in God," she said.

"They must have been pretty shaken up by the blackout," I said.

She sighed. "The Lord moves in mysterious ways. We must not question His decision to black out New York at a most inopportune time. He must have been very angry at the city or He would have never sent down those bolts of lightning to smite our power lines."

"Then you people believe that it was God who did it?"

"As Mr. Flaherty wrote in his brief yesterday, 'The Lord giveth light and He taketh it away. The power of Con Edison is in His hands.'"

"So you are not looking for any other reason for the blackout?" I asked.

"What other reason could there possibly be? Every safeguard known to man was in operation at the time. But there is no failsafe when the Lord turns His wrath against sinners."

"Is it Con Edison's position that New Yorkers are sinners?"

"Verily," she said. "You have only to walk down 42nd Street or Eighth Avenue to know why God was enraged. We are living in a virtual Sodom and Gomorrah," she said.

"Why didn't God just black out the porno shops and theaters showing X-rated movies if He was so mad?"

"Even the Lord cannot smash one of our circuits without putting the others out of commission. Besides this happened in the summertime and there was sinning going on all over the city, particularly in apartments and houses where the wives were away on vacation."

"I forgot about that."

"Con Edison knew about the sinning, and our engineers feared the wrath of God for a week before the blackout. But we felt that, as a power company, it was not our place to warn the populace that if they continued their behavior the Lord would loose the fearful lightning of His powerful swift sword."

"Do you think the 'Act of God' defense will hold up in court?"

"We can only pray it will. If the courts decide against us, then no one will ever believe the Lord is trying to tell the people something. As Mr. Bradley said to his Bible class yesterday, 'If this blackout doesn't make people believers nothing will.' "

I heard an organ in the background.

"What's that?" I asked.

"It's the beginning of Vespers. Con Ed has Vesper services for its employees every day."

"Is this something new?"

"We started them the day after the blackout. It was the legal department's idea."

"Is it an electric organ I hear?"

"No, it's manual. The Lord only knows when He will strike us again."

## THE END OF THE DREAM

"Can I help you, sir?"

"Yeh, fill up the tank."

"With what, sir?"

"I'd like some of that beautiful Alaska petroleum I've been seeing on television."

"I'm terribly sorry, but we don't have any Alaskan gas. We have some lovely fresh Saudi Arabian fuel that just came in a few days ago."

"How come you don't have any Alaskan Gold? The stuff's been coming down the pipeline for months. I've been looking forward to burning it ever since they made the first strike."

"It's not as easy to come by as one might think. You see, sir, once it comes out of the ground it has to be shipped by pipe. The pipeline was only just completed. It was supposed to cost less than a million dollars. It finally cost between seven and eight billion dollars. Then after it was built, there was some question about the welding, and there was an explosion along the line, and then a truck went into it and the whole thing has been a mess. I'm not sure Alaskan fuel will be available to many Americans for some time to come. Would you like to try our Kuwaiti-No Lead? It's very popular for a car of your size."

"I thought once we got the Alaska pipeline built our fuel problems would be over."

"Oh, no. Actually it's created new problems. We may have an oil glut on the West Coast as more and more of the oil comes down the pipeline. There aren't enough refineries to handle what we're shipping. Would you like to try a little unassuming Persian gasoline? It doesn't come from one of the famous oil fields, but it's very good for everyday bumper-to-bumper driving."

"If it was up to me I'd say put Libyan gasoline into the car if you want to. But my wife says we should buy American. She says the less money we give the Arab states the less co-operative apartments they can buy in New York City."

"Well, what about some Venezuelan Crude? It has a lovely black texture to it and smells rather nice in a tunnel."

"Look, my wife sent me out for Alaska Premium and she's going to be furious if I fill up the car with something else. We've been led to believe that by August 1 we could buy all the Alaskan gasoline we wanted to, and at a reasonable price I might add. It isn't fair to get people's expectations up and then not be able to deliver."

"It's true, sir, we did expect to sell the Alaskan oil in August but so many things have happened since then."

"What happened?"

"They built the pipeline to the wrong place. They should have built it to the Midwest. It's actually cheaper to sell Alaskan oil to Japan than it is to the lower 48 states."

"You wouldn't sell Alaskan oil to foreigners and keep us Americans from having any of it."

"There is a lot of talk of it. We'll give you Nigerian oil instead."

"I don't want my car to drive on Nigerian fuel!"

"What about Algerian Regular?"

"I don't see why as a consumer I can't get what I want."

"It's nobody's fault, sir. As I said, they built the pipeline to the wrong place. It could happen to anybody. The Alaskan oil companies feel worse about it than you do."

"All the buildup, all the hopes of Americans using their own Alaskan slope petroleum have gone down the drain. How long can our cars keep running on Iraqi British petroleum? Suppose the Sultan of Oman starts mixing his oil with Muscat? When President Andrew Johnson bought Alaska he had only one thing in mind, and that was that someday every American, rich as well as poor, would be able to pull up to any service station in the United States and say, 'Give me ten bucks worth of Super Alaskan Ethyl.'

"I feel the way you do, sir. It is the end of the American dream."


## IT'S ALL IN THE HEAD

It was not given much publicity, but the Department of Energy has now come to the conclusion that the greatest amount of energy lost in this country is caused by heat escaping from people's heads.

The original discovery was made by a Washington lawyer, named David E. Weisman, when he noticed his brother-in-law, who never wore a hat, complained he was always cold. Then one Sunday, during halftime of a particularly bitter Redskins game, Weisman actually saw steam escaping from his brother-in-law's ears!

He put two and two together and reported his observations to ERDA, the research arm of the Department of Energy. The research people had suspected that heat was escaping from people's bodies, but up until then no one had thought the loss was going out of their heads.

So the researchers dressed up rats in warm clothing, but left their heads uncovered. Then they placed them in refrigerators. Sure enough the tests showed an appreciable energy loss depending on the size and shape of each rat's head.

Encouraged, they proceeded to test volunteer Energy Department employees. The data were confirmed. A pointy-headed person lost 10 percent of his body heat when he did not wear a hat, and a flat-headed person lost 20 percent. Also, volunteers with hair managed to be more insulated from the cold than those who were going bald.

Once all the results were in, they were turned over to the Department of Energy's Policy Committee. After making an environmental impact study, the Committee recommended new legislation which would assure the conservation of America's body heat.

The first recommendation was that a new law be passed requiring every American to wear a hat. Knowing that this might put a burden on many bald people, the Committee suggested that as an incentive, a tax credit be given to each bald person who purchased a new hat. The credit would be limited to the purchase of one hat per person, with not more than four deductions per family.

The third suggestion was that the President wear a hat at all his press conferences and state dinners to set an example to the rest of the country.

These recommendations were sent up to the Secretary of Energy, James Schlesinger, who immediately ordered his lobbyists on the Hill to add them to the energy bill.

Unfortunately, the Hat Manufacturers' lobbyists got wind of the new legislation and immediately went to work sabotaging it. They testified that they had no objection to making everyone in the United States wear a hat. But they attacked the tax credit plan maintaining that the money set aside for rebates to bald people should go instead for the exploration of new felt.

They also demanded complete deregulation on the price of new hat bands. As one lobbyist put it, "Unless we get $2.25 per cubic yard for our hat bands we will be unable to find new sources of domestic material to supply all the head gear that will be needed this winter."

To complicate matters the shoe industry got into the act and said they should also get tax credits for conserving energy. "If we didn't make shoes," one of their lobbyists said, "body heat now rising from people's heads would escape out of their toes."

Despite the intensive lobbying pressures, an Administration spokesman said he was optimistic that Congress, in its wisdom, would keep a lid on the price of hats, rather than overheat the economy. And he predicted that if both the House and Senate kept working at their present pace, everyone in the country would be wearing a warm hat by July.

## TO CLONE OR NOT TO CLONE

For some reason, which is hard to explain, my mind keeps wandering these days to cloning. I guess it all started when I read about the book revealing that an anonymous multimillionaire had paid to have a child cloned in his own image.

The author of the book says the millionaire, a lifelong bachelor, wanted to leave a son to posterity, but had found no woman whose genes he considered worthy of his own. He hired a scientist who took one of the man's own cells, had it hatched by a woman, cleansed it of all the woman's genetic material and then produced an identical likeness of the rich man. (I'm not making this up—it's all in the book.)

Reputable scientists have scoffed at the story, and so far neither the author nor the publisher has produced any proof that it really happened.

My concern is that perhaps it didn't this time, but who is to say in the future that it couldn't? Cloning could soon become as common as the Asian Flu. Once we have the knowledge to reproduce exact duplicates of ourselves, with just one cell, it's a whole new ball game as far as the human race is concerned.

I wouldn't mind reproducing a thousand persons just like myself, because I think the world needs them. But I definitely would be against one more Codsmather. He lives down the block and he's really a mess. He never washes his car, he lets his dog wander all over the neighborhood, his kids skateboard in the middle of the street, and from the empty bottles in his garbage, he's really into gin.

There is something wrong with Codsmather's genes, and if we permitted his cells to be cloned the neighborhood would really go to hell.

On the other hand there's Sara Lee, who works down the hall from my office. Sara Lee is beautiful, bright and a joy to behold. Everyone on the floor has always said that it was a pity that there was only one Sara Lee to go around.

Columnist Robert Novak just told us the other day during a coffee break, "Wouldn't it be wonderful if there was a Sara Lee for everybody?"

I told him, "Some day when they get cloning down pat there will be."

Our coffee steamed with the thought.

But there are many things that enter into the moral aspects of cloning which we all must take into consideration.

If there was more than one Reggie Jackson would baseball be as interesting? Can the world afford two Ilie Nastases? Or, for that matter, two Robert Novaks? Would Farrah Fawcett Majors mean as much to all of us if there were 500 of her walking around at the same time? Is there a limit to the number of Billy Carters the country will put up with?

Once cloning becomes the "in" thing, teen-agers are going to want to try it. I don't know of any parents who could survive with an exact duplicate of the teen-ager they have now.

Another worrisome thing is that in the beginning, cloning is going to be very expensive and only rich people will be capable of duplicating themselves. Therefore, until they get the price down, all we'll be able to reproduce wholesale will be oil and gas tycoons who, as they multiply, will lobby for higher and higher prices, with the excuse that they have so many more mouths to feed.

Once the middle class can afford cloning they will probably get Congress to pass laws forbidding poor people from doing it, because they won't want to pay the extra welfare costs.

The whole thing will be a shambles unless we start thinking it out today. Each person must search his own heart and ask, "Do I want an exact duplicate of myself to take my place when I'm gone, or am I willing to abort my cells for the good of mankind?"

## ASK THE ENERGY MAN

Q—Why is there an energy shortage?

A—Because not enough dinosaurs died so they could rot and make oil to last us beyond the year 2040.

Q—Why don't we raise more dinosaurs and kill them and bury them in the ground so they will rot and provide oil for us?

A—Because the environmentalists won't let us kill dinosaurs. They are a protected species.

Q—What about foliage and other fossils? Why can't we bury them so we can have more oil?

A—It takes a billion years for vegetation and fossils to rot and turn into oil. Most people don't want to wait that long.

Q—What happened to all the oil we were supposed to get from Alaska that would make us independent of the Middle East?

A—That oil is going to be shipped to Japan and we will get the oil that Japan would ordinarily buy from the Middle East.

Q—Won't that make us more dependent on Middle East oil than we were before?

A—No comment.

Q—What does President Carter propose to do to solve the energy crisis?

A—Declare moral war on it.

Q—How do you fight a moral war?

A—By taxing people who use gasoline. He expects to raise the price of gasoline by five cents per gallon until people use less of it.

Q—Won't that be a burden on people who need their automobiles to go to work?

A—They will get rebates providing they don't have gas-guzzling cars.

Q—How will I get my rebate?

A—By filling out IRS Energy Form 19876 listing your name, address, Social Security number, number of dependents, as described in Paragraph C. You will add the weight of the car to gallons of gas consumed, and then divide the total by the number of cylinders you have in your engine, and then multiply this figure by your earned income, making an allowance for state and city taxes as described on page eight of the amended IRS Energy Form 1218, Article 3A. This figure will then be noted on page three, line 6B and subtracted from your date of birth on line 6C. Once the form is filed, no later than April 15, or unless you ask for an extension, under the IRS Energy Act S-304 you will receive a rebate of as much as $50 or pay a penalty of $200, which of course can be appealed.

Q—Will the oil companies benefit from the President's plan?

A—Only to the extent that the price they will receive for their "new" oil will be competitive with what we are now paying the OPEC nations.

Q—Does this mean the price of gasoline will go up for the consumer?

A—Does the sun rise in the morning?

Q—What is a gas guzzler?

A—A gas guzzler is any car that gets less miles to the gallon than the car you own at present.

Q—The Supreme Court just ruled that you could spank children in school. Does President Carter plan to spank people who drive gas guzzlers?

A—Not at the moment. But the Department of Energy has a standby plan in case its goals on the purchase of small cars are not met. They would set up a Government Spanking Bureau and before you would be permitted to buy a big car you would have to go there and get 20 whacks on your backside.

Q—There are some people who like to be spanked and who might buy a big car just to get beaten. What will you do about them?

A—The government has their names in a computer, and if it finds out they bought a big car just to get spanked they will be refused the privilege and will be asked to pay an excise spanking tax instead.

## HAVE A COOKIE

Washington is going to need a wailing wall after President Carter's energy proposals. I have never seen so much crying and anguish in a city since the President addressed Congress.

I was walking by the White House when I saw a man in a pinstripe suit sitting on a curb sobbing uncontrollably.

Usually I don't like to get involved, but in this case I sat down next to him and gave him my handkerchief. "What's the matter, fellow? Are you lost?"

"No," he said. "I'm the President of a Detroit automobile company and I've come to Washington to tell them we can't do it."

"Can't do what?"

"We can't make small cars that run efficiently and are comfortable and get good gas mileage."

"Why can't you?" I asked him.

"We don't know how!" he cried. "And even if we did no one would buy them."

I put my arm around him. "Surely you can. Detroit can do anything if it sets its mind to it. After all, you are the motherland of automobiles. Why don't you say to your designers and engineers, 'We're going to make the best small car that money can buy. And with our vast advertising resources we're going to persuade the American public it's to their advantage to buy one.' Rex Harrison could do it all by himself."

"But it would mean retooling our factories, moving assembly lines, changing consumer attitudes. Our people are not up to it."

"You just say that. But why don't you think of it as a new challenge, a test of American industrial ingenuity. Remember the story of the little train that couldn't? Well, you know what happened to him."

"But that was a train. We make cars."

"It's the same thing. You could pretend your car was a train."

He sniffled. "I'll think about it," he said.

"Here," I said, "have a cookie."

I got up and walked a few more blocks. Then I saw a man sitting on a bench. He was wearing a hair shirt and seemed to be in agony.

"Why are you wearing a hair shirt?" I asked him.

"I'm in the oil business," he said. "Everyone in the oil business is wearing a hair shirt since Carter announced he wanted to tax gasoline and give the money back to people."

"Doesn't the shirt hurt?"

"Of course it hurts," he said, "but what would you do if the President wanted to raise the price of your product but refused to give you enough profit to search for new oil? How are we going to eat and support our families?"

"I understand the oil business is very good."

"That's because you read the newspapers and watch television. If you knew the real story, you'd know we can barely exist on the few trickles of oil we get out of the ground and an occasional foot of gas we can sell on the side."

"Here," I said, "have a cookie."

I wandered up to Capitol Hill and saw a man wailing against the wall of the Sam Rayburn Building.

"Why me?" he said, looking up at the sky.

"I beg your pardon."

"Go away," he said, "unless you're a congressman."

"I'm not a congressman, but maybe I can help you."

"I'm in the coal business. Carter wants the country to switch to coal."

"That should make you very happy."

"Happy?" he wailed. "He wants us to mine the coal without wrecking the environment. He wants us to fill in the holes we dig in the landscape and plant trees and flowers. He wants us to clean the coal before it's burned. Oh, woe is me to be cursed as the owner of a coal mine."

Next to him was another man wailing just as loud.

"What's his problem?" I asked the owner of the coal mine.

"He has to haul my coal on his railroad and he says the government won't let him raise his rates."

I opened my paper bag and gave them each a cookie.

## "IT'S OUR OIL"

The argument that President Carter gives for energy conservation is that if we keep using up the petroleum reserves we have now there won't be any left for our children.

It's probably strong logic with many people, but Clemstone, my gas-guzzling friend, isn't buying it.

"Let the kids find their own oil," he said after the President's address on television.

"How can you say that?"

"We found it, didn't we? We dug in the ground and we brought the stuff up with our own hands. Why should we give the kids our oil on a silver platter?"

"We have to think of future generations who may suffer because of our waste and abuse."

"Why?" Clemstone asked me.

"Because," I said weakly.

"Look, do you think they'll appreciate the oil and gas if we just leave it to them? I know kids. The only things that have any meaning for them are those they worked for themselves. What we should say to them is, 'We're using up whatever petroleum we've found in the ground. You want some for yourselves, go out and find it.' That's the kind of challenge that will grab them."

"But you can't use up all our reserves in ONE generation."

"Sure we can. It's OUR oil and gas. Why should we freeze so some rotten kids can have gas to tool around in their cars 20 years from today?"

"There's something wrong with your argument," I told Clemstone, "but I can't put my finger on it."

"There is nothing wrong with it. Each generation should fend for itself. Do you think we'd be where we are today if we depended on handouts of oil from our parents? No sir, we worked to get that petroleum. We drilled holes in Texas and Oklahoma. We sweated for it in the Gulf of Mexico and froze our tails off on the northern slopes of Alaska. We kissed the feet of desert sheiks to get our oil. And, by heaven, when we got it we appreciated it.

"Now Carter wants us to say, 'Here, kiddies. We won't use up the oil so you can have it.' Well, I say 'bulldozer!' You can give them your oil reserves if you want, but I'm not giving them mine."

"You make a strong argument against conservation," I told my friend, "but you forget one thing. You can't take it with you."

"I'm not taking it with me," he yelled. "I'm going to use it right here, today, tomorrow, next week, next year. When I go there won't be a quart of the stuff left."

"What will your kids think of you? What will they say about a father who doesn't leave his kids a quart of oil after he's gone to that big Exxon station in the sky?"

"They'll bless me. They will eventually say, 'Thanks, Dad, for not making it easy on us. Thanks for having the faith in us so we could find our own Alaska slope. You found your oil and we found ours, and our kids can find their own.'"

"I'm not sure that was the message the President was trying to get over to the American people," I said.

"Of course, it wasn't," Clemstone said. "But he doesn't have the confidence in the next generation that I do. He doesn't think they have the moral fiber and the pioneer spirit to go out and drill for their own fuel."

"But suppose it's true that there aren't any more reserves of gas and oil left?"

"If my son came to me and said, 'Dad, I can't find any oil,' do you know what I'd do? I'd hand him a shovel and say, 'Okay, go out and dig for coal.'"

## "MORE SNOW?" IT DOESN'T PAY TO ANGER GOD . . .

People used to talk about the weather, but now they just sit in front of their TV sets and curse it.

Everyone has his own theory why this country has had such horrible winters, One was advanced by a friend named Merkin, and while I don't personally buy it I feel obligated to pass it on.

Merkin believes all the bad weather in the United States began just after Anita Bryant attacked America's gay population.

"God," said Merkin, who is very devout, "got very angry with Miss Bryant when she said He doesn't like gays, and He's been punishing us ever since."

"How do you know this?" I said.

"I talk to God every night," Merkin said. "Right after Miss Bryant's attack He became very upset and decided to teach us all a lesson. You see God loves us all, and He doesn't distinguish between heterosexuals and gay people. As far as He's concerned we're all His children, and when one person says He doesn't like a certain group of people He becomes furious."

"But Anita Bryant talks to God too, and she says God is against homosexuals and believes they're sinners."

"She doesn't speak to the same God I do," Merkin said. "My God is too busy to get involved in people's sex lives. As long as they don't hurt anybody my God believes everyone should be left alone."

"But Anita Bryant has to be speaking to the same God," I protested. "After all there is only one."

"Maybe she's not hearing Him the same way I do. Everyone hears God differently. My message from Him is that there are a lot of straight people who are sinning and are on their way to Hell, and there are a lot of homosexuals who will be allowed in Heaven. What's getting God really sore is that there are more and more people in this country telling other people what He does or does not like. That's why we're having such bad weather."

"Merkin, has God told you this Himself?"

"I'm afraid He has."

"When?"

"The other night just before I went to bed."

"What exactly did He say?"

"He said everyone is using His name these days to plug his or her own cause. People are making fortunes telling the rest of us what's good and what's bad. He says He's being sold on television like soap or toothpaste. What's even worse is that anyone who has a political ax to grind says that God supports him. If there is one thing we know from the Bible it's that God doesn't like people cashing in on His name."

"Did he tell you He was going to drop a pile of snow on the East Coast?"

"Yup."

"What did you do about it?"

"I went out and bought up all the rock salt at Sears Roebuck."

"That was good thinking," I said. "Did God say He was going to continue giving us all these bad winters?"

"He did indeed. He said He was going to keep it up until everyone stopped saying terrible things about their fellow Americans."

"How do I know what God told you is any more valid than what Anita Bryant says God told her?"

"Why don't you ask Him yourself?" Merkin said.

That's exactly what I did. That night as I knelt by my bed I said, "God, did You tell Merkin You were punishing all of us because everyone was using Your name for his or her own purposes?"

There was a pause, and then God said, "Merkin talks too much."

## DISINFORMATION IS DANGEROUS

*The New York Times* has run a series of articles on the CIA and the media. One of the revelations is that the agency had its own "disinformation department" charged with planting false stories in the newspapers through foreign correspondents. The idea is to wreak havoc on an unfriendly country or political system.

The Soviet KGB has a similar department charged with counterfeiting news stories. Therefore I'm sure many Americans are saying, "If the Russians are doing it, why shouldn't we?"

I'll tell you why.

Official Washington gets most of its information from three newspapers: *The Washington Post, The Washington Star* and *The New York Times*. It's true that men in power also get cables from their overseas embassies, but since these are official communications, people in Washington tend to disbelieve them, especially if *The Washington Post* reports otherwise.

Now let us suppose the CIA plants a story in a local Nonomuran newspaper that the Cubans have sent 10,000 military advisers into the bush to help Nonomuran rebels oust the legitimate Nonomuran regime. The object of the plant by the CIA station chief is to get military aid for the Nonomuran prime minister, with whom he plays poker every night.

*The Washington Post* stringer in Casablanca picks up the story in good faith and sends it back to his paper, after checking with the Moroccan CIA station chief to make sure of its credibility.

The next morning it appears on the front page of the *Post*.

The story is read at breakfast by Pentagon chiefs, high State Department officials, CIA people, not clued in that it is a plant, and the White House.

That morning at a White House briefing several correspondents demand to know what President Carter is going to do about the "Nonomuran situation." Jody Powell insists the Administration is "on top of it."

After the briefing he calls up the Pentagon which has been working on contingency plans all morning. The Joint Chiefs are arguing whether to send an aircraft carrier, a military airlift of U.S. marines or a squadron of the American F-4 fighters to Nonomura.

The State Department produces six position papers on the Nonomuran "problem" and three evacuation plans for Americans. All three news networks send camera crews there. The print media are not far behind.

Henry Kissinger, under contract to NBC, gives a pessimistic assessment of the situation on the "Today" show. Barbara Walters gets an exclusive interview with the prime minister of Nonomura, and John Chancellor digs up an opposition leader now working as a waiter in Chicago.

Soviet Ambassador Anatoly Dobrynin is called to the State Department to explain the Kremlin's role in what has now become a "crisis." The Soviets take a hard-line position on Nonomura and threaten to pull out of the SALT talks.

The covert part of the CIA, which doesn't talk to the disinformation branch (because they eat on different shifts in the cafeteria), decides the present prime minister is too weak to fend off the rebel forces. They finance a coup and turn the government over to a military junta led by a Nonomuran Fort Bragg-trained colonel.

President Carter is urged to visit Nonomura on his next five-day trip around the world to show the United States really cares.

The crisis finally abates when another CIA disinformation officer plants a story in a neighboring Ulfoona newspaper that the Cuban military advisers have been withdrawn to Upper Gambling for rest and recreation.

The scenario I have just described is not as farfetched as one would believe. The difference between the Soviets and Americans is that, when it comes to disinformation, the Russian leaders don't believe anything they read in their own papers and therefore have no problems discounting it. On the other hand, American officials in Washington *have* to believe a story in their papers whether it's true or not, because even if they don't the people they work for do.

# III.  The Gas Man Cometh

## "THE OTHER WOMAN"

"I am getting sick of 'The Other Woman' in every famous man's life," my wife said to me one morning as she read about Kay Summersby's revelations of her love affair with General Dwight Eisenhower during World War II.

"Why do you say that?" I asked her.

"Because every biography coming out these days indicates that the real love in a man's life was not his wife, but either his secretary, his housekeeper or his chauffeur. Apparently the publishers won't print a book about a famous person unless there was a secret scandal that nobody knew about before."

"Wives don't sell books," I made the mistake of saying.

"Isn't that *too* bad. Most of the great men in this country owe everything they were to their wives. The wives took care of them when they were sick; they raised their children; they were with them in defeat; they nourished them during their depressions, and when the book comes out it sounds like some woman who spent three hours a week in some hideaway with him was responsible for all his success."

"What you say is true," I told her, trying to recoup some ground, "but you have to look at this not from an historical point of view but a business one. Publishers are in the business of publishing books that will titillate the public. Who is going to buy a biography of a famous personage if he had a happy married life? Mistresses are what best-sellers are made of."

"The whole thing is sick," my wife said. "The people who write these biographies paint the wife as an old hag who is constantly driving her husband to drink. The mistress is always described as a beautiful understanding woman who is tender and kind and willing to listen to the great problems the poor personality faces. Have you ever read a book about an ugly mistress who drove her lover up the wall? Or a lover who is a constant nag? Oh, no. It's always the wife who is portrayed as the heavy—and the mistress as the raving beauty who brought happiness to the great man in the bedroom."

I knew the ice was getting thinner, but for some reason I kept skating on. "Everything you say has validity," I said. "But when people plunk down $10.95 or $12.50 for a great man's life, they don't want to read how he and his wife went bowling every Thursday evening. They also don't want to read about the founding of the United Nations. You have to appeal to their prurient interests. No newspaper is going to pick up a story about the revelations of an ex-President if the headline reads PRESIDENT X NEVER CHEATED ON HIS WIFE WHILE HE WAS IN THE WHITE HOUSE."

"So that's why wives have to take it on the chin? Just to sell books. Does it really matter if someone had a torrid correspondence with some filly in Kansas City? Is that what history is all about?"

"My dear," I said, "you're getting overwrought. People by nature are romantics. There's nothing romantic about a great man who spent his afternoons feeding pigeons in the park with his wife. But put the man in the park with his mistress and everyone suddenly hears violins."

"The whole thing stinks," my wife said. "I'm going to find some great man who never cheated on his wife and write a book about him."

"Good heavens," I said. "I'm your subject. I fit all of your qualifications. I never had a mistress and everything I am or ever hope to be I owe to my wife."

You'll have to admit even President Roosevelt wouldn't have thought of that one.

## THE GAS MAN COMETH

In all the fuss about the gas shortage no one has mentioned the gas man. When I say the gas man, I mean the fellow who comes to your house in a nice uniform and goes down into your cellar to read your gas meter.

For years no one has paid any attention to him. He would ring your doorbell and yell, "Gas man to read your meter!" and you'd let him in and he would disappear downstairs for five minutes, come up again and you'd shout at him rudely, "Shut the door when you leave!"

But now he has become the most important person in the lives of many of us.

Just the other day we were all eating dinner when the doorbell rang. My son answered the ring and came into the dining room, his face white. "It's the gas man. He wants to read our meter."

"Oh Lord," my wife said. "How did he ever find us?"

"Be calm, everybody," I warned. "Pretend nothing has happened. Ask him to come into the dining room."

The gas man came into the dining room carrying his clipboard. "Where's the meter?" he asked.

"Would you like to have some dinner?" I asked in what I hoped was a hearty voice.

"Nope. I've been offered dinner in every house I've been to tonight. I'm stuffed. Just tell me where the basement door is and I'll be out of here."

"You don't want to go down into the basement," my wife said. "It's *so* messy. We'll tell you anything you want to know."

"I have to check your meter," he said.

"I checked it yesterday," I assured him. "It's working fine."

"I have to read it."

"I'll send my son down to read it," I said. "He's great at reading gas meters. Here, have a glass of wine."

"I'm sorry, but I have to read it myself. It will only take a minute."

"Do you have a search warrant?" my wife asked.

He looked surprised. "I don't need a search warrant to read your meter."

"I think you had better check the Constitution. You can't just barge into somebody's house and look at his gas meter," she said.

"Well, if you feel that way, we'll just shut off your gas," he replied.

"It's all right, Mother. The man has not come to do us harm," I said. "I'm sure he won't take advantage of a family that is probably eating its last meal unless our food stamps come through."

"Could you please direct me to the basement?"

I took him to the door and opened it. Then I said, "Be gentle with us. Be good to us."

"Where have I heard that before?" the gas man asked.

"Barbara Walters said it to President Carter on her show," I said.

"Oh yeah," he chuckled, and he went downstairs.

The family all waited in the kitchen.

"Why is he taking so long?" my wife asked nervously, as she twisted the dish towel.

I put my arm around her. "It's all right, dear. The man is only doing his job."

"What kind of person would sneak into somebody's home and inform on them as to how much gas they had used?" she said.

"Hush, he'll hear you and add a couple of hundred cubic feet just for spite."

"I can take him, Dad," my son said. "Let me use karate on him."

"Will you all shut up! He's got us over a barrel. Gas meters never lie."

The man came up whistling.

"Give it to us straight," I said. "We can take it."

"You used 87,900 cubic feet of gas this month," he said.

My wife almost collapsed.

I blanched. "Does the gas company have to know?"

"Yup," he said cheerfully.

My wife gazed at him. "I just pray your mother never finds out what you do for a living."

## FATHER'S DAY FANTASIES

Most people don't believe it, but fathers have fantasies about their children, too. Here are a few I've collected from fathers I've spoken to.

"Hello, Mr. Guilford. This is Nat Lefkowitz of the William Morris Theatrical Agency. I just saw your 12-year-old daughter perform in the school play at Holton Arms as the wicked stepmother in the production of 'Cinderella,' and I was so impressed with her performance that I was wondering if you would consider letting her play the lead in the road show of 'Annie,' the Broadway hit musical. It would pay $2,000 a week and we would, of course, see that you and her mother would be able to travel with her during the run."

"Mr. Minow, this is the chairman of the Coca-Cola Company. Your son's science teacher sent us a formula for a new diet soft drink which we were so impressed with that we would like to buy it from him. Since he is still a minor we thought it best to talk to you. We are prepared to pay $100,000 for the formula and one cent royalty on every bottle sold. I'll give you my home number if you arrive at a decision."

"Hello, is this Mr. Harold Lachman? This is Police Sergeant Kelly at the 33rd Precinct. We have your son here. Before you get upset, let me explain that he dove into the river fully clothed and saved an 8-month-old baby from drowning. I was wondering if you would bring a dry set of clothes to the police station for him?"

"Dad, I just wanted to tell you that you were right, and I was wrong. I'll never question your judgment again."

"Mr. Wanamaker. This is Dr. Winstead. Our laboratory made a terrible mistake on the pregnancy test and got the rabbits mixed up. Your daughter is suffering from nothing more than a bad stomachache. I'm terribly sorry to have gotten you and your wife all upset—but you know how those things are."

"Dad, I'd like you to meet my new boyfriend, Arnold Rockefeller. He doesn't drink or smoke pot and is now working for his Uncle David in the bank. Because of his hours, he has to bring me home no later than eleven o'clock at night. Arnold is interested in scouting. He has never had a traffic ticket for speeding. He loves to play golf and tennis. He would like you and Mom to visit his family at Newport this summer. They could send their private plane for you any time you would like to do it."

"Hello, my name is Patrick O'Brien and I'm a scout for the Notre Dame football team. I just saw your son out there throw a football. I was wondering if he would be willing to go to Notre Dame on a four-year athletic scholarship. I can't promise you that he'll play first string in his freshman year, but from what I've seen so far, I would be amazed if the coach would want to keep him on the bench."

"Dad, I know this may not be the time to talk about it, but I just wanted to reassure you that when you retire I have every intention of supporting you in your old age. I'm only starting out in business, but I've set aside a part of my salary for a trust fund for you and Mom. As I rise up the ladder of success, I will put more and more in it. I hope you will be able to live on the interest from the fund, but I've set it up so you can touch the principal any time you and Mom want to take a trip or buy something. It's just my small way of saying 'Thank you for everything you've done.' "

"Mr. Melton, this is *Time* magazine calling. We're doing a cover story on your daughter, Jeannette, who has been named 'Person of the Year,' and we were wondering if one of our reporters could come out and interview you for it?"

"Mr. Sanford, this is the White House calling. The President would like to know if it would be all right for your daughter, Nancy, to sleep in the tree house with Amy overnight?"


*INDIANS!*

As if Martha's Vineyard didn't have enough trouble trying to figure out whether or not to secede from the United States, it is now faced with another problem: INDIANS.

Yes, the Indians who were here way before the white man want their land back, and obviously everyone who owns a house on the Island is somewhat nervous about it. Rather than struggle with weapons the Indians have chosen the white man's most powerful medicine—the law.

The legal basis for the suit is the Indian Nonintercourse Act of 1790, a treaty with the United States that said no land could be sold or taken from the Indians without the specific approval of Congress.

(Unfortunately, most home owners on the Island thought the Act had to do with not having sexual relations with Indians.) The Act was ignored through the years until recently, when tribes in Maine and Massachusetts claimed their land had been illegally taken from them and they wanted it back.

In the case of Martha's Vineyard the Indians want Gay Head, Cranberry Acres and Herring Creek. People on other parts of the Island are willing to give up this land, since they don't own it. But they fear once the Indians get their appetites whetted they may go for the whole Island.

It was not long ago that everyone was glad to see a Wampanoag Indian. But lately if one shows up, particularly with a lawyer, the cry goes out, "INDIANS!" and everyone draws their station wagons in a circle.

I didn't believe it myself until I was sitting on Bill Styron's porch in Vineyard Haven drinking a gin and tonic.

An Indian came riding up on his Moped and Styron gathered the entire family and his guests into the house. We each took a window.

The Indian carrying the flag of the Vineyard Haven Yacht Club marched up to the porch.

"I come in peace," he said. He gave Styron a pipe of grass and the two men smoked.

"This is nice land you've got," the Indian said.

"It's really not a good place," Styron said nervously. "There are mosquitoes and hornets and the wind blows the roof off the house every winter. The taxes are very high and our cesspool overflows twice a week."

"My ancestors used to fish from this very beach."

"There must be some mistake," Styron said. "The fishing is lousy. We haven't caught a minnow in fifteen years. Now if you really want nice land you ought to see Kingman Brewster's property. If I were an Indian that's the place I'd sue for."

"It's nice?"

"This land can't hold a candle to it."

"Where is it?"

"I'll drive you over," Styron said hurriedly.

Kingman Brewster, who is now on home leave from being Ambassador to the Court of St. James, told the Indian that the water in front of his house was filled with man-eating sharks. "If you're really looking for a good house you ought to go over to Edgartown. Walter Cronkite has the perfect place for an Indian reservation. He even has room for a tennis court. I'll drive you over."

Kingman and the Indian drove over to Cronkite's house in Edgartown. But someone had tipped off Walter and Cronkite was standing at the entrance of his dirt road. "You can't go any further," Cronkite said. "There's quicksand all the way to my dock. Besides, the whole family has malaria."

"I didn't know there was malaria on the Island," the Indian said.

"It's just around my property. I must have brought the mosquitoes with me when I sailed back from Panama last week. You'd hate it around here, and your people would die like flies."

"That's a pity," the Indian said. "We were hoping to find something close to town so we could walk to our lawyer's office."

"I know the perfect spot," Walter said. "Barbara Walters rented it two summers ago. It not only has fresh water and grazing land but the last time I was there it had herds of buffalo as far as the eye could see."


*HELP!!!!!!!!!!!*

What happened was that a few years ago people started giving us houseplants instead of cut flowers. The children gave their mother a palm tree for Mother's Day; they gave me a philodendron for Father's day and three dieffenbachias for Christmas.

My wife put them in the living room. Then relatives brought a snake plant a few months later, and a friend presented us with a fatsia plant which my wife put in the library to help "cheer" it up.

She dutifully watered them and talked to them and they started to grow . . . and grow . . . and grow. Then she decided the living room looked bare and bought some grape ivy which she wrapped around the fake balcony and some aspidistras which she placed in the corner near the television set.

Someone sent us a schefflera for an anniversary, and friends who have a farm in the Shenandoah trucked in two spider plants which were put in the dining room. A future son-in-law presented us with three rubber plants, and on my birthday I was given a potted elephant's-ears all of my own. My daughter, who was going away to college, asked us if we would keep her weeping fig plants while she was away, and someone, I can't remember who, sent us a box of screw pines.

The house looked green and lovely for a short while. But then a strange thing happened. The plants kept getting larger and larger. First they took over the living room. We realized this when the man who came to fix the TV set got lost and was never heard from again. My wife wanted me to search for him, but I said to her, "Are you kidding? That living room's a jungle."

One Saturday I bought a machete and tried to chop a trail through the living room to my library. But after four hours I realized it was hopeless. The more I hacked away the faster the houseplants grew. We closed off the living room.

We were sitting in the dining room one evening when I noticed I couldn't see anyone at the table. It was an eerie feeling as I shouted through the palm leaves: "Is anybody there?" I thought I heard a voice coming from the end of the table saying, "You Tarzan, me Jane," but it could have been the wind. I looked up and saw one of my children sitting in a branch of the palm tree. "What are you doing up there? Sit down and eat your dinner."

"Where can I sit?" she wanted to know.

"In your chair," I said.

"I can't find my chair," she said.

"Do you think they'll ever send a rescue ship to find us?"

That night I said to my wife, "We've got to move out of the dining room. It's not safe to eat there any more."

"They're only plants," she said.

"What about scorpions and snakes? You can't have that much foliage without scorpions."

We put some defoliant down between the dining room and kitchen and started to eat all our meals in the kitchen. Occasionally, a kangaroo vine or the grape ivy tried to sneak in, but I kept an ax by my side and every once in a while I chopped off a length of it before it crawled to our food.

My doctor warned me to stay out of the library unless I wanted to take a gamble on catching malaria or yellow fever.

Despite our efforts to keep the plants from getting into the kitchen a yucca tree crushed the door down and in a matter of a week the kitchen was a forest.

One evening I lost my wife for four hours, and only by luck stumbled over her next to the Waring blender. Worse, both the dog and the cat had become wild and we decided to free them to live the life of their ancestors, before they had been domesticated by man.

Two weeks later we moved everyone up to the second floor of

the house but the plants followed us. At first we kept them at bay by starting small forest fires and removing the staircase, but the vines began climbing the walls.

I am now writing this from our attic on the third floor. If anyone reads this please send help! We have enough food to last us one more week. Tell the helicopter pilot we have a gray mansard roof. That's the only thing he can see from the air.

## CONVERSATION-STOPPERS

Every once in a while I provide my readers with conversation-stoppers that they can use to attract attention at cocktail or dinner parties or family gatherings. They are packaged so you can cut them out and stuff them in your wallet.

Here are just a few that are guaranteed to make everyone turn in your direction.

"I saw the first Nixon TV show and I don't have any opinion on it."

"I bought a pound of coffee for $1.98 this morning."

"Amy Carter hit my son in the head with a book yesterday."

"Joe Califano's cook gave me the recipe."

"My daughter married a doctor who makes $300,000 a year from Medicaid."

"I'm related to Alex Haley through Kunte Kinte's daughter."

"Spiro Agnew has asked me to be his campaign manager."

"My 18-year-old son was given a citation by the mayor for safe driving."

"I just got my electricity bill and it was $25.90."

"The Concorde flies over our house and the noise lulls us to sleep."

"My daughter sells carnations for Rev. Moon at the airport."

"I'm a housewife."

"The CIA rented our home for the summer."

"I called my college son collect the other night."

"The tree surgeon came out to the house the other day and told me all my trees were healthy."

"My husband is in Charles Colson's Bible class."

"Farrah Fawcett Majors hates me because I style my hair the same way she does."

"My broker is E.F. Hutton and he said he's as perplexed about the state of the stock market as everybody else on Wall Street."

"I just had a booster for my swine flu shot."

"A guy rammed into my car three days ago and his insurance company sent me a check yesterday."

"My nephew was the first pupil in Public School No. 35 to be spanked since the Supreme Court made it permissable."

"My priest asked me to be best man at his wedding."

"Would anyone like to see a photograph of my grandson taken by Margaret Trudeau?"

"I went to the King Tut exhibit in Chicago and it was all junk."

"George couldn't come tonight. He's exhausted after capping the oil blowout off Norway last week."

"My wife deals in commodity futures."

"We hated 'Rocky.'"

"Warren Werthheimer had a sex operation and her tennis is still lousy."

"My niece got thrown out of West Point for cheating."

"I think the ozone is overrated."

"David Frost wants to interview me."

"They're tearing down the movie theater on Main Street and building a nuclear power plant in its place."

"Tongsun Park used to be in our car pool."

"I filled out my IRS Form in 20 minutes."

"My secretary doesn't know how to type or take shorthand."

"Did anyone read the article about Anita Bryant in Hustler magazine?"

"Idi Amin is coming to my son's bar mitzvah."


## THE NIXON SHOW, PART I

It's very hard to get the family together these days. We only seem to gather for graduations, weddings and when Nixon goes on television.

Last week it was our turn to have everyone over to the house because Cousin Edith had us over to her house when Nixon resigned. We all gathered around the TV set—Cousin Edith, Uncle Harold, Aunt Alice and Granny.

Granny is the only one in the family who is still 1,000 percent for Nixon. She thinks the press drove him from office and she doesn't mind saying it to me. "You and Robert Redford and Dustin Hoffman are responsible for that poor man being driven into exile."

I keep explaining to her that it wasn't just Robert Redford and Dustin Hoffman who did it. If Jason Robards hadn't backed them up they would have never been able to do it.

Anyway, after dinner my wife gave each person a box of Kleenex and we waited for the show to begin.

As it opened up, Granny said incredulously, "Oh, my goodness. He's developed an English accent."

"That isn't Richard Nixon," I explained to her. "That's David Frost."

"What's an Englishman doing interviewing Richard Nixon on American television?" she wanted to know.

"Frost offered Nixon $600,000 plus 10 percent of the profits to appear on TV."

"Nixon would never take money for appearing on television." Granny said. "That would be checkbook journalism."

"Well, he did."

"Hush," said Cousin Edith, "or we'll never know the truth about Watergate."

Frost started to ask about the tapes and what was said on them.

Nixon replied that everyone could put their own interpretation on them, but he could categorically say he did nothing to obstruct justice.

"I believe him," Uncle Harold said. "I never did before, but a man wouldn't go on television for $600,000 and lie."

"Why not?" I asked.

"Because if the FCC found out about it, they could take the station's license away."

Frost kept zeroing in on what Nixon said to Haldeman, Ehrlichman and Colson about the hush money.

Granny started to get mad. "What right does an Englishman have to ask him questions about American hush money?"

"He's only doing his job, Granny," I said. "There does seem to be a discrepancy between what Nixon said and what he really meant."

When Nixon was asked what was on the 18½ minutes of tape that had been erased, he said that it was merely a discussion between himself and Haldeman on a public relations offensive to counteract the political slopover of Watergate.

"I believe him," Cousin Harold said. "What else could they have possibly talked about?"

As the show went on. Nixon switched from details to what was in his heart. He said if he had any fault it was that he wasn't a good butcher.

"I didn't even know Nixon was a butcher," Granny said.

"That's just a figure of speech," I told her. "He was quoting a prime minister of Great Britain who said a leader has to be a good butcher."

Nixon admitted he lied to the American people, but they were little lies and he did it to protect Ehrlichman and Haldeman because he didn't want to do to them what Eisenhower did to Sherman Adams.

"I believe him," Uncle Harold said. "The man was only trying to protect his loved ones."

At the end of the show Nixon said he would never grovel before the American people, and if he had made mistakes they were of the heart and not the head. It was at this moment that everyone grabbed for their Kleenex boxes.

Granny was the most moved, of course. Finally, she pulled herself together and said, "Well, I hope Robert Redford and Dustin Hoffman are satisfied. They not only destroyed the best President we ever had but they made him go on television to bare his soul to an Englishman."

All Uncle Harold could say between sobs was "I believe it. I believe it. I believe it."

## HOW SAD IT IS!

I think for me the saddest thing about Watergate is that members of the old Nixon gang have turned against each other. Who would have ever dreamed that on the David Frost show former President

Nixon would have implicated John Ehrlichman and Bob Halde-man, whom he considered his "sons," in the coverup of a third-rate burglary?

Who would have thought that John Ehrlichman would write a fiction novel based on President Nixon showing him in such an un-favorable light? How could anyone have predicted that Bob Halde-man, one of the great White House stonewallers, would let down his hair and blow the whistle on Nixon, Charles Colson and Henry Kissinger?

Whatever they did in the past I always said to my wife, "At least you have to admire them for their loyalty to each other."

I always dreamed the Nixon crowd would meet together on the Tenth Anniversary of Watergate and have a nostalgic reunion, re-living those wonderful days when they were all fighting in the White House bunker. They would kid each other about putting on weight and tell outrageous lies about their Watergate War experi-ences. It would be a scene out of "White Christmas," with John Dean calling up everybody and saying, "Let's go out to San Cle-mente and show the old man that, while the rest of the country may have forgotten him, those of us who fought with him still really care."

I could see them gathering on the lawn overlooking the blue Pacific and everyone would break into "Hail to the Chief" as Nix-on came out in the suit he wore when he was President. There would be tears in his eyes as he looked at those familiar faces, and then he'd say, "I want you all to shape up. I've never seen such a bunch of sloppy White House aides in my life."

Then they would all sit around the pool drinking California wine and listening to the tapes, once again thinking back on those won-derful days when it was "us" against "them."

But apparently the reunion will never come off. And once again the Nixon Administration people have the media to blame.

If the newspapers, magazines, TV and book publishers hadn't dumped all that money on them, this great group of honorable men might never have ratted on each other.

The tragedy of post-Watergate is that in order to pay their law-yers, all those involved in the break-in and the coverup had to go their own way to make their stories worth the megabucks their agents had gotten for them.

It is sad for all of us who sat on the sidelines to see these men who went through so much together now at each other's throats.

Those of us who thought that Watergate was behind us now realize that the wounds are too deep and the book advances too high for any of the people involved to stick together.

My wife has taken it harder than I have. When the Haldeman excerpts from his book were printed, she said tearfully, "How could he have done it to Nixon?"

I said, "How could Nixon have done it to him?"

Then she said, "How could Colson have done it to Haldeman?"

And I said, "How could Dean have done it to all of them?"

Perhaps it's futile for people who weren't there to speculate why these fine, outstanding men would turn against each other at this stage of the game. My own theory is that it never would have happened if Checkers had been alive.

## SPRING BREAK

There was a time when the college "spring break" took place during Easter vacation. Parents could plan on having all their children home at the same time. This cut down the cost of food and made it possible for the owners of the house to make appropriate plans to handle all the refugees at the same time.

But this has all changed and now each school in the country has its spring break at a different time, which means you wind up with one or more children at home any time from January to June.

This is how it goes now.

Mrs. Baker tells her husband: "George is coming home for spring break two weeks after Easter."

"When does Ellen go back?"

"Her spring break ends on Good Friday."

"She's been here for a month."

"I know, they've had a longer spring break than usual because the school ran out of gas."

"When does Marsha get her spring break?"

"She had hers in January. She'll be home in April."

"Does she get two spring breaks?"

"No, she'll be home in April for the summer. Her school closes the day after Easter."

"What are we going to do with her in April? Our summer doesn't start until July."

"I have no idea. All her friends will still be in school and she'll probably drive us nuts."

"When is Freddy coming home?"

"He arrived last night. He said his spring break ends May 15th."

"What are we going to do with him?"

"He wants to go skiing in Colorado, but his girl's spring break starts in two weeks and he also wants to see her. He hasn't made up his mind what to do."

"I can't afford to send him skiing," Mr. Baker said, "and also pay his tuition at school."

"He's not sure he wants to go back to school after his spring break. He says he has only two more weeks before the summer vacation and it hardly seems worth it."

"Then why doesn't he get a job?"

"He says if he gets a job and then decides to go back to school he'll be cheated out of his spring break."

"What about Sarah?"

"I thought she was coming home next weekend, but it turns out she has the choice of a spring break or going with her class to Heidelberg. She decided to go to Heidelberg."

"Well, that's a break."

"The trip costs $2,000. She needs the check by Thursday."

"I'm not going to lay out $2,000 for her to go to Heidelberg."

"She says if you don't her teacher will flunk her in German."

"It was my understanding that when we sent our kids off to college we would see them at Christmas, Easter and in July and August. I think that's enough for any parents."

"Well, don't get mad at me. I don't make up the holiday schedules. Oh, by the way, your nephew Jody called this morning."

"What did he want?"

"He said his spring break starts on April 25th and he wanted to know if we could put him up with three friends when he comes to visit Washington."

"Wasn't it great," Mr. Baker said, "when all the kids lived at home and went to high school and we never saw them at all?"

## UNREALITY OF TV

Dr. Heinrich Applebaum recently completed a study on the effects of television on children. In his case, though, he wasn't concerned with violence, but how television gives children a false sense of reality.

Dr. Applebaum told me, "The greatest danger of television is that it presents a world to children that doesn't exist, and raises expectations that can never be fulfilled."

"I don't understand, Doctor," I said.

"Well, let me cite one example. Have you ever seen a television show where a person in an automobile doesn't immediately find a parking place on the very first try?"

"Come to think of it," I said, "I haven't."

"Not only is there always a parking spot available but the driver doesn't even have to back into it. There are *two* parking spaces available whenever someone in a TV show needs one. Children are being led to believe that when they grow up they will always be able to find a parking place when and where they want it. Can you imagine the trauma when they discover that in real life you can drive around a block for three hours and still not find a place to put your car?"

"I never thought of it but it's true. What else do they show on television which gives a distorted picture of the real world?"

"Have you noticed that whenever a character walks out of a restaurant or office building or apartment and says to the doorman, 'Get me a taxi,' the taxi immediately arrives? Millions of children are under the impression that all a doorman has to do is blow his whistle and a taxi will be there. I have never seen a show where the doorman has said, 'I'm sorry. I can't get you a taxi. You better take the bus.' "

"Of course," I said. "I never knew before what bothered me about those TV action programs, but now I do. There is always a yellow taxi waiting offscreen."

"Now," said Applebaum, "have you ever said to a taxi driver, 'Follow that car and don't lose him'?"

"Not really."

"Well, if you had, the driver would have told you to blow it out your ear. No taxi driver is in a mood to follow another car because that means he's going to get involved. But on TV every cabdriver looks as if he'd like nothing better to do than to drive 90 miles an hour through a rain-swept street trying to keep up with a carful of hoods. And the worst thing is that the kids believe it.''

''What else have you discovered?''

''Kids have a perverted sense of what emergency wards of hospitals are really like. On TV shows they take a kid to an emergency ward and four doctors come rushing down to bandage his leg. In a real life situation the kid would be sitting on the bench for two hours before he even saw an intern. On TV there always happens to be a hospital bed available when a kid needs it. What the kids in this country don't know is that sometimes you have to wait three days to get a hospital bed and then you have to put a cash deposit of $500 down before they give it to you.''

Applebaum said the cruelest hoax of all is when TV shows a lawyer defending someone innocent of a crime.

''On the screen the lawyer spends day and night digging up the evidence to clear his client. In real life the lawyer says to the defendant, 'Look, I've got 20 minutes. Tell me your story and then I'll plead you guilty and make a deal with the DA.' In real life the defendant might say, 'But I'm innocent.' The lawyer would say, 'So what? I can't afford to find that out. I'm not Perry Mason.'''

''Then what you're saying, Dr. Applebaum, is that it isn't the violence on TV but the fantasy that is doing harm to children.''

''Exactly. Even the commercials are taking their toll. Children are led to believe that when they grow up if they use a certain mouthwash they'll find the mate of their dreams. When they don't find him or her after gargling all night, they go into a tailspin and many of them never come out of it.

''What do you think is the biggest fear little girls have?''

''I have no idea.''

''That someday when they get married their husbands will have ring around the collar.''

''What about boys?''

''Boys worry that they'll only go around once in life and they won't have all the gusto out of their beer that they deserve.''

## FOR YOUR VACATION PLEASURE

The problem after a Christmas vacation is that parents of college students can never be quite sure if their children had a good time or not.

I've taken a leaf from Holiday Inns, Howard Johnson motels and Hilton to solve this problem. In many motel and hotel rooms there is a form the management asks the guests to fill out regarding the service of the establishment.

As a public service I am printing a similar form that parents can mail to their children at school to find out if they were satisfied with their vacation visit. Just clip it out and stick it in with the next check you send to your loved ones.

Dear Guest,

In order to improve our service at_____(write in address) we are asking you to fill out the following form. Your answers will help us in our desire to improve our guest operation and to guarantee that you will come back again. A stamped return envelope is enclosed for your convenience.

1. Were you happy with the hotel service you received from your mother?_____. Your father?_____. Other members of the family?_____. If you weren't please tell us where you felt they let you down in the blank space on the back of this form.

2. Were you satisfied with the meals? Please rate them as (a) Excellent  (b) Good  (c)  Fair  or (d) Poor.

3. Could your friends find everything they wanted in the icebox? Yes_____. No_____. Was there enough beer, wine and liquor available for them when they dropped by? Were they satisfied with their accommodations when they decided to sleep over? Yes_____. No_____. Were there any complaints about the room service?

4. Did you find the house quiet enough when you slept late in the morning? Were you disturbed by anyone coming into your room asking when you were getting up? Was your room cleaned up satisfactorily while you were in the kitchen having breakfast?

5. How did you find the laundry service? Were there always fresh clothes in your drawers and did our staff pick up the dirty ones every day which you threw on the floor?

6. Was there enough hot water for your bath or shower? Did you find your father's hairbrush when you needed it? Were you

happy with the brand of cosmetics you borrowed from your mother's dresser? Did you have enough clean towels every day? Did your mother pick up the dirty ones after you bathed, in a satisfactory and cheerful manner?

7. What was your opinion of our limousine service? Was there a car always available when you needed it or did you have to wait until a member of the family completed an errand? Did the doorman park your car or did you have to do it yourself?

8. How would you rate the help? (a) friendly and on the job; (b) willing to drop everything to resolve a request, no matter how demanding; (c) surly and unco-operative. In this respect were you made to feel at home, or did you get the impression the help would be happy when your vacation was over?

9. Did you find our cashier co-operative and willing to dispense funds at any time of the day or night? Or did he hesitate to give you cash when you needed it?

10. Finally, did we at Hotel_____ (fill in your name) provide you with the school vacation you dreamed of? Did it live up to your expectations? Will you come back as our guest next Easter? How many people do you expect to bring with you? Would you recommend us to your friends?

Our existence depends on your patronage and our only purpose is to make you happy. If we have done so we're very pleased. If we have failed in any way, no matter how small, we would like to hear from you. Remember: "Our Casa Is Your Casa."

> Sincerely yours,
> (Name of Mother),
> Housekeeper and Director of Catering
> (Name of Father)
> Manager and Chairman of the Board

## A FESTIVE MEAL

Holiday eating can be divided between large festive lunches and dinners, and meals served during football games. The football fare has been largely ignored as the food pages of newspapers and magazines devote all their space to how to stuff a goose, how to baste a turkey or how to roast a rib.

And yet football eating is far more important to the welfare of the family, and has much greater significance for most people during this merriest time of year.

Here is the perfect football TV menu, one that has been handed down in my family through the generations.

For appetizers we always have a selection of potato chips, in a low glass bowl. (We disdain Pringles which come in a tube with each one the same size. We want a potato chip assortment so our guests will be surprised every time they put one in their mouths.)

Next to the potato chips should be placed a large deep dish (four inches) of salted peanuts. The peanuts should be shelled, otherwise there will be a mess all over the living room as people in their excitement toss the shells all around.

Another hors d'oeuvre which we traditionally serve is M&M's, a colorful candy that looks like medicine pills. The beauty of M&M's during a football game is the surprise factor. You never know whether you're going to get one with chocolate inside or one with a nut. Also, you can hold at least 40 in your hand at one time while watching the tube.

All right, that should take care of the appetizers. In some families the lady of the house adds a guacamole or an onion dip for the potato chips, but very few football watchers have time to dip, and usually get furious at their wives and girlfriends for serving something they can't grab with their fingers without taking their eyes from the set.

The main course of a football dinner is always the traditional can of beer. In order to prepare the beer, you place it in the icebox for six hours so it will be properly chilled. The beer is then put on a tray and brought into the living room. The lady serving the beer must be very careful in carrying it into the living room or den, as the slightest shaking of it will cause the beer to foam when opened.

The serving of beer during a football game can either make or break the traditional football dinner. If the lady of the house walks in front of the set when placing the tray on the coffee table she can ruin the holiday spirit she has worked so hard to achieve. ALWAYS serve the beer BEHIND the viewers and make yourself as unobtrusive as possible. Never say, as you place the beer on the table, "What's the score?" or "Who are the men in the white jerseys?"

After the main course of beer is served—we prefer cans in our house as we find pouring bottled beer into a glass messy—you can serve the traditional condiments that go with it such as buttered popcorn, Fritos and bacon-flavored chips. This should be followed by pistachio nuts, hard candy and Hershey kisses.

For dessert I recommend Poppycock, a unique popcorn covered with molasses and mixed with walnuts. It is absolutely perfect for a third down situation when the ball is on the fifteen-yard line and it's four yards to go for a first down. Poppycock comes in a can so you can keep it on your lap and not have to reach for it during a crucial play.

The thing to remember while serving the traditional TV football dinner is that, while beer is served as the main course, it can also be drunk with appetizers, dessert and as an after-dinner drink. The lady of the house must always make sure the empty cans are removed and replaced with full ones while the game is in progress. The best way to spoil this nutritious festive occasion is to make one of the TV spectators go to the icebox and get his own beer.

When it's done right, the TV football dinner can be the highlight of the holiday season and one every man and male child will remember for years to come.

## TOO MANY HOSPITAL BEDS

Hospitals are getting more efficient these days and have cut down the time it takes to get a bed for you. The reason for this is that there is a surplus of beds, and in order to survive a hospital must keep them full. This is good and it's bad.

I went to visit a sick friend at the hospital the other day. I had to go to the information booth which also handled the admitting procedure.

Before I could ask what room my friend was in the lady took down my name, age, occupation, filled out a slip and rang a bell. I was just about to tell her I was only visiting a friend when two attendants arrived with a wheelchair, placed me in it and started pushing me down the hall.

"I'm not sick," I yelled. "I'm just looking for a friend."

"When he comes," one attendant said, "we'll send him up to your room."

"He's here already," I protested.

"Good. Once we have you in bed he can come up and see you."

I found myself in a small room marked "Private. Check With Nurse Before Knocking." The attendant stripped me, gave me a weird, short nightgown that tied in the back, a water pitcher and turned on the television set hanging from the ceiling. "If you need anything, press the button."

"I want my clothes back."

"Oh, you can trust us," the attendant said. "Even if the worst happens we will see that your widow gets everything."

I was trying to figure how to escape out the window when Dr. Ward came in with several of his students.

"Thank heavens you finally came," I said.

"It hurts that bad?" he asked.

"It doesn't hurt at all," I retorted.

Dr. Ward looked worried. "If you don't feel any pain that means it's much more serious than we thought. Where did it originally hurt?"

"It didn't hurt anywhere."

Dr. Ward nodded sympathetically and turned to his students: "This is the toughest kind of patient to handle because he refuses to acknowledge that he is ill. He will never be well again until he gets over the delusion that he is in perfectly good health. Since he won't tell us where it hurts we'll have to do exploratory surgery to find out for ourselves."

"But I don't want an operation."

Dr. Ward nodded. "No one does, but wouldn't it be better to get it out now rather than later?"

"There's nothing to get out! Everything is in order."

"If it was," said Dr. Ward, writing on a chart, "you wouldn't be here."

The next morning they shaved all the hair off my chest and refused to give me breakfast.

Two attendants arrived and placed me on a rolling stretcher. The head nurse walked along beside me. A minister brought up the rear. I looked for help from anywhere. There was no one.

Finally, I was wheeled into the operating room. "Wait," I said. "I have something to tell you. I'm deathly sick but I HAVE NO

MEDICAL INSURANCE! I can't even pay for the anesthesiologist."

The anesthesiologist turned off the valve on his machine. "And I have no money to pay the doctor," I said. The doctor started to put his instruments away.

Then I looked at the head nurse. "I can't even pay for the room."

Before I knew it I was back in my civilian clothes and out on the street, thrown there by the two attendants who had first wheeled me in.

I went back to ask what room my friend was in but the admitting clerk looked at me coldly and said, "We don't ever want to see you in this hospital again. You're sick."


## BUT HE WASN'T INVITED!

These are desperate times for newspaper people in Washington. The most we can come up with around the holiday season is that the Carter people refuse to come out of the closet and mingle with the Establishment in this town. The few times they have come out, they've made social faux pas of such proportions that their remarks cannot be printed in a family newspaper.

There are two sides to every story and while, under ordinary circumstances, it is not the job of a paper to print both, I think the Carter people should be heard.

I received a telephone call last week from one of President Carter's speech writers who said, "The reason we never get out in Washington is that we've never been invited anywhere."

"I find that hard to believe."

"It's true," he insisted. "The only people that ever get invited to an Establishment affair are Ham Jordan and Jody Powell. I don't think the Carter Administration should be judged on the table manners of these two people when there are over 500 of us working in the White House who are dying to go to a Georgetown salon."

"But would you be up to mingling with the Washington Establishment?" I asked him.

"You bet I am. My wife and I have been studying etiquette since we came to town. We have pictures of Evans and Novak and Joe Kraft, and Clark Clifford and Averell Harriman and Liz Taylor on our walls, just so we can memorize their faces in case we ever run into them. But so far we haven't got the call."

"What about clothes? Do you have the right clothes for an Establishment party?" I asked.

"The best. We took all our money from the last White House pay raise and invested it in every type of outfit you can think of. We're even prepared to go fox-hunting if the right invitation comes along."

"And still you've struck out?" I said.

"I would say so. We only got four Christmas cards this year and three were from merchants we do business with."

"And the fourth?"

"It was from President Carter."

"Well, you certainly can't consider him Establishment," I told my friend. "It seems to me that except for Ham and Jody everyone in the White House has kept such a low profile that you're uninvitable."

"What exactly does that mean?" he wanted to know.

"If you were invited to one of our soirees no one there would know who you were, and you'd just be taking up a place that could be filled by someone from the Ford Administration."

"How are we going to get known if no one ever invites us out?" he said angrily.

"Don't get upset," I told him. "It's not your fault. But you see Washington operates socially on the revolving door principle. You go into the White House and then when your man loses, you go into a law firm or become a lobbyist, and then after four or eight years you're back in the government again. That's how it works.

"When Joe Califano worked for President Johnson no one ever heard of him and he was never invited anywhere. Then he went into law practice, and finally he came back as secretary of HEW, and now he's very much in demand. But it took ten years for him to make it in this town.

"You can't expect to break bread with Joe Alsop just because you've been working in the White House for a year."

"All right," he said. "Then why do they keep writing that we Carter people are unsociable?"

"What would you write if you had a deadline and had to get to the British Embassy for Christmas carols and egg nog by eight o'clock?''

## TO BE READ ON CHRISTMAS DAY

If you weren't sure what to get your mother and father this Christmas, perhaps you could read them this column, which I'm sure would mean more than any gift you could have bought in a store.

"Please, dear Mother, why don't you go into the living room and watch television with Father, while we, your devoted children, will clear the table, and do the dishes, and see that all the leftovers are put away in the icebox, so you will not have to cook tomorrow.''

"Do not worry, Father, we will clean up all the mess around the tree, including the torn wrapping paper and cartons and boxes and other trash. It is our responsibility because, after all, we were the recipients of all these wonderful presents.''

"Mother, I want you to know that everything you bought me fits perfectly, and you will not have to go back and stand in line on Tuesday and exchange any of your purchases. You are indeed a wonderful person for getting not only our sizes right but selecting the perfect colors for each item of clothing.''

"Father, Brother has asked to play with the trains you bought me for Christmas and I, of course, said I would be very happy if he would. He in turn has urged me to take his radio-controlled racing car outside and use it as long as the batteries hold out. Father, I wish to thank you and Mama for giving me such a wonderful younger brother to share my Christmas gifts. He is a joy to be with at this time of year.''

"Dearest Mother, do not fret because the beds have not been made and it is four o'clock in the afternoon. Although we have plans to see our friends, we shall cancel them so we can clean up our rooms. Why don't you relax here by the fire with a hot toddy while we proceed to bring some order out of this tumultuous day.''

"No, Father, I will not need the car this afternoon. Why don't you and Mother go for a drive on this festive day and see some of the lovely decorations? Please do not protest. A son does not take the family's only mode of transportation on Christmas Day and leave his parents in the lurch. I shall be very happy to take the bus and even transfer twice in the icy cold so I may visit my girlfriend on the other side of town."

"No, Mother, I shall not be going out tonight. Christmas should be spent with one's family, and I wish to share these happy hours with my wonderful relatives who will stop by to visit us today. I hope *all* my aunts and uncles and cousins come so that I may wish them a Merry Christmas, and they may do the same to me. We are lucky to have so many people related to us, and I couldn't stand the thought of being away for an hour knowing they were here."

"Dearest Father, although I am home on vacation, I will not need any money as I managed to save several hundred dollars from my allowance in anticipation of my visit for the holidays. Although you have never deprived me of anything during the holiday season, it is my belief that when one goes off to college one should try to be independent of one's parents, particularly when it comes to asking for money just to have a good time."

"Mother, I have canceled my trip to Florida with my sorority sisters next week so I can stay home and take down the Christmas tree and put away all the decorations."

"Father and Mother, would either one of you have any objection to our giving all our hi-fi speakers and rock records to the Salvation Army or Goodwill Industries? The noise seems to be interfering with our homework, and we don't want anything to hurt our grades in the upcoming year."

## WHO NEEDS A COMPUTER?

There is a great deal of publicity these days about the advent of the home computer.

Futurists are predicting that in a few years there will be a computer in everyone's home which will store all sorts of useful information in its memory, such as birthdays, anniversaries, bank balances and inventories of household effects.

The computers will also be used to turn on lights, turn off furnaces and adjust air conditioners, open and shut doors and record what time your children come in at night.

When it comes to information retrieval I doubt if there really is the market out there that home computer manufacturers think there is. The American wife has a memory far superior to any computer, at least she does in my house.

My wife can recall things in seconds that I have forgotten for years.

An example: The other night we were having a discussion over some remark I had made about an attractive lady sitting next to me at a dinner party.

I said, "I don't see anything wrong in admiring a pretty girl at a dinner as long as you don't make a pass at her."

"That's just the point. You can't admire a pretty girl without making a pass at her."

This got me really angry and I said, "When have I ever made a pass at a girl at a dinner party?"

"September 6, 1963, at the Stevens' house. You were sitting next to Hope Lange and as the chocolate soufflé with the coconut-meringue cookies was being served you put your arm around her. I believe it was 10:14 P.M."

"Are you sure it was chocolate soufflé? I thought that night Liz Stevens served a vanilla mousse with fresh raspberry sauce."

"Don't avoid the issue," my wife said. "And what about midnight, June 12, 1957, when we were in Paris at the Crazy Horse Saloon and you made a fool of yourself dancing to 'I'll Never Smile Again' with that lady in the green-beaded dress and pale-green chiffon scarf and gold shoes and dyed blonde hair."

"You remember *that?*" I said.

"She was 5-feet-5, weighed 115 pounds, spoke with a Swedish accent and had a silver handbag shaped like a turtle."

"You do remember it."

"While we're on the subject, I suppose you've forgotten April 9, 1969, at 7:40 P.M."

"What happened that night?"

"The cocktail party at the Federal City Club when you were telling Barbara Lipscomb of Area Code 212 Boulevard 3-2376 if you ever came to New York you'd give her a call."

"Was that her name?"

."Brunette," she said, "with a beauty mark on her right upper cheek, three fillings on the right side of her mouth, two on the left.

False eyelashes and flaming red Revlon nail polish. Known to her intimates as 'Bobby.' ''

"Wow, what a memory!" I said more in admiration than anger.

"Do you want more? Remember the night it snowed on Feb. 13, 1971, and we were at the Hartwells and you offered to drive Ginny Southern home because she had no snow tires on her 1970 green and white Thunderbird with the white vinyl roof?''

"What was wrong with that?''

"You didn't have a driver's license at that time.''

"Are you sure?''

"You didn't get one until March 6, 1974.''

I looked at my driver's license and darned if she wasn't right.

"Is there anything else you have in your memory bank?" I asked her.

"Would you like to talk about VJ night, 1945, at the Astor Hotel?''

"But I was still in the Marines," I protested. "I didn't even know you then.''

"Yes, but you told me about it on Sept. 26, 1952, the first time you took me out for a drink at the Cafe Flore in Paris.''

## A MIRACLE AT YALE

A very interesting experiment took place at Yale University.

Because of an employees' strike of 1,400 service workers, the students were faced with cleaning their own bedrooms and bathrooms, as well as their dormitories.

While most of the 10,000 students were prepared intellectually to cope with the tough Yale curriculum, very few knew anything about how to clean a bathroom or make a bed. It has changed all of them as I discovered when I visited a family who had a Yalie home for Thanksgiving.

His mother said proudly while we were sitting in the Whitman living room, "Ezra knows how to hang up a suit in a closet.''

"Aw Ma," said Ezra. "Don't make such a big deal of it.''

But Mr. Whitman chimed in. "Not only that, he knows how to clean a bathtub, and he's only a junior.''

"You must be very proud of him," I said.

"Proud isn't the word," Mrs. Whitman said. "Do you know that this morning he put his socks, his shirt and his underwear in the laundry hamper without being told?"

"And they say the kids aren't getting an education these days," I said.

"Ezra, would you like to show everybody how you make your bed at Yale?"

I could tell Ezra was embarrassed. "I'm on vacation, Mom. I don't want to think about school."

"Before Ezra went to Yale this fall he always threw his coat on the floor at the front door," Mr. Whitman said. "Now he hangs it on the banister. I wouldn't have believed it if I hadn't seen it with my own eyes."

"I wish my kid could do that," I said.

"It sounds difficult," Ezra said. "But actually, once you get the hang of it it's not that hard. You see, instead of just dropping your coat on the floor, you take it off and carry it to the banister. Of course it takes practice."

Mrs. Whitman said, "The kids who go to Harvard, Princeton and MIT still throw their coats on the floor. Only Yale has a program in coat hanging."

Mr. Whitman said, "Ezra knows how to wash a frying pan."

"I don't believe it," I said. "And he's only 21 years old. Doesn't the pressure get to you sometimes?"

Ezra replied, "Sure it does, but when the going gets tough you rise to it. Frankly, I never thought when I went to Yale that I'd ever have to wash a frying pan, and neither did any of the other kids. But the one thing I've learned is that food tastes lousy if you don't wash your frying pan. Our chemistry teacher showed us why."

Mrs. Whitman beamed. "I know you're not going to believe this but Ezra now knows how to put the garbage out to be picked up by the trash men."

"I thought you didn't do that until you went to graduate school," I said.

"We didn't in the past. But Yale has a remedial program in garbage," Ezra said. "They found for the first time that undergraduates could handle it. My college advisor said I ought to think about going into the trash business. He says I have a natural bent for it."

I looked at Ezra's proud parents. "I never thought I'd live to see the day when a college student could hang up his own suit in the closet, put his dirty laundry in a hamper, wash a frying pan and know how to take out the garbage."

"And make his own bed," Mrs. Whitman added.

"Yale has made a man out of you, Ezra," I told him.

"We have a lot to be thankful for on this Thanksgiving," Mr. Whitman said contentedly.

"Say, Ezra, how are you on cleaning dirty windows?"

"I'm sorry," Ezra said huffily, "I don't do windows."


## JAMMING THE COURTS

Attorney General Griffin B. Bell warned in a speech in San Francisco recently that an "explosion of lawsuits has plunged federal courts into a crisis that is already hurting the quality of justice people receive."

What he didn't say was that lawsuits were also overwhelming state, county and city courtrooms as well.

The reason is quite simple, and whether Mr. Bell can do anything about it is anyone's guess.

There was a time when a town had one or two lawyers who were very respected citizens, and you only went to see them when you were going to buy a piece of property or draw up a will.

But now practically everyone in the country has either a brother-in-law, a son, a niece or nephew who is a lawyer.

It stands to reason that they must be kept busy, and the business should, if possible, stay in the family.

Let me give you an example. Mrs. Givern has just arrived at her son's for Thanksgiving dinner. She is limping.

"Why are you limping, Mom?"

"I slipped on the ice in front of McGooley's Hardware Store."

Mrs. Givern's lawyer nephew hears this and takes out his yellow legal pad. "McGooley's Hardware Store. Why that's negligence of the highest order. We'll have to get you to a doctor right away so he can testify you suffered from extreme pain and loss of your right leg."

"It's the left leg," Mrs. Givern says, "and I feel fine. I don't want to go to a doctor. I just want to have my Thanksgiving dinner."

"But you've got to go to the doctor. His testimony will be very important in the lawsuit."

"I don't want to sue Mr. McGooley. He's a nice man."

"We're not going to sue Mr. McGooley. We're going to sue his insurance company. McGooley has to be insured."

"But won't we get Mr. McGooley into trouble?"

"We'll have to prove McGooley was negligent in not cleaning off the ice."

"On Thanksgiving Day?"

"That's McGooley's problem. Listen, Charley Efrom is McGooley's insurance company's lawyer. I'll call him now."

"I feel fine," Mrs. Givern protests.

The nephew dials the phone number. "Charley, I think I've got a good one for us. My aunt just slipped on the ice in front of McGooley's Hardware Store. We won't settle for less than $25,000. . . . That's what I thought you'd say. Well, we're going to demand a jury trial. It could tie up both of us for months. . . . I knew you wouldn't mind being bothered on Thanksgiving Day to hear the good news."

"Is Charley mad at me?" Mrs. Givern wanted to know.

"Mad? He's thrilled. It made his dinner. He says he'll probably countersue if any damage has been done to McGooley's sidewalk."

Finally, everyone sits down to dinner. Mrs. Givern's son carves the turkey with an electric knife. The blade flies off and hits Mrs. Givern's daughter Harriet in the head, slightly cutting her ear.

Everyone rushes to Harriet. "Never mind Harriet," the nephew yells. "I want the name of that electric knife company. They'll rue the day they let that carver out of the factory."

These are only examples of what is going on in the country since relatives started becoming lawyers.

If Attorney General Bell really wants to ease the overloaded court calendars he's going to have to get Congress to pass a law making it a felony for an attorney to solicit business from any member of his own family.

## PRINCE CHARLES MUST CHOOSE

If Prince Charles believes his visit to the United States was a good-will trip, he's sorely mistaken. His appearance on American soil caused nothing but hard feelings and bitter recrimination among the mothers of eligible daughters in this country.

I was sitting between two of these mothers the other night at a dinner party and this is exactly what happened.

"I wish Prince Charles would come to Washington," one of the mothers said. "I know he would love to meet Mitzi."

The other mother scoffed.

"Why would Prince Charles want to meet Mitzi?"

"Because he's looking for a wife, and Mitzi would be the perfect princess. She has beauty, education and she understands the British pound."

"I never heard of anything so ridiculous. If Prince Charles was really looking for an American wife, he would be much happier with my Caroline. When she was born, the nurse said, 'She's beautiful enough to be a queen.'"

The first mother said, "Caroline has asthma. She wouldn't be able to live in Buckingham Palace."

"That's a stupid thing to say. If Caroline married Prince Charles she would install a new furnace with an air-purifying system that would take care of her asthma."

"I'm quite certain that Queen Elizabeth wants Prince Charles to marry somebody who is completely healthy. After all, the whole purpose of him getting married is to have a male heir. Now Mitzi hasn't even had a cold in her whole life. She is the picture of good health. The Windsors do need new blood."

"In all due respect, I don't think Mitzi is regal enough to be a queen," Caroline's mother said. "It takes tremendous *savoir faire* to open Parliament."

"Mitzi would not have to open Parliament. Prince Charles, when he became king, would open it. The least you could do is read up on British customs if you want your daughter to marry into the royal family."

The discussion was becoming rather heated, so I tried to add a light note. "Why don't we do it like the TV show, 'The Dating Game.' Prince Charles could sit behind a screen and ask Mitzi and Caroline questions. Then at the end of the show, without seeing them, he could choose one of them for his bride."

"That would be very undignified," Mitzi's mother said.

"For Prince Charles?"

"No," she replied. "For Mitzi. After all, if she's going to be a princess she can't do anything commercial."

"I wouldn't allow Caroline to do it either," her mother said. "I believe Prince Charles should marry for love."

"Do you really think that Prince Charles would fall in love with Caroline?"

"There is no doubt in my mind," Caroline's mother said. "Besides, I know that Prince Philip and Queen Elizabeth would enjoy having us as in-laws. Jim and I are very comfortable with royalty."

"You forgot one thing," Mitzi's mother retorted. "A British queen is expected to ride a horse on her birthday. You told me yourself that Caroline was allergic to horses."

"There is nothing in the Magna Carta that says the queen has to ride a horse," Caroline's mother said angrily.

Finally, Mitzi's mother turned to me. "Let's leave it to Art. Which do you think would make a better match for Prince Charles—my beautiful Mitzi or her asthmatic Caroline?"

I choked on my mousse au chocolate. "What a question!" I said. "All I can say is I don't think Prince Charles is worthy of either of them.

"Now, if you'd like to talk about my daughter, Jennifer. . . ."

# IV. Clean Bomb For Sale

## THE HORN OF AFRICA

Recently after we watched the evening news my wife said, "Would you explain to me what's going on in the Horn of Africa?" It was a very reasonable question and it showed she trusted me.

"The Marxist junta of Ethiopia," I said, "is fighting the Marxist junta in Somalia over the Ogaden desert which Somali rebels have invaded."

"I thought we were friends of Ethiopia," my wife said.

"We were before Haile Selassie was overthrown. For a long while we were against the Somalis because they had allowed the Soviets to use their ports in the Indian Ocean. But then the Somalis kicked the Russians out, and we made a promise to arm them in their fight with Ethiopia. When the Soviets were booted out of Somalia they decided to help the Ethiopians kick the Somalis out of the Ogaden desert."

"How did they do it?" she wanted to know.

"By bringing in the Cubans to fight with the Ethiopians against the Somalis. They also gave the Ethiopians a billion dollars in arms. In that way the Soviets hope to shift the balance of power in East Africa."

Her eyes started to glaze.

"Western allies in the area, particularly Iran and Saudi Arabia, are worried that if Ethiopia becomes strong, it will not only drive the Somalis out of the desert but will invade Somalia itself. But the United States has been assured by the Soviets that they won't per-

mit this to happen. At the same time, we don't want to give Somalia arms because we're afraid it will escalate the war."

My wife started dozing off and I had to poke her gently in the
ribs.

"What really complicates the situation is that Israel is also helping Ethiopia, even if it means they have to be on the side of the Soviets."

"What has Israel got against Somalia?"

"They don't have anything against Somalia except that it affects
their shipping into the Red Sea which they're afraid could become
an 'Arab lake' since Somalia is being supported by the majority of
Moslem countries, except for South Yemen."

"What are the Cubans doing in Ethiopia?"

"They're the Hessians of the Horn of Africa. The Soviets don't
want to do the fighting because that might get us involved on the
Somalian side. So they let the Cubans do it instead. Since the Cuban pilots are tied up flying MIG fighter planes in Africa, the Soviet
pilots are flying MIG fighters in Cuba."

She was starting to close her eyes again. "Let's go to bed," she
said.

"Wait," I said. "You have to get the whole picture. Not only are
the Ethiopians fighting the Somalis, but they are also fighting the
Eritreans, who want their independence from Addis Ababa. You
see Eritrea was an Italian colony until Ethiopia took it over after
World War II.

"The Arabs are supporting Eritrea which is predominantly Moslem. Kenya, on the other hand, is supporting Ethiopia even though
they hate the pro-Moscow regime that is now in power."

"Could we talk about this in the morning?" she wanted to know.

"It's not that simple," I told her. "The Soviets are not investing
in Africa because of the climate. They hope to get airfields in Ethiopia for their Backfire bomber, which would be a threat to Western
oil lifelines."

"What can we do about it?" my wife asked.

"Sit tight until Andy Young settles the problems of Rhodesia."

"Can I go to bed now?"

"Yes," I said. "I'll sit up and watch the eleven o'clock news and
wake you up in case there is any change in the situation."

## HOWARD IN JERUSALEM

The role that Walter Cronkite, Barbara Walters and John Chancellor played in the Sadat-Begin talks in Jerusalem cannot be underestimated. By bypassing the State Department and going directly to the three anchorpersons of American television, Sadat and Begin agreed to meet, which was the breakthrough that everyone had been hoping for.

It might have been different, though, if Roone Arledge, the president of ABC News, had chosen to have Howard Cosell conduct the interview between the two men instead of Barbara Walters.

This is what I mean.

"Good evening, ladies and gentlemen. This is Howard Cosell bringing you an exclusive ABC Sports spectacular live and in color from the ringside here in Jerusalem. Tonight we are presenting another star-studded fight with the incomparable Egyptian heavyweight, Anwar Sadat, who is risking his title as champion of the Arab world, to meet with one of the toughest little sluggers in the Middle East, Prime Minister Menahem Begin, a comparatively unknown backbencher until he knocked out the formidable Yitzhak Rabin in the last Israeli elections.

"I spoke to Anwar in the locker room in Cairo a few days ago, and he told me that he would go anywhere, any time, to meet with Menahem. I then passed this message on to Menahem, who revealed he was ready to take on Anwar even if it meant fighting his whole Israeli cabinet.

"And so the two gladiators are here tonight, which I will have to admit, in all candor, I must take full credit for.

"Anwar, forgive me for asking this question, but I feel it incumbent on my part to do so for the benefit of the TV audience. Why did you decide to fight Begin at this time?"

"I decided to come to Jerusalem to show I was interested in peace."

"But surely, Anwar, Egypt, with its Russian-made tanks, missiles and MIG airplanes, is a match for Israel. Are you trying to say, and correct me if I'm wrong, that you couldn't march into Tel Aviv at any time you wanted?"

"That is not the point. The point is that war is no longer a solution to the problem of the Middle East."

"It sounds to me, Anwar, that you're afraid of tiny Israel."

"I am not afraid of Israel."

"All right, Anwar, forgive me, but I have to tell it like it is.

"Now, let's have a word with Begin. Menahem, I must say, in all frankness, that it has been said you have lost some of the spunk and verve that made you such a formidable threat during the memorable Mideast wars in 1948, 1956 and 1967. You don't seem to be the same Begin that we all remember from the Irgun days."

"I wish to say, Howard, I welcome Anwar Sadat to Jerusalem and I hope that we can find a peaceful solution to our differences."

"And yet, if you don't mind my own observation, you told me only a few months ago that you could still go the whole distance and get to Cairo if you wanted to. Perhaps I'm speaking out of turn, but I would be remiss if I didn't ask this question: Are you chickening out because you are not in condition?"

"I am not chickening out of anything. Sadat knows I'm not chicken."

"Anwar, are you ready to say in front of millions of people watching this telecast by satellite that Menahem is not chicken?"

"I don't think we should talk about chickens at this time. I am here to give my position and listen to the Israeli position."

"If you don't mind my saying so, and I must intercede at this time, it appears to me that we have here a total absence of aggression in both parties, which I perceive will disappoint everyone who was tuned in because we promised them a fight.

"This is not the show we expected to bring you from the Middle East.

"I hope that the World Boxing Commission will take note of it and hold up the purses of both Sadat and Begin until a full investigation is forthcoming.

"This is Howard Cosell from Jerusalem telling it like it is."


## THE LAST DITCH BATTLE

Americans haven't had a good "gut" foreign issue in several years. Finally one has come along that will divide brother against brother, family against family, conservative against liberal, hard-hat against student, and Senator Strom Thurmond against President Jimmy Carter.

The issue, of course, is the Panama Canal and the battle has started already. I was in the Purple Onion bar one night when the issue erupted after the seven o'clock news.

"Dammit," said Planter, "if the Panamanians want the Canal they're going to have to fight for it."

Ellstrom said, "Let them have the bloody ditch. The only thing it's good for any more is sailboats."

Planter got red in the face. "How can you say that and call yourself an American? We bought it, we paid for it and we died for it."

"That's how much you know about it, Ellstrom said. "We stole it from Colombia and forced the Panamanians to sign a treaty they wanted no part of."

You could see Planter was getting mad. "You didn't learn that in no American school. You must have read it in some Commie paper. The Panama Canal was built with American blood. Twenty thousand of our boys died to join the Atlantic and Pacific oceans."

"They weren't American boys," said Ellstrom. "They were mostly West Indians hired to do the dirty work. All we put up was our know-how and money. It ain't worth fighting about."

Planter rolled up his sleeves. "Well, I'm ready to fight about it. We were given the Panama Canal in perpetuity. That means for life or forever, whichever comes first."

McCarthy, the bartender, said, "Let's have no fighting in here about the Canal. You want to fight about it you buy a ticket to the Canal Zone and slug it out there."

Someone tried to bring up the Washington Redskins, but Planter wouldn't be deterred. He turned to Ellstrom. "How can you sleep at night knowing some banana republic is occupying our Canal?"

"Very easily," Ellstrom said. "If you would read up on it you'd realize nothing of value can go through it any more. Our aircraft carriers are too big for it, and most oil tankers can't get into it. All we're doing is supporting a bunch of Americans in the Zone who are living the life of Reilly."

Ellstrom didn't realize it, but Reilly was in the bar. "What's that? Who's living my life in Panama?"

"The Americans who work down there," Ellstrom said.

"Well, it can't be much of a life," Reilly laughed. "Would anybody like to buy me a beer?"

"Giving up the Panama Canal is nothing to laugh at," Planter said. "I say if the Panamanians try to take the Canal from us we should drop the bomb on them."

McCarthy, the bartender, said, "That wouldn't be a bad idea. At least it would widen it enough for American Navy ships to get through."

Ellstrom stuck to his guns. "I'm not about to go to war over Panama."

Planter said, "Well, you might not be, but there are millions of Americans who are. Teddy Roosevelt must be turning over in his grave now, knowing that the President of the United States is going to give away the greatest man-made body of water in the world."

I didn't want to get into the discussion, but I couldn't help myself. "I suggested a compromise some time back. And that is we fill in the Canal with dirt and give it back to the Panamanians just the way we found it. Would that satisfy both of you?"

Ellstrom sipped his drink and said, "I couldn't care less."

We all turned to Planter for his reaction. "I might go for it, but I'll have to check it out with Ronald Reagan first."

## CLEAN BOMB FOR SALE

"Knock, Knock. How do you do, sir. Could I interest you in our latest enhanced neutron bomb?"

"What do I want with a neutron bomb?"

"This is the best thing to come along since the invention of synthetic potato chips. The neutron bomb is not really a bomb, but an artillery shell with a low-yield atomic capability."

"Thank you very much but I've got all the atomic weapons I need."

"Please don't shut the door until you've heard me out. The neutron bomb is a clean weapon."

"What does that mean?"

"It means, sir, that it kills people but it doesn't destroy property. You can fire one of these into a city or town and walk in the next day and find almost every building intact. Since this has just been developed, you would be the only one to own a clean bomb on your block. You would be the envy of everyone in your neighborhood.''

"I don't know. It sounds interesting but I've been spending so much money on weapons lately I'm not sure I could afford a clean bomb.''

"Let me show you our catalog. Look at the size of the neutron bomb. You can put it in your station wagon, and fire it from any U-Haul. This is not a luxury item, but an absolute necessity. As a major power you can't do without it.''

"That's what you told me about the B-1 bomber.''

"Forget the B-1 bomber. Think of the environmental aspects of the neutron bomb. You don't have to worry about dirty fallout any more. You don't have to mess with a lot of rubble or deal with radiation for years. After you kill everyone you can walk into a town in 24 hours and it will be as clean as a whistle. Your troops can set up an officers' club and a USO in a matter of days.''

"It does sound interesting, but isn't there some arms limitation about a clean bomb?''

"Absolutely not. There is nothing in the SALT agreement about owning a neutron bomb. This is not a strategic weapon such as a missile. It is nothing more than an artillery shell that can be used by your ground forces in the same manner as a flame thrower or a tank.''

"Does the other side have a neutron bomb?''

"They do not. That's what makes it such an appealing weapon. We're the only ones manufacturing them and we have the patent on it. If you buy it we assure you that you will be ahead in the arms race.''

"There is only one problem. If I have a clean bomb and the other side doesn't, what would prevent them from using a dirty bomb to get even with me?''

"That would be against the rules of nuclear warfare. After all if you're not destroying their property why should they get mad enough to use a dirty bomb?''

"You make it sound so simple. But there must be a catch in it somewhere. If I was the other side and I didn't have a clean bomb, I'd use everything I had, just to get even.''

"But that would be all-out war. The beauty of the clean bomb is that the war could be limited to just armed combatants. You can pinpoint a neutron bomb to just hit the target area. Think of all the civilian lives you could save.

"How much is it?"

"It comes to only a few cents a day for every man, woman, and child in the United States. One small war and it will pay for itself."

"All right. I'll buy it. But if I use it, how can I be sure that the other side won't throw a dirty bomb at me?"

"We guarantee it. If you use a clean bomb and the other side retaliates with a dirty one, we'll give you your money back with no questions asked."

## TIP AND TEDDY AND ED

If you're wondering why it's impossible to keep defense costs down in this country, perhaps I can help you.

The U.S. Navy wanted a new plane and, after budget considerations, opted for the F-14 made by Grumman Aerospace Corp., in Bethpage, Long Island.

The F-18 designed by McDonnell-Douglas was scrubbed because it was too expensive and too controversial. This might have been the end of it except that the engines for the F-18 would be made by General Electric in Lynn, Mass. Strong rumor has it that House Majority Leader Tip O'Neill of Massachusetts and Senators Ted Kennedy and Ed Brooke leaned on the White House and the Pentagon to keep the F-18 alive, and after several telephone calls Defense Secretary Harold Brown decided the F-18 might not be a bad plane after all.

Four hundred and nineteen million dollars has been set aside for "Research and Development" for the F-18, but a spokesman for the secretary said the decision was made "on its own merits" and had nothing to do with Representative O'Neill and Senators Kennedy and Brooke's interest in the project.

I believe it.

The reason is that I talked to an expert who advises O'Neill and Kennedy and Brooke on military affairs, and he advised me the last thing any of the three legislators would want to do is waste money on an airplane the Navy said it didn't want.

"The Navy needs this plane," he told me. "In the worst way. They just don't know they need it. But once it's sitting on their flight decks they'll be grateful to Tip and Teddy and Ed for persuading them to buy it."

"What makes the F-18 so great?" I asked.

"The General Electric engines which are produced in Lynn, Mass., by the finest technicians and engineers in the country."

"How do O'Neill, Kennedy and Brooke know that?"

"They all have GE appliances in their homes and they're aware of what a great product GE makes."

"Some people have said that if the engines for the plane were not made in Massachusetts, none of the three would have gone to bat for the F-18."

"That's ridiculous. Tip has always wanted a multi-mission fighter that could outfly anything the Soviets have. Teddy has dreamed of this country someday having an aircraft with an increased wing area and a wider and longer fuselage to provide greater internal fuel capacity. And I've heard Ed Brooke say many times, 'What this country needs more than anything else is a fighter plane with a radar dish on its nose.'

"When it comes to national security these three men would never let politics stand in the way of the Navy getting the best plane that money can buy."

"Even if the Navy doesn't want it?"

"What does the Navy know about fighter planes? Tip and Teddy and Ed have been making airplane models since they were six years old."

"But if the Navy has already ordered the F-14 from Grumman what are they going to do with the F-18?"

"They can sell their F-14s to the Shah of Iran. He'll buy anything that flies."

"I never thought of that," I admitted. "The whole thing makes sense when you explain it. The Navy gets a plane it doesn't want, GE's Massachusetts plant gets to build the engine, McDonnell-Douglas gets to build the plane, and the security of the country will be safe for years to come."

"Tip and Teddy and Ed couldn't have put it any better."

"What will it cost the taxpayer?"

"If you have to ask what it costs to have a new fighter plane you shouldn't own one."

## BE IT EVER SO HUMBLE

I recently read in the newspaper that they resettled 75 natives on Enewetak (which, incidentally, was formerly spelled Eniwetok) Atoll in the Marshall Islands. A pang of nostalgia went through me when I read the story. I was stationed on the Enewetak Atoll for twelve months during World War II with a U.S. Marine fighter squadron, and while it sounds like a short period of time to us now, it felt like an eternity.

Ever since then I have always considered myself a native of Enewetak, and when I heard the United States was letting people return I was sorely tempted to pack up and move back.

After World War II Enewetak probably would never have been heard from again except that the United States decided to use it as an atomic testing ground. As a matter of fact, they blew the island of Engebi, where I was stationed, right out of the water and right off the face of the earth.

There were about 2,000 or 3,000 men stationed on Engebi consisting of Marines, Seabees and U.S. Army personnel. In a few months we had gone native and wore nothing but shorts, hats and sandals. Our skin became very dark and we developed an island mentality. Anyone who didn't live on Engebi was a white stranger who was not to be trusted. There were also tribal feuds on the island. The Marines and the Seabees managed to get along, but the Army personnel were considered "Dogfaces" who could not be trusted and, according to our Navy chaplains, had never really accepted the existence of *one* God.

The main industry of Engebi was making home-grown brew from raisins. Each tent had its own still, and with the help of good ole boys from the South we vied with each other to see which tent could make the most powerful raisin jack. This was more dangerous than one might think because if you didn't pour it out in time the still could explode, setting off air raid sirens all over the island.

I have always believed the atomic testing at Engebi was never accurate. While the scientists measured the power of the hydrogen bomb device they set off, they never figured how much of the destruction was caused by old fermented raisin juice which all of us left behind when we got our orders to ship out.

A second cottage industry from which we all profited was the manufacture of "Japanese flags." The lagoon was used as an anchorage for allied merchant and Navy ships, and every time one came into harbor we went out in boats and sold the flags as war souvenirs to the crews. We made the "Japanese flags" from white sheets and red paint which we had our parents ship us from the States. After carefully drawing the Rising Sun on the linen, we then splattered red paint around it to indicate the flag had been captured during a bloody battle. We circled the ships as natives do, waving our flags and negotiating for meat, fresh vegetables or medicinal brandy. Our "Japanese flags" are probably still decorating basements all over America.

Despite what you see in the movies and on television, not all the islands in the Pacific had beautiful panting nurses on them.

There wasn't one woman on Engebi and after six months we forgot all about them. Then Bob Hope came in with a USO show and he had some strange-looking people with him that he kept making jokes about.

One of the fellows in our tent insisted they were girls, and that they were very nice to touch and do other things with.

But the rest of us didn't believe him. "Why would you want one of them in place of a good batch of raisin jack?" someone in the tent asked.

I must admit, though, that after we saw the girls on stage with Bob Hope for a couple of hours, the peace and tranquility of Engebi was violently disturbed. People started fist fights for no reason, other "natives" refused to clean up their tents, and mistrust, suspicion and other strange feelings grabbed many of us.

But in a few weeks we forgot all about "girls" and went back to making raisin jack and Japanese flags and looking for seashells in the lagoon.

I could go on about this glorious period of my life on Eniwetok but I'm too choked up. It's nice to read that the real natives have now returned to their islands. I know everyone in my Marine Corps outfit wishes he could be with them now.

## THE KREMLIN BACKS DOWN

The Soviet colonel came into the situation room of the Kremlin. He was holding in his hand a photograph of the United States taken from a Russian spy satellite.

"Look, comrades, the Americans are digging holes all over the country. Why are they digging so many holes unless it's for missiles?"

The Joint Soviet Command studied the satellite map.

"Is true," said a marshal. "Hole is here, hole is there. No one makes as many holes unless they going to put in launchers. We must speak to KGB chief for North America immediately."

A button was pushed and Boris X came in.

"Why," a general demanded, "you have not reported United States is digging holes for new missiles to be aimed against U.S.S.R.?"

The KGB man took a look at the satellite photograph.

"Those are not rocket launcher holes, comrades. Those are potholes made by American cars and trucks."

"What are potholes?" another Soviet general demanded.

The KGB man said, "In America there is winter, yes?"

Everyone agreed.

"In winter," he continued, "there is snow and ice, yes?"

"Get on with it," the marshall said.

"To break up ice and snow on roads they put salt on them. Salt not only breaks up ice, it also breaks up road. When road breaks up there is hole. Americans call it pothole," the KGB man said.

"Why don't Americans fill in potholes?" the marshal demanded.

"Because there are so many of them it's impossible to fill them all in. Is better to let them stay as holes until municipal elections."

"What are these yellow lights and pieces of wood around these holes: Surely they must be for missiles," a general said.

"Is not for missiles. Traffic police put up these lights to warn people there is a pothole," the KGB man said.

"Why don't they put them up around all the potholes?" a general asked.

"They don't have enough yellow warning lights."

"How do they decide which holes to put lights on and which holes not to put lights on?"

For the first time the KGB chief was nervous. "We haven't been able to find out why they choose to put lights on some holes and not others. There doesn't seem to be any pattern to it."

The marshal said, "There must be a reason for it. Americans wouldn't just mark some potholes and not others. If they did that they would wreck their automobiles."

The KGB man said, "That's just it. They are wrecking their automobiles. My people are trying to find out why police mark certain potholes and don't mark others but is impossible to get information so far. No policeman will explain why he chooses one pothole over another."

"Is possible," said a general, "that ones with yellow blinkers are really dug for missiles."

"But," said another general, "suppose they put yellow blinkers on to make us think those potholes are missile sites, when in fact unmarked potholes are real missile launch pads?"

The KGB man said, "Comrades, as you know I have lived in America for a long time. It's true that from the air American potholes look like missile pads. But I have driven over them and I assure you that they are rarely more than six feet deep. A car can fall in one, but a missile can't be fired from it. We must not come to conclusion from one satellite photo that Americans are building launching pads all over their highways."

"But," said the marshal, slamming his fist on the table, "how can we be sure?"

"Here is car bill from Soviet ambassador to U.S.," the KGB man said. "Is bill for four new suspension systems in one winter, and that is only from driving around Washington. Comrades, missile sites don't do that kind of damage to cars—but American potholes do."

## WALL STREET MADNESS

There is a certain insanity going on in the country at this moment which cannot be diagnosed by any doctor. If you don't believe me, take a look at what happened on Wall Street last Friday. All week long we saw and heard nothing but bad news about the economy, inflation, the national deficit, the fall of the dollar etc., etc.

Then on Friday, Wall Street went ape, traded 52 million shares of stock in one day, and the market went through the roof. It was hard to believe that the men and women who drove up the Dow Jones by 20 points were watching the same economic news as the rest of the country.

As soon as I heard about it I called a friend on Wall Street to find out what was going on.

He sounded very giddy on the phone. "They're buying," he cried. "They're buying everything. Zip a dee dooda!"

"I know that," I said. "But why are they buying?"

"You know Thompson, who manages all of Glutton Insurance Co.'s investment portfolio?"

"No, I don't know him," I said.

"He started it. He'd been sitting on $2 billion worth of cash, and not doing a damn thing with it. Well, he went to the health club on Friday morning and suddenly started screaming, 'I can't take it any longer. I've got to buy *something.*' Then he went running down Wall Street in the nude yelling, 'Buy! Buy! Buy! I'm going to buy everything.'"

"Did they lock him up?"

"Lock him up? I should say not. Everybody started taking off their clothes, too. They figured Thompson knew something they didn't.

"Pretty soon we were all dancing in the street. The big guys from the mutual funds, the pension trusts and the banks were running around naked screaming at their brokers to buy any stock they could get their hands on. Panic broke out, and money managers, who were playing gin rummy for a penny a point, were throwing orders for millions of dollars out their windows. The brokers got on their phones to the little guys and told them the big guys were buying. That's all the little guys had to hear, and they started buying, too. I've never seen anything like it."

"You mean to say because one person went nuts in a steam room the entire financial community went berserk?"

"Right. We always knew that's all it would take. If we could just get one of the big guys to go off his wagon, everyone else would follow suit. Nobody likes to be left behind on Wall Street when someone takes his clothes off and starts buying stocks. When the word got out that Thompson of Glutton Insurance had lost his marbles it started an avalanche of business the likes of which none of us has ever seen."

"Where is Thompson now?" I said.

"Someone threw a blanket around him so he wouldn't catch a cold."

"But doesn't anyone up there know what's going on in Washington now?"

"We don't care what's going on in Washington. We were desperate for action. An investor can't sit on billions of dollars forever—something has to give. If it hadn't been Thompson, it would have been somebody else. Everyone was cracking up from the boredom, but Thompson was the first one to completely flip."

"What's all that noise I hear in the background?"

"Merrill Lynch has just unleashed a thundering herd of cattle on Wall Street, and they're goring everyone in sight."

"Why did they do that?"

"Because Merrill Lynch is bullish on America again."

"It all seems too good to be true," I said. "What happens when Thompson sobers up and decides he wants Glutton Insurance out of the stock market again?"

"Don't ask."

## CHARLEY AND THE FOXBAT

When Lieutenant Viktor Belenko of the Soviet Air Force delivered a spanking new MIG-25 "Foxbat" fighter plane to the Japanese there was tremendous excitement amongst all Western military commands. The Foxbat is considered the world's fastest warplane and everyone, especially the U.S. Air Force intelligence people, were dying to have an opportunity to examine every toggle switch on it.

The Japanese knew the Soviet Union would put tremendous pressure on them to have the MIG-25 returned immediately so they asked the United States how they could stall for time. Pentagon officials huddled for a few days and then a general came up with the answer. "What we need is an expert in stalling—someone who can keep the MIG from being sent back and at the same time not offend the Soviets."

"Whom do you have in mind?" the secretary of defense asked.

"Charley Muleback."

"Who the hell is Charley Muleback?" another general asked.

"I can't tell you now," the general replied.

Muleback was flown out that evening. He arrived at Hakodate airport and was taken to the Foxbat which had been completely sealed off by the Japanese and under heavy guard. In another part of the airport an angry Russian Embassy official was screaming at the Japanese officials that the Soviet Union wanted its MIG back immediately, and if they didn't get it there would be serious consequences.

The Japenese introduced Muleback to the Russian.

"Tell him," Muleback said, "that the plane's been completely totaled and we're going to have to start from scratch to rebuild it."

A Japanese official translated this to the Russian.

The Russian protested that the plane was in perfect condition and there wasn't a scratch on it.

Muleback shook his head. "That's what all MIG-25 owners say, but they never look underneath the plane where the real damage is. Besides, we're going to have to replace the two afterburning jet engines. At the impact of landing, they were wrecked beyond repair and I believe they wouldn't last another 500 miles. Tell him I personally called the spare parts factory in Lansing, Michigan, and they promised they would air freight the engines in two months."

The Russian made a telephone call to his superiors and then returned. "We'll take the plane as it is," he told the Japanese, "and make our own repairs."

Muleback, when told what the Russian said, replied, "Even if the afterburning engines worked, we're going to have to put in all new air intake valves. They're a mess. And we have to replace the grill on the radar nose cone and the wheels will have to be realigned. And we have to change the oil filters which means removing the radar equipment from the cockpit. We found some dirt in the gaskets that control the air-to-air missiles, and we'll have to send away to Shreveport which is the only place that still makes them."

The Russian was screaming at the Japanese, "Just give us the plane as it is!"

Muleback listened to the translation and shook his head.

"I'm sorry, mister. It's too late now because we've got the whole thing torn apart. We were under the impression you wanted your MIG plane fixed up so no one would ever know it had been totaled on a Japanese runway."

The Japanese officials were horrified to see the Russian Embassy official beat his head against the ticket counter.

That night the general in the Pentagon received a cable which said, "I did like you said. Regards, Muleback."

The elated general showed it to everyone at the meeting.

"All right," the secretary of defense said. "Who the hell is Muleback?"

The general replied, "He runs a body shop in Alexandria. My kid smashed up my Mustang and it took Muleback six months to repair it. I figured if it took him six months to repair a Mustang, it would take him three years to patch up a MIG-25, providing he can get all the parts."

## SALES MEETING

It was reported in the New York *Times* recently that the Pentagon has set as one of its highest priorities the sale of U.S. military equipment to foreign countries. Chief sales manager is Deputy Defense Secretary William P. Clements, and the *Times* reported he held a pep talk sales breakfast meeting to tell his people the Pentagon sales program was one of the most important missions of the Defense Department.

I wasn't invited to the breakfast, but I like to think this is how it went.

"Gentlemen, we've moved $10 billion worth of arms this year, but I am disappointed in many of you. We were hoping to have a $12 billion year. Now, we're here to speak frankly. Why isn't the stuff moving?"

"I can only speak for Africa, sir, and my people have done a fine job there. We sold a squadron of F-5 fighters to Kenya, and tons of stuff to Zaire. Ethiopia is talking about buying a missile cruiser."

"What's holding up the sale?"

"Since she's landlocked, she doesn't know where to put it."

"I don't want excuses. I want sales. Your people should have figured out some way of persuading Ethiopia that it was essential for a Third World power to have a missile cruiser whether she was landlocked or not. They have lakes in Ethiopia, don't they?"

"Yes, sir."

"Then let them keep the cruiser in one of their lakes. All right now, what about the Seychelles Islands. Why haven't they bought anything from us?"

"They only got their independence last week. We're waiting for the prime minister to appoint a minister of defense."

"What are you pushing?"

"We thought we'd talk them into some aircraft carriers, submarine chasers and possibly antiaircraft guns."

"That's all? A country has just gained its independence, and all you're going to sell them is a couple of lousy carriers and a few sub chasers. What kind of a salesman are you?"

"Well, sir, it's a question of money. They want to put what little money they have into industry and agriculture."

"Your job is to persuade them that defense comes first. What good is it to have industry and agriculture if they can't protect themselves from an attack by Kenya."

"Kenya?"

"Listen, you tell them we just sold Kenya a squadron of F-5 fighters, and if the Seychelles Islands don't buy a squadron of our F-15s they'll never be able to repulse an attack."

"I got you."

"All right now, what about South America?"

"I left two samples of Trident missiles with Ecuador just to whet their appetites. I told them to try them, and if they didn't live up to their expectations, they wouldn't have to pay for them."

"What about Brazil?"

"We told Brazil that Ecuador is ordering the Trident missiles and advised them to order the anti-Trident missiles that could shoot them down."

"That's just a drop in the bucket. Why isn't Brazil ordering Cruise missiles? I'll tell you why. Because you all think like Avon Women. You make one sale and believe that's all you have to do. Well, let me tell you, gentlemen, the Pentagon is not going to stay in business unless we sell, SELL—SELL! I want those warehouses emptied by Christmas, and if you people can't do it I'll find generals and colonels who can. All right now, take your order books and get out of here. The first man who sells a complete nuclear weapons system to a Third World power gets an all-expense-paid trip to Bermuda."

"Woweeee!!!"


## LAUGH-IN AT WEST POINT

A Pentagon commission has just released a study recommending, among other things, that West Point cadets develop a sense of humor, something it found the academy was lacking. As anyone who has dealt with military officers knows, this is easier said than done. But I'm sure that if the Pentagon recommends it, West Point will give it the old school try.

"All right, cadets, we will now devote the next hour to developing a sense of humor. Brinckley, are you prepared?"

"YESSIR!!!!!!!"

"At ease, Brinkley. You don't have to stand at attention. Just tell us a joke."

"A WHAT, SIR?!!!!!"

"A joke. You know, something to make us all laugh."

"YESSIR!!!!!!!"

"Well, go ahead, Brinckley."

"IN THE ARMY THERE ARE THREE KINDS OF FOOLS, SIR. FOOLS, DAMNED FOOLS AND VOLUNTEERS."

"Very good, Brinckley. Very amusing. What is it, Grunback?"

"SIR, I TOLD BRINCKLEY THAT JOKE LAST NIGHT IN THE MESS HALL. HE STOLE IT FROM ME."

"If that's true, Brinckley, this is a serious violation of the Honor Code. West Point has a rule that a cadet will not lie, cheat or steal a joke from another cadet."

"SIR, GRUNBACK HEARD THAT JOKE FROM SOMEONE IN THE SECOND BATTALION. HE STOLE IT FROM THEM."

"Why didn't you report it under the rules of the Honor Code?"

"I INTENDED TO, SIR, IF IT DIDN'T GET A LAUGH."

"That's not very funny, Brinckley. I'm afraid you'll have to go on report. The academy will not condone joke stealing, nor the failure to report another cadet who stole one. When you lead men into battle, they will expect you to make up your own jokes, and they will not follow an officer who takes jokes from someone else in the field. Have I made myself clear?"

"YESSIR!!!!!!!"

"All right, now let's keep our sense of humor in spite of this tragic affair. O'Reilly, can you make the class laugh?"

"YESSIR!!!!!"

"Well, go to it."

O'Reilly takes a banana cream pie out from under his desk and flings it into the captain's face. The captain, wiping the cream off his starched uniform, says, "That was very good, O'Reilly. I'm giving you an A in the course."

"THANK YOU SIR!!!!!!!"

"I am also going to have you court-martialed for striking an officer, insubordination and insulting the uniform of the United States Army under Article 12, Section 8 of the Military Code."

"BUT SIR, YOU TOLD ME TO MAKE THE CLASS LAUGH. THEY'RE HYSTERICAL."

"Good, then I am also adding the charge of mutiny. What is it Grimstead?"

"SIR, YOU STILL HAVE SOME WHIPPED CREAM IN YOUR LEFT NOSTRIL."

"Do you want to go to Leavenworth, too?"

"NO SIR, THAT WAS A JOKE. I JUST MADE IT UP."

"How would you like to march around the parade grounds in full battle dress for six hours?"

"THAT'S VERY GOOD, SIR. YOU'RE VERY FAST ON THE REPARTEE."

"This class will not be given weekend leave for the rest of the year."

"WHY, SIR?"

"Because, dammit, you don't have a sense of humor. And I'm going to see that you get one if I have to break every bone in your bodies."

# V. You All Spoken Here

## NO SOUTHERN JOKES

"You should have a ball with the Carter Administration," many people have told me.

"Why do you say that?" I always ask.

"Well, it's the first time in ages we've had a President from the Deep South, and there has to be endless material in that."

There probably would be except that Carter's election, instead of giving some Southerners a feeling of self-confidence, has made them even more sensitive to any levity about the South.

Even my Southern friends in Washington see no humor in Carter and Plains, Georgia.

I have a friend, a distinguished newscaster, who comes from Georgia and he doesn't want to read any allusions to the South for the next four years.

"Making fun of Carter's Southern background is just a cheap shot," he told me.

"But we used to make fun of Johnson and his Texas background," I protested.

"Texas isn't Georgia," he replied. "Texans are used to being made fun of—Georgians aren't."

"Why not?"

"Because it's taken us such a long time to get respectable again, and we're not going to blow it just because the next President of the United States comes from there."

"But," I protested, "it's an American tradition to make fun of a man's background. Look what we did with John F. Kennedy's Hyannisport and Johnson's Pedernales ranch and Nixon's Watergate.''

"Nixon didn't come from Watergate," my friend said.

"We still aren't sure of that, are we?" I said.

"It was different with those men. What you're dealing with when you write about Carter is a man who comes from the red clay of a Southern state, who rose to the highest office in the land despite prejudice and suspicion. You don't heal the wounds of a Civil War by writing about grits and peanuts and good ole' boys."

"Then what do you write about?"

"A new South that has risen on the ashes of the old one—a South that takes pride in its tall buildings and its paved highways and its great football teams."

"There is nothing funny about that," I said.

"That is exactly my point. There is absolutely nothing funny about the South, and if you say there is you're just making it up."

"There must be something humorous about the South. It can't be the only part of the country that isn't funny."

"We're not going to stand for it," he warned me. "The South is not a joke. Jimmy Carter proved that."

"I guess that means we can't laugh for the next four years, then?"

"I didn't say that. I just said it's going to be harder, because we Southerners don't think jokes about the South are funny."

"Don't Southerners tell jokes about themselves?" I asked.

"That's different. It's all right for us to tell Jimmy Carter jokes amongst ourselves. What we resent are Northerners telling Jimmy Carter jokes to us."

"Boy, you people are no fun at all."

"That is a typical example of your prejudice. Just because we don't like Northerners to tell Southern jokes you accuse us of no sense of humor."

"Okay, no jokes about Carter and his Southern background. Did you hear the one about the traveling salesman whose car got stuck in the snow in Mondale's hometown in Minnesota?"

"No," he said, laughing for the first time. "What happened?"

## CARTER, PLAYBOY AND LUST

The day that Jimmy Carter's famous quotes from *Playboy* were released was also the same day he issued a paper on how to save the American family. Mr. Carter has said that he is very concerned about what is happening to the American family, and if he becomes President one of his priorities will be to bring it back together again.

Well, I must say the *Playboy* interview didn't do much in our family to heal any wounds.

For those who have been down in a coal mine and haven't read what Mr. Carter told *Playboy*, he admitted that he has looked at a lot of women with lust. But he said God forgives sinners, including adulterers. "This is something God recognizes I will do," he was quoted as saying, " . . . and I have done it . . . and God forgives me for it. But that doesn't mean that I condemn someone who not only looks on a woman with lust, but who leaves his wife and shacks up with somebody out of wedlock."

The problem with this thinking is that while God is willing to forgive men for lusting thoughts, most wives aren't—at least not where I live.

The night after Mr. Carter's views were publicized I went to a dinner party at a friend's house where there were some very attractive wives and single women.

When we got home my wife said, "I saw you lusting after Florence Pennyweather."

"I wasn't lusting after her," I protested. "I was talking to her about tax cuts for the median class of American who makes an average of $12,000 a year."

"You were lusting while you were talking."

"How do you know that?"

"I saw it in your eyes."

"That wasn't lust," I protested. "The look was caused by my eyeglasses. You see, when you wear bifocals they give off this odd effect that some people could interpret as lust. Ask any optometrist."

"Are you trying to tell me you weren't committing adultery in your heart when you sat on a stool at her feet?"

"Adultery was the furthest thing from my mind. I was breathing heavily because I had too much chicken cacciatore."

"Jimmy Carter says he's committed adultery in his heart many times."

"But he's from Georgia. They have nothing else to do down there. I live in Washington where none of us has time for such thoughts."

She said, "Well, he says God forgives him when he does it, but I'm telling you right now, if I ever catch you committing adultery in your heart you can pack your bags."

"You'll never catch me," I assured her. "There are some men who lust after women and there are others who don't. You're fortunate to be married to one who doesn't."

"Don't tell me you've never had a fantasy about having an affair with another woman?"

"What's an affair?"

"What President Ford said he would never approve of his daughter Susan having."

"Oh, *that* kind of an affair," I said. "The answer is no. The Lord said to think of having one is the same thing as having one, and frankly since I've been playing tennis, I tire easily."

"Well, at least Jimmy Carter is man enough to admit his sins," she said bitterly.

"That's unfair. Just because Carter confessed he lusts after women in his heart doesn't prove everyone in the country does. Gerry Ford bumps his head every time he gets out of a helicopter. That doesn't mean every other man has to bump his head."

"There were several other husbands at the party lusting after women," she said.

"If they were, I can't criticize them," I said, "because that would be a sin of pride, which Carter said is worse than lust."

"How can I believe that whenever we go out to a party you are not committing adultery in your heart?"

"As Carter would say, 'Trust me.'"


## CRUEL PUNISHMENT

The Board of Education of the State of Virginia has issued an edict that in order for a student to receive a high-school diploma he will have to be able to prove he can read, write and perform basic arithmetic computations.

If other states follow suit this radical step could eventually affect every high-school student in the country. Although the Virginia board won't put the rule into effect until 1978, many students are already claiming that the decision violates the Constitution as cruel and unusual punishment.

"Like," a Virginia high-school student told me, "I think that's an awful lot to expect of someone going to school. I mean they're asking us to prove we can read and write and also figure out decimals. How do they expect any of us to finish high school if they're going to make it that tough?"

"It does seem rather harsh," I admitted, "particularly since for ten years high-school graduates have not been required to prove they could do any of these things."

"It's not that we can't do *any* of them," he said. "Like in my class some kids can read, and I know some can write and others can add and subtract. But there's only about six that can do all three, ya' know?"

"I guess this will put more pressure on the teachers," I said.

"Yeh, they'll probably ruin the best years of our lives. I think a lot of kids will drop out of school if they're going to be expected to read and write and multiply and divide to get a diploma."

"Why do you think the board got so tough at this time?"

"They probably don't like kids. They're jealous of us because we have so much fun in high school. They're trying to turn us into robots."

"Perhaps," I said, "the colleges and universities have been putting pressure on them. I've heard that most universities are complaining that they have to spend so much time teaching high-school graduates the fundamentals of reading and writing that they don't have time to devote to higher education subjects."

"What do they expect of us anyway?" he said. "After all, we're only kids. I'm not saying reading and writing don't help you in some situations, but I think it should be optional until you get to college. A lot of kids don't want to go on to universities, so why should they be required to learn skills if they're never going to use them?"

"I don't have the answer," I said frankly. "Perhaps there are some taxpayers who feel that for all the money they spend on high schools in this country they would like to see the students come out of them with just three basic skills."

"Like maybe they feel that way, but a high school shouldn't be a prison where they tell you that you have to do this and you have to do that. It's a place where you should be able to expand your mind, ya' know. You're not going to learn about life out of books. A high school is a place where you make friends and learn how to drive a car, and go to concerts and stuff. A high school is where you root for the football team and the basketball team and have school spirit. That's what it's all about. Now they're going to load us up with homework and make us read books and write compositions and do math problems, and we're not going to have time for any of the things that really count."

I said, "The only thing I can say in the Board of Education's defense is that they have the decency to give you until 1979 to learn to read and write."

"They had to," he replied. "The Class of 1978 never would have been able to do it."

## WHY AMY CAN READ

To show you what a crazy town this is, President Carter recently presented his new budget to Congress and it provides for a $59 billion deficit. Hardly anyone raised an eyebrow. But when people in Washington read that Amy Carter had attended a state dinner for Prime Minister Trudeau, and read a book between courses, everyone went into a frenzy.

The capital is now divided between those who think it's outrageous to allow a 9-year-old child to read books at a state dinner, and those who believe if you get a kid to read these days, let her do it anywhere she wants to.

I'm on Amy's side. I haven't attended many state dinners in Washington, but there are many times I wish I had a book to read at the dinner table. There have even been embassy dinners where I wouldn't have minded perusing Hustler magazine.

But the anti-Amy reading people argue that the President's daughter is setting a bad example for children all over America.

One mother told me: "If she wants to read, why don't they feed her in the kitchen?"

Another said: "My daughter now brings her homework to the table. I told her it was forbidden and she replied, 'Amy can read at the table,' and I told her, 'When we have the Trudeaus over for dinner you can read, too.' "

I believe that most people are overreacting to Amy sticking her nose in a book between courses. I also am quite certain the Carters know what they're doing.

Every time a head of state comes to Washington he is testing the new President. He wants to see how far he can push President Carter. The President is too smart to admit he knows what the head of state is doing, and he's too much of a political animal to react to the testing directly.

So he invites Amy to attend his state dinners. While the head of the state is trying to get down to business he keeps glancing at the President's 9-year-old daughter with her nose stuck in a book. It's very disconcerting and throws the prime minister completely off balance. Even Brezhnev would have a tough time making a point for the Soviet Union to President Carter with Amy sitting at the table reading "The Mystery of the Black Lake with Nancy Drew."

Some paranoids in Washington have another theory. And that is Amy isn't really reading, but listening to everything everyone at the table is saying. After dinner her father and members of the CIA go up to her bedroom and debrief her. People will say anything that comes to their heads when they see a child reading, and Amy may be providing the President with some of his most vital national security intelligence.

I, for one, don't buy this. I believe that Amy has decided that most state dinners are a waste of time and if her parents make her attend them under duress, she's going to use the opportunity to catch up on books that she's been wanting to read for years, but which weren't available to her in Plains, Ga.

My wife, who is a literary agent, has even come up with an idea that could make the both of us wealthy. She wants to start an "Amy Book-of-the-Meal Club." People would be asked to subscribe to the club and would receive a book-a-meal which would be selected by Amy. There would be an alternate book selection for milk and crackers after school. If you purchased a week's supply of books for mealtime reading, you would get a free book for Sunday brunch.

After all the publicity about Amy's reading habits at state dinners my wife feels a "Book-of-the-Meal Club" is an idea whose time has come.

## WHAT IS OBSCENITY?

Mark Shields, a philosopher friend of mine, said the other night, "This country has come to a pretty pass when Harry Reems of *Deep Throat* and Larry Flynt of *Hustler* magazine have become the Sacco-Vanzetti of 1977."

What Mr. Shields was talking about was the fact that Mr. Reems and Mr. Flynt have been tried in Memphis and Cincinnati respectively on obscenity charges, and we civil libertarians have to defend them to protect ourselves.

Since the Supreme Court, in a cloudy decision, has left the question of obscenity up to local communities, it is getting more and more difficult to define exactly what it is.

For example, I have an aunt who lives in Boston and she thinks *Vogue* magazine is obscene because it has printed photographs of topless models.

One of my best Catholic friends believes *Ms.* magazine is obscene because it publishes stories advocating abortion.

I have a cousin in Tucson who canceled her subscription to *Time* magazine because it did a long takeout on pornographic films *with photographs* and my sister in New York thinks *Cosmopolitan* articles on how to steal somebody else's husband are the height of obscenity.

I must confess I'm rather loose about these things. I occasionally write for *Playboy* magazine, usually about tennis. But my wife won't read the publication and thinks I shouldn't be earning money from an obscene publication.

I did walk out after the first five minutes of *Deep Throat* because it made me queasy, but Russell Baker of *The New York Times*, with whom I went, stayed to the bitter end and got a column out of it. I told him later the column was obscene, but he just laughed at me.

My nephew, on the other hand, doesn't find anything in *any* magazine obscene. He thought the Vietnamese war was obscene and had no redeeming feature.

A brother-in-law in Cincinnati is not disturbed by the sale of *Hustler* on magazine stands, but thinks the advertisements urging people to buy bigger and bigger cars, when there is an energy shortage, are obscene.

A liberal friend of mine has told me he considers Bill Buckley's *National Review* obscene, and a columnist colleague who works across the hall from me keeps telling me my humor appeals to people's prurient interests.

In California, Frank Sinatra thinks most gossip columnists are obscene, and many gossip columnists say Frank Sinatra is obscene.

A school library board in New York State has decided Kurt Vonnegut is obscene and has voted to withdraw his books from its shelves.

Several parents' organizations have protested that a lot of black poetry is really filth, and their children shouldn't be exposed to it.

Thanks to the Supreme Court ruling, many local prosecutors have decided obscenity is the fastest steppingstone to higher political office and have become national TV personalities overnight.

So everyone in this country and many in the same towns and cities have their own definition of what obscenity is.

The problem is that people are being thrown in jail because of it.

The excuse is that the communities are trying to protect their children. This makes a lot of sense except for the fact that these same children are exposed to about 80 hours of violence each week on television, and many people consider violence the ultimate in obscenity compared to bare bosoms and the other junk that people have to pay a lot of money to see and read.

If they're going to throw Harry Reems and Larry Flynt into the slammer, I think they ought to go after Russell Baker, too. A guy who sits through the entire uncut version of *Deep Throat* is, in my opinion, a menace to the community.


## "ROOTS"

Ever since the tremendous impact of Alex Haley's "Roots," people all over this country have been searching for clues to their own ancestry. Mr. Haley was fortunate to find the history of his forebears through a "griot" (storyteller) in Gambia, and archives of the slave trade as well as stories his grandmother had told him.

The rest of us have not been that lucky. If our family is typical of many in this country the genealogy is going to be messed up forever. The problem is that my three sisters and I each remember the stories we heard from my father and his brother and sister differently.

At a recent family gathering we tried to reconstruct our roots, to pass on to our children.

"Our family came from Austria," one sister said.

"No, it was Poland," the other sister objected.

The third sister was adamant, "It was a town in what is now Czechoslovakia."

"I thought we came from Galicia, which doesn't exist any more," I said.

"Pop told me his father was a foreman on a large estate," my oldest sister told the children.

"That was his stepfather," my second sister said disgustedly. "His real father worked in a dry goods store before he died."

"I thought that was his uncle," my younger sister said.

"I heard he was a shoemaker."

"Pop's father begat five children," I said.

"No, he didn't. He begat two, Pop and Aunt Sarah."

"His stepfather begat Aunt Molly and Uncle Oscar."

"I'm sure there was another one," I said.

My sister said, "You always were known to exaggerate."

"Well, I know one thing for sure," I said. "We were distantly related to the Rothschilds."

"That was always one of your fantasies," my older sister said. "During World War I the Rothschilds supported a home in Vienna where Aunt Molly and Uncle Oscar were placed for safety."

"Well, it would have been easier if we were related to the Rothschilds. At least we could trace our ancestry by going to the movies."

"Our mother came from Hungary," my second sister said, "and had three sisters."

"No she didn't," my youngest sister objected. "She had a sister and brother."

"Who were her mother and father?" one of my nephews asked.

"Her father was named Kleinberger and he was a printer."

"He was not. He was a farmer."

My nieces and nephews were becoming bored. Nancy said, "Who is my father?"

"It's Harold," I said.

"No it isn't," Nancy's mother said. "It's Arthur."

"I'm Arthur," I said.

"My husband's name is Arthur, too," she replied.

"Then Harold is David's father," I said.

Harold, who was sitting there, said, "That's correct."

Michael, my nephew, said, "Then I was begat by my father."

"Right," his mother replied.

"Well, at least we have our generation straightened out," I said.

"I had Eric first," my older sister said.

"I thought I had David first," my second sister said.

"No," my older sister said firmly, "my husband begat Eric before you were married."

The kids left the room in disgust.

Alex Haley had many things going for him in the writing of "Roots" but I believe the most important is that he was smart enough never to discuss his lineage with his immediate family.

## A NEW EDUCATIONAL PLAN

There is a tremendous concern in this country about our educational system. At least 1,567 commissions are studying it; 18,732 professors are now writing books critical of it, and every politician running for office is demanding a change in it.

I myself have opted for the Makepiece Plan, put forward by Harvey Makepiece of the Society for the Abolishment of the Three-Chocolate-Milk Lunch.

Makepiece told me, "It's obvious that 5- and 6-year-olds are not ready for grade school. Their minds and bodies are too fragile to take on the difficult tasks that their teachers assign to them. They should have more leisure and fun before they get down to work."

"What do you suggest?" I asked him.

"We send them to college first and let them work off their high spirits."

"I'm not sure I follow."

"Let first graders have their first taste of school in college. Give them a chance to join sororities and fraternities, go to football games, frolic on the campuses and have panty raids in the dorms.

College is not the time for serious schoolwork, and it is the perfect place for children from the ages of 5 to 9 to have a good time and get used to attending classes, where they can sleep, flirt or cheat on their studies.

"Very few demands are made on college students. They can cut classes, spend their days in the student union and their evenings listening to rock music."

"And then what?" I said.

"After four years of college, a child is ready to tackle high school. High school, as you know, is just a little tougher than college, and a child would have to get down to work. Not too much work, but enough to get him or her interested in books. The student would still have an opportunity to attend football games, date once in a while if he or she wanted to, go to an occasional dance and drive around in a car after three o'clock.

"But high school would still give the youth a feeling that life is not a bowl of cherries and that he or she is going to have to take education seriously.

"Also, the student would have to work hard because he or she knows that there are only a certain number of places open in grade school, and to be able to go on to the school of his or her choice would mean making the grades to qualify."

"Then," I said, "what you're advocating is that grade school be the last one a student must attend."

"That's correct. After the pleasures of college and the joys of high school, a student should be mature enough to face life in the tough world of grade school. There are no fraternities or sororities to distract them. Social life is at a bare minimum, teachers in grade schools don't take any back talk from their students, and corporal punishment is permitted. Lower public schools have no football teams or extracurricular activities. If the truth be known, it's an eight-year grind, and no one accepts any excuses from a kid who can't make it from grades one to eight."

"But grade school is so long," I protested. "Do you think teenagers could go the distance without dropping out?"

"No one drops out of grade school. All of them are prepared to come to grips with it, particularly when a grade school diploma will be the highest one that any student can receive. A grade school education under my system is what every parent in this country will want for his kid."

"But what about graduate school?" I asked.

"Those who want to go on to graduate school could enroll in kindergarten."

"You're advocating a complete reversal of the American educational system," I said. "Do you think this country is ready for it?"

"After what we've seen of our students for the past ten years, this country is ready for anything."


## BILLY, SAY IT AIN'T SO!

Mr. Billy Carter
Plains, Ga.
Dear Billy,

I just read in the newspapers that you have signed up with a high-powered agent from Nashville, Tennessee, to represent you in the area of personal appearances and the media. Your agent claims you're the hottest personality in America and he's going to package you and make you a potful of money.

Say it ain't so, Billy. Say you ain't sold out for a mess of pork chops. You were the greatest free spirit we had in this country. As far as we working stiffs were concerned you were the first folk hero to come along in decades. We identified with you, Billy Boy. All you seemed to need was a can of beer and an oil barrel to sit on, and you could spit at the world.

You told them dumb newspaper people anything they wanted to hear. Your gas station was a beacon of truth which lit the skies of a new South. You didn't give a hoot for Washington or all them big shots who were snickering at you behind your back. You made jackasses out of them at the Inauguration, and we were counting on you to make jackasses out of them for the next four years.

You know why, Billy? Because we knew you couldn't be bought. People in bars all over America said, "Jimmy may not be able to save the country, but Billy will."

So when I read you signed up with some outfit called "Top Billing, Inc.," I couldn't believe it.

Do you have any idea what they're going to do to you? Look

what the William Morris Agency did to Mark Spitz. They had him selling milk. That's what I said, Billy, MILK! Suppose your agent signs you up to become the spokesman for the dairy industry? Do you know what that could do for your image? You're not only going to have to push the stuff on TV commercials, but according to the law you're going to have to drink it when you're not on TV. Think of it, Billy, they're going to make you consume a quart of milk a day.

You saw what they did to Joe Namath when they packaged him. They made him dress in women's nylon pantyhose. How are you going to face the boys back in Plains after you've done a pantyhose commercial? Every hard-hat in America will turn against you.

And what about O.J. Simpson? Suppose they sign you up to run through airports with your suitcase and jump over barriers so you can rent a Hertz car? You're just not in condition for that sort of thing, Billy. That could kill you before you got the keys to the car.

Besides commercials, your agent ain't going to let you talk to newspapermen any more for free. He's going to charge for every word you utter. You're going to wind up in Reader's Digest telling people how you learned to love the FBI and found God. They'll have you doing pieces for the Ladies' Home Journal on your favorite chicken recipes, and Family Circle will probably name a diet after you.

They'll book you at state fairs and have you play a Yankee carpetbagger in the sequel of "Roots." Everyone will own a piece of you and you'll be working so hard for your agent you won't have time to go fishing or dig for earthworms or even roast a bag of peanuts.

Before you know it, Billy, you'll be escorting Hollywood starlets to motion picture premieres and having your photo taken with Raquel Welch and Ann-Margret.

And then you'll wind up putting Aqua Velvet on yourself and some girl will slap your face and they'll make you say, "Thank you, I needed that!"

Yes, Billy Boy, they'll make you rich, but they'll break your heart. I'm pleading with you. Us working people have always looked up to you because you were your own man. I ask you, Billy, what profiteth a man if he gains the world's riches but loses his six-pack of beer?

## REMEDIAL COLLEGE

The Timkens sent their child Laura off to college with a check for $7,000 in tuition and thought that was the end of it. But soon after they received a letter from the Dean of Studies.

"We are happy to announce that we have instituted a remedial reading class for college freshmen and strongly advise that your daughter Laura participate in it. If she doesn't, it is our opinion that Laura will not be able to keep up with her studies. The cost will be $250."

Timken read the letter. "I thought Laura could read," he said to his wife.

"So did I. I think the problem is she can read, but she has no comprehension of what she reads."

"What did they teach her in public school and high school?"

"I have no idea, but if the college says she needs remedial reading we better see that she gets it or $7,000 will go down the drain."

A few days later they got another letter from the dean.

"The English Department has brought to our attention the fact that your daughter Laura cannot write. They have recommended that she enroll in the remedial writing class which we started two years ago when we discovered this was a common problem for most college students. If you agree that Laura should get this special help, please send a check for $250."

Timken was now very angry.

"How did she get in college if she can't write?"

Mrs. Timken was much more sanguine about it. "Laura can write. She just can't write complete sentences."

"She went to school for twelve years and she can't write a sentence?"

"Don't you remember? They were much more interested in Laura's thoughts than they were in how she put them down. The teacher's main concern was with expanding her consciousness."

"That's hogwash," Timken said. "They made an illiterate out of my daughter."

"I believe that's a bit strong. Laura graduated with honors in analytical consciousness-raising."

"But she can't write."

"I'm sure the college can help her learn to write. After all, it is an institution of higher learning."

"So now we have to pay $250 for something they should have taught her in grammar school?"

"Don't you remember when we went to the PTA meeting years ago, and the principal said it was the school's responsibility to make good citizens out of the students, and the parents' responsibility to teach the children how to read and write? Carlton, we're the ones who failed."

Timken sent in the check, and was not surprised to find another letter waiting for him a week later.

It read: "It has come to our attention that no one in the freshman class can add, multiply, subtract or divide simple sums. We feel it is urgent that this deficiency be corrected early in a student's college career. Therefore, we are setting up a special remedial arithmetic course. The fee will be $250. If you do not want your daughter to take this course we cannot guarantee she will graduate."

Once again Timken went through the ceiling. "I thought Laura got A's in math in high school."

Mrs. Timken said, "That was conceptional math. Her courses had to do with the advanced integration of numbers. She never could add or subtract them. Don't you recall when you complained once about it and Laura's teacher told you, 'She can always learn to add and subtract when she gets to college.'?"

## NO PARKING

As the fall college term is about to begin, faculty members in every part of the country are asking the same question: "Will I get a decent parking space at my school this year?"

It is not generally known outside of academic circles, but most professors are more concerned with their place in the Reserved Faculty parking lot than they are with any of the educational problems they have to deal with during the school term.

One of the reasons for this is that a faculty member's standing at his or her university is usually based on where the professor is assigned to park.

I heard of a tragic story that took place the other day at a leading Eastern university. A professor, I shall call him Rubloff, came back to school to discover that he had been assigned to Faculty Parking Lot B, which was 1,500 yards from the Administration Building. For five years, Rubloff had a space reserved for him in Faculty Parking Lot A, which was only 100 yards from the Ad Building. He couldn't believe it, so he immediately demanded an appointment with the chancellor of the university.

"I want to know why I've been placed in Parking Lot B when I've always parked in Lot A," Rubloff said.

The chancellor said, "It was not my decision, Rubloff. As you know, we have a Faculty Parking Lot Committee, and they make all the assignments."

"On the basis of my seniority, I have the right to keep my car in Parking Lot A."

"That's true," the chancellor said, "But seniority no longer plays a role in parking lot assignments."

"That's ridiculous," Rubloff said. "What other standard can be used?"

The chancellor said wearily, "We've had to change the criteria. It seems most of the women faculty members found they had to park in Lot B. The Women's Faculty Caucus demanded equal parking privileges with the men. They said if they didn't get it they would sue the school. We had no choice but to change the system of assigning places. I'm sure you'll be very happy in Parking Lot B. The longer walk will be good for your health."

"But why me? I notice Seagram is still in Parking Lot A and so is Teetoler. They got their tenure three years after I did."

"If you want me to be frank with you, Rubloff, the committee discovered you hadn't written a scientific paper in several years. They felt you're more interested in writing letters to *The New York Times* than you are in furthering your academic research. There was also the question of the unfavorable book review you wrote on Professor Carstairs' 'Root Canal Work of the 14th Century.' Carstairs is chairman of the Faculty Parking Committee."

"So that's it," Rubloff shouted. "Carstairs is getting back at me for saying his book had no bite to it. I stand by my review."

"And Carstairs stands by your parking lot assignment."

"Don't you realize what you're doing to my academic standing?" Rubloff asked. "When the students find out they have a professor relegated to Parking Lot B they'll laugh me out of the classroom. Those kids can be cruel when they want to be."

"Rubloff," said the chancellor, "if it were up to me you could have my reserved parking place which is covered and also up against the building. But I'm only the chancellor, and I cannot interfere in faculty parking matters. Your peers are the only ones who can decide what kind of sticker to put on your car."

"Don't I have a right of appeal?"

"It's too late for this term. Your place has been given to Dr. Mary Ogelthorpe."

"But she's only an associate professor."

"She also happens to be in charge of the Faculty Tow Truck Pool."

## YOU ALL SPOKEN HERE

I'm grateful to Roy Wilder Jr. and David Moffett of the "Gourd Hollow Press" in Raleigh, North Carolina, who sent me two little books titled *You All Spoken Here*, devoted to how country people speak in the South.

Nobody knows how many people from the Deep South Jimmy Carter will bring with him, but the dictionaries will be invaluable to help us know what they're talking about.

For example, if the Carters are throwing a dinner party at the White House and there is a discussion of the guest list, one of Mr. Carter's aides might say, "He's too poor to paint, and too proud to whitewash." They would be discussing, of course, a member of the Southern aristocracy.

If a Southern member of the staff says to you, "Don't get cross-legged," he is telling you not to get angry, or your wires crossed, or your signals mixed, or upset without knowing the situation.

There will be occasions when someone in the Carter entourage gets mad at a congressman or a senator. He may then tell the press, "He's three pickles shy of a barrel." This means he doesn't have all his marbles or "He's three bricks shy of a load" or that "his traces ain't hooked up right."

If the same person says the congressman or senator is "Passin' gas faster'n he can cap it," it means the person in question is a windbag.

A cabinet officer may be in trouble with the President. If someone says he "pulled through" it means his sins have been forgiven and "he's ready for deep dip baptism."

Despite a Carter Administration there will always be sex scandals in Washington. A man caught in one will be known as a person who is "wild as a boar in a peach orchard," which means he is unrestrained in his sexual passion.

If the President has not seen one of his appointees for a long time he might ask him, "Did you winter well?" which is what someone in the Deep South asks a person in the spring that he hasn't laid eyes on since Christmas.

Since Mr. Carter has never been to Washington he is not acquainted with too many members of the Establishment. He might be asked, for example, if he knew Clark Clifford. The President could reply, "We've howdied but we ain't shook," which would mean that the President knows the name, but he was never introduced.

Some Presidential appointments may get more power than others. In this case, the person in question will be referred to in the Administration as a "big dog in the meat house."

If you are invited to the White House for dinner you can tell your friends: "Last night I ate the President's salt." The worst thing is to "eat another man's salt" and then knock him in public. If word gets out that you did, it could make the President angry and his press secretary might say, "The President is as mad as a rooster in an empty henhouse."

If you apologized publicly, that "would put spit on the apple" and end the argument.

Suppose the Secretary of State is confused about a diplomatic problem. The White House aides might leak the fact that the Secretary is "like a rubber-nosed woodpecker in a petrified forest."

When someone comes back from a trip overseas and brags about it he will be known as "journey proud."

If he lies to the President they will say of him, "His mouth ain't no prayer book."

If he failed to give the President the information he wanted, a White House aide might say, "He never said pea turkey" or "We got what the bear grabbed at," which means they got nothing out of the conversation.

How will you know if Mr. Carter is angry? If he ever says "That takes the rag off the bush," Brezhnev better watch out, because the lowest thing someone can do in the Deep South is steal someone's washrag that he left on a bush to dry.

## $64,000 IS TOO LOW

The news item that rocked America a short time ago was that it now costs parents $64,000 to rear a child, including education at a state-supported university. A low-income family can rear one for $44,000 if you forget about his or her schooling.

According to Professor Thomas J. Espenshade of Florida State University, this is a 60 percent increase over what it cost in 1969.

With all due respect to Professor Espenshade, I think his figures are too low. While he threw in the usual things such as food, clothing, housing and education, I think he failed to take into consideration the following items:

—Automobile insurance for a teen-ager: $1,000 a year.

—Automobile insurance for the parents, when the company cancels everyone's policy because of the claims filed for the teen-ager's accidents: $3,000.

—Repairs to interior of the house after a party given by teen-ager for 50 of his or her "dearest" friends: $2,000.

—Food and drink dispensed to non-members of the family, who for one reason or another are always at the house: $6,000.

—Rug and furniture damage caused by teen-ager's untrained dog: $2,500.

—Rock concert tickets for children starting at age 11 and lasting until they get a job, which could be age 30: $3,800.

—Orthodontist bills for straightening teeth by braces: $2,000.

—Orthodontist bills for replacing braces that were accidentally lost on overnight camping trip: $1,200.

—Replacement of lost winter gloves, shoes, socks and overcoats left at a friend's house, whose name child cannot remember: $800.

—Hi-fi equipment, absolutely essential to the peace of mind of a young person: $100 to $1,000, depending on whether child pays cash or uses family credit card.

—Birthday presents for friends who are having lavish parties their parents can't afford: $1,200.

—Birthday parties you give for your own children that you can't afford: $2,000.

—Collect telephone calls from children at camp, school or gas station on the highway, to find out why kids have not called collect in three weeks: $5,600.

—Unpaid tickets for illegal parking sent to parents because car is registered in their name: $780.

—Fines for library books overdue: $150.

—Cost of hiring someone to cut lawn because children don't have "time" to do it: $3,400.

—Football, baseball, hockey uniforms (now both male and female): $890.

—New clothes for Barbie and Ken dolls: $4,500.

—Gas and oil used for car pools for student and athletic activities: $3,000 (and expected to go higher).

—Records and tapes that children will die if they don't own: $4,700.

—Visits to hospital emergency rooms: $2,000.

—School prom tickets, as well as rental of tuxedos for boys, purchase of dresses for girls and money to "go out after the dance": $600.

—Replacement of wine and booze stolen from liquor cabinet or closet by persons unknown: $1,500 to $5,000, depending on what kind of wine you keep and how well you hide the key to cabinet or closet.

—Miscellaneous items not covered in the study by Professor Espenshade: legal fees for pot busts and arrests for disorderly conduct or sit-downs to protest building of nuclear energy plants; damage to neighbor's property done by your children; abortions; purchase of church or school raffle tickets your children have been unable to sell; parcel post packages; ski trips; remedial reading; Christmas. To be on the conservative side, we'll put down $8,780.

Professor Espenshade did a good job, but I suspect he just didn't talk to the right people.


## THE AMY-MISS LILLIAN THREAT

Republican strategists met recently to discuss the Democratic National Convention and the Carter-Mondale ticket. They were worried about what they had seen on television.

One of them said, "I think we can handle Carter and Mondale, but what are we going to do about the kid and the mother?"

"What kid and what mother?" someone else asked.

"Amy Carter and Miss Lillian. A 9-year-old kid and a 77-year-old mother are a tough combination to beat, particularly when they're both eager to campaign."

"Our research people have been trying to dig up stuff on them. You know the kid doubled the price of lemonade she was selling to reporters in Plains, Ga., from a nickel to a dime. Can we do anything with that?"

"Only if we want to knock the free enterprise system. Don't forget one of the planks of our platform is to let the businessman charge whatever the lemonade market will permit. By doubling her price when there was a shortage, Amy was following the Republican philosophy. If we attack her on the lemonade issue, it could backfire on us."

"I guess you're right. Are there any skeletons in her closet that we can leak to the press?"

"We found one skeleton, but it was from a Halloween party she went to last year. We can't do anything with that."

"There's got to be something. A 9-year-old kid is always getting into trouble. Has she hit any kids in school?"

"If she has, they aren't talking. You know how Southerners clam up when someone comes around asking questions."

"Okay, let's forget the kid for a moment. What have we got on the mother?"

"Nothing. She looks like everybody's mother, or at least like everybody would like his mother to look. Frankly I think we better lay off Miss Lillian or we could get a lot of voters angry at us."

"Good grief. This woman is dangerous. She could wipe us out on the talk shows. We can't stand by and let her steal the election from us."

"We better tread carefully," one of the strategists said. "Miss Lillian is a personal friend of Walter Cronkite's. She spent the whole evening with him in the booth on nomination night. If we go after her, Walter's going to be furious."

"We can't allow Walter to get mad at us," someone agreed.

"All right, wise guys. We can't touch Amy, and you say we have to lay off Miss Lillian. At the same time you all agree the combination of the two of them could murder us. What do we do?"

"We have to find our own Amy and Miss Lillian."

"Impossible. Ford's kids are too old and so are Reagan's."

"Yeh, but don't forget neither one of them has chosen his Vice President yet. They've got to choose a VP who has a 9-year-old daughter and a 77-year-old mother. I say we start a search now for a Vice Presidential candidate who can provide both."

"That's not going to be easy." someone warned.

"But it's possible. I want you to go over every Republican list you have and find someone who can fit the bill."

"I found one Vice Presidential possibility, but his kid has never sold lemonade in her life."

"Well, she can start learning. We'll get the Marriott Corporation to build her a lemonade stand."

"Okay, but we may have trouble with the mother. She doesn't believe her son should be Vice President. She says politics is a dirty business and she wants no part of it."

"How does she feel about Walter Cronkite?"

"She never watches him. She prefers Brinkley and Chancellor."

"We better scratch her and start looking for somebody else."

# VI.  The Wasps Are Restless

## CARTER IS GOOD FOR US

A meeting of the American Society of Humorists, Satirists and Political Cartoonists was held in the basement of the First Baptist Church of Washington one morning to discuss the effects of the election on our profession.

Everyone was bullish about the results, believing that Jimmy Carter would provide us with excellent material for the next four years. (Our society always asks what our country can do for us, not what we can do for our country.)

"Any guy who says 'I will never lie to you,' " said one cartoonist, "can't be all bad."

"I'm sorry for Gerry Ford," said another cartoonist, "but I needed Carter's teeth. No one ever knew whom I was drawing when I sketched Ford."

A political satirist said, "The beauty of Carter is that he's the first President we've had that we know lusts after women in his heart. That in itself is a big plus. We've had Presidents who did it and Presidents who didn't do it. But this is the first President we'll have who doesn't do it but thinks about it a lot."

"What I'm looking forward to," said another political satirist, "is the family. Billy Carter, Jimmy's brother, Miss Lillian and Amy, his daughter, should keep us in business for a year."

A political cartoonist said, "And don't forget we have Sunday school and Plains, Georgia, to work with. All we have to draw is a peanut and a Bible and everyone in the country will know whom we are talking about."

"Carter's Administration could be a Camelot for humorists and cartoonists," someone said.

"Of course, we're going to miss Rockefeller," someone else said. "Fritz Mondale is a nice guy, but he's no Rockefeller."

"You can say that again," a columnist said. "But then again Rockefeller was no Agnew."

"You can say that again."

"What are we going to do with Mondale?" a cartoonist asked.

Another cartoonist said, "When we draw him we'll have to write on his coat, 'Fritz Mondale, Vice President of the United States.' "

"Dole was easier. All you had to do was draw a guy who looked like Nixon, holding a hatchet in his hand, and everyone knew who he was."

"I don't want to throw a wet blanket on this meeting," another cartoonist said, "but do you realize we're not going to have Henry Kissinger to kick around any more?"

"I forgot that," someone said. "What are we going to do without Kissinger? He was great for laughs."

"And so easy to draw."

I said, "I'm sick about losing Henry. He put bread on our table."

"There'll never be another Kissinger," someone said.

A stand-up comedian tried to cheer us up. "Forget Kissinger. We've got Pat Moynihan and S.I. Hayakawa in the Senate. They could make up for Henry. We never expected Kissinger to last forever."

"It's funny. I did," I said.

The president of the society stood up. "Can we get on with the business of this meeting? I propose we send a telegram of congratulations to Jimmy Carter and wish him well and tell him that if he makes as many boo-boos in the White House as he did in the campaign, he'll get no complaints from us."

"I second it," someone said.

"All those in favor say aye. Opposed? The ayes have it. Herb Block will now lead us in the closing prayer."

## TO SECEDE OR NOT

The decision of Martha's Vineyard and Nantucket to secede from the United States is no idle threat. It has been in the works for some time. As a matter of fact, a group of us discussed it one night two years ago at a cookout on William Styron's beach. Lots of lobster had been eaten and daiquiris consumed when the question of secession from the mainland came up.

I think it was Lillian Hellman, or possibly John Hersey, who mentioned that something had to be done to stop the illegal immigration of people from Cape Cod who came over to the vineyard in the daytime, left all their trash there and then took the ferry back at night.

Styron said that Bostonians had been investing in real estate on the Vineyard, and before we woke up to it the entire island would be infested with rich Harvard professors and claim adjusters from the John Hancock Life Insurance Co.

Jules Feiffer said that fishermen from Hyannisport were encroaching on Vineyard waters and stealing all the bluefish which swam under his pier. Jules was for instituting a 200-mile fishing limit around the Vineyard or 20 feet from his pier, whichever was greater.

Bob Brustein, head of the Yale Drama School, felt that the sailing ships from the New York Regatta should not be permitted to come into Edgartown. "The crews are a bad influence on our children," he said. "They throw their money around, get into fights in bars and the stockbrokers steal our women."

I pointed out that while the tourists brought money to the island they also insisted on taking our pictures, plying our daughters with nylons and Hershey bars and dressing in whites to play tennis.

More daiquiris were passed around and then the question of secession came up.

The first question was asked by Phillip Roth: Could Martha's Vineyard and Nantucket go it alone?

Rose Styron, Bill's wife, thought we could.

"What about fuel for the island?"

James Reston, who owns the Vineyard Gazette, said, "That's no problem. There are oil spills from tankers off the coast at least twice a year. The oil that floats ashore is more than enough to take care of our needs."

"What about food?" James Taylor asked.

"Simple," said Rose Styron. "If we're independent from the United States they would be obligated to supply us with everything we needed under the Food for Peace program."

"We would also be entitled to a Peace Corps," someone added. "They could cut our lawns."

"Don't forget military aid," Brustein added.

"We can't get military aid unless we have a Communist threat."

One of the writers who was eating a lobster claw said, "I was once a Communist in the '40s."

"That solves *that* problem," Brustein said.

"Okay," John Hersey said, "it's obvious that once we become independent we'll get American aid which will keep us going. But we'll have to have a leader. We need someone who will stand up to the United States and tell them that even though we're accepting their aid we're not going to be pushed around. Whom can we get?"

We passed around the daiquiris as we thought.

Then someone jumped up. "I've got it. Let's make Katharine Graham, the owner of *The Washington Post*, our prime minister. She has been called the most powerful woman in America. If she becomes the prime minister of Martha's Vineyard and Nantucket she could become the most powerful woman in the world."

"I'll drink to that," I said.

And so the seeds of independence were planted that night on William Styron's beach. In years to come the beach will be known as the Munich Beer Hall of the First Republic of Martha's Vineyard and Nantucket. The name will probably be changed to Martha's Tucket as soon as a Declaration of Independence is written by Phillip Roth, who has provisionally titled it, "Martha's Complaint."

## HOORAY FOR CONGRESS

Congress is criticized for a lot of things it does to waste the taxpayer's money. But you rarely read about what it does to save us all money. I think it's time we newspapermen printed something nice about our lawmakers when they deserve it.

A story in a recent paper, buried on the inside pages, is an illustration of what I'm talking about.

The Agriculture Department announced it was cutting down on its free milk program for 1.4 million needy schoolchildren. Starting on February 1, an Assistant Secretary of Agriculture announced that needy children would no longer be given a second helping of milk at school mealtime if they requested it. They would get only half a pint and if they wanted any more they would have to pay for it.

The secretary explained that the edict was put into effect because a recent law "expressed the concern of the Congress that some of the free milk was being wasted."

A spokesman said that taking away the second free serving of milk for needy children would save the government $25 million a year.

Now this is the kind of tax-saving that every American can applaud. I don't know which congressional committee discovered that kids need only half a pint of milk with their meals, but these men and women legislators should be congratulated for putting their feet down and saying, "Enough is enough. We will not support a program which gives needy children more milk than they can drink. As watchdogs of reckless spending it is our duty to cut down on waste and, if you can't do it with free milk, where can you do it in the federal budget?"

What amazes me is how Congress got wind of the fact that some needy kids were trashing their second half-pint of milk.

Since the newspaper story didn't say, I can only guess it came from either an informer planted among the schoolchildren or from garbage pails dug up by the staff of the Joint Congressional Committee on Milk Waste.

There are some bleeding hearts in this country who will probably write to me and suggest that Congress pass a law saying that if the kids ask for second half-pints they should have to drink it all. But you don't save taxpayers' money that way. All you do is encourage needy children to drink more milk.

The worst thing you can do in this country is give a needy child a second helping at school mealtime. For one thing it raises expectations, and they will start to believe that they can get seconds any time they want them. By limiting the milk intake of each poor schoolchild, Congress is saying in no uncertain terms that it will no longer tolerate this kind of overrun in government spending. It's one thing to vote money for tanks that don't move and planes that don't fly and dams that don't dam, but when it comes to blowing money on half-pints of milk the elected officials of this country are on the ball.

A saving of $25 million out of a national budget of $400 billion may not sound like much to some people, but as a taxpayer I can't think of a more worthy place to cut back spending than in a school milk program.

As someone who has been critical of the way Congress throws our money around, it is a pleasure to give them credit when credit is due.

The men and women responsible for this bill deserve high marks for serving notice on the schoolchildren of America that we tax-payers are sick and tired of giving them second half-pints of milk, and if they aren't careful we might even take their first half-pint away from them, too.

It's about time someone in this country said to its poor children, "There's no such thing as a free lunch."


## SOUTH KOREA AND GIFTS

I don't believe that the House Ethics Committee can truly understand the Korean investigation unless they read a book entitled, "Korean Patterns," by Dr. Paul Shields Crane, distributed in this country by the University of Washington Press.

Dr. Crane has spent most of his life in Korea and wrote the book as a guide for Americans and other foreigners who are not acquainted with the customs of this Far Eastern ally.

The chapter that is relevant to the Korean scandal is called, "The Problem of Gifts."

It begins, "Koreans are among the most gracious and generous people one will meet. They are thoughtful and considerate, and try by every means to establish personal relationships before they conduct any business . . . . The giving and receiving of gifts are considered the normal operating commission for services rendered. In this context, every gift-giver expects something in return."

Dr. Crane says Koreans are very friendly and have the ability to work their way into the affections of foreigners which, at some later date, might prove embarrassing. "Many Koreans," he writes, "expect to use their friendships and connections for personal advantage and see nothing amiss in this approach as long as they are the main recipients of the favors." The only time a Korean becomes truly angry is when another Korean gives a foreigner a better gift than he does. Then he becomes critical of the foreigner "who has been so stupid as to allow himself to be taken in by a group of thieves."

The part of Dr. Crane's chapter that should be studied by the House Ethics Committee has to do with the manner in which Korean gifts are dispensed.

For example, it is a Korean custom, after a death in the family, to present the grieving relative with a white envelope stuffed with cash.

It seems to me that, since the main thrust of the investigation in the House has to do with congressmen accepting white envelopes of cash from the Koreans, Leon Jaworski should investigate to find out how many U.S. legislators had deaths in their families at the time they accepted the money from the Korean CIA.

This is what could have happened. A Korean agent on instructions from his government could have met a congressman in the halls of the Capitol and said, as he handed him the white envelope, "I'm sorry your mother died."

"My mother didn't die," the congressman might have replied, giving him back the envelope.

"Well, has anyone in your family died recently?"

"I had a second cousin in Canoga Park who died a month ago."

The Korean agent would hand back the envelope, "Then please accept this with President Park's personal condolences."

"I wasn't too close to my second cousin."

"If you were, the envelope would be twice as full."

I'm not saying this happened, but it's worth looking into. If any congressman or aide accepted a white envelope at the time there was a death in the family, I believe he should be given immunity from prosecution.

For the bereaved to refuse condolences in the form of a sealed white envelope is the worst insult you can inflict on a South Korean, and could not only make him lose face but destroy an endearing friendship forever.

## THE AMERICAN DREAM

I walked into my son's room as he was stretched out on his bed watching a basketball game on television.

"Son," I said, "I'd like to talk to you about the American dream."

"Yes, Dad."

"Remember when I told you a few years ago that someday you would have everything you ever wanted in life, thanks to the American dream?"

"Yes, Dad," he said, "and I've been counting on it ever since."

"Well, son, I just heard President Carter talk about energy on TV and he said no one can count on the American dream any more. It's a whole new ball game, and we're going to have to make sacrifices and give up many things that we've gotten used to."

"Why us, Dad?" my son asked.

"Because we're consumers, son. We're using up energy faster than it can be produced. We're slothful, wasteful people who haven't given a thought to the future."

"But we're Americans, Dad," he said.

"I know. It's hard to believe Americans would do anything bad, but it turns out even America is running out of fuel much faster than we ever dreamed we would. No one ever thought it would happen to the good guys. Son, I don't know how to tell you this, but someday, when you become successful and achieve the wherewithal to enjoy the fruits of your labor, you will probably not be able to buy a large Cadillac."

My son bit his lip to keep from crying. "But you promised!" he cried.

"I know I promised you a Cadillac but it isn't my fault I can't deliver. This country, despite its power and greatness, can no longer afford the luxury of gas guzzlers that only get twelve miles to the gallon. You're going to have to be satisfied with a small car which Detroit will have to make if we are to survive as a viable and free nation."

"How small?" he wanted to know.

"Very small," I told him. "But that isn't all. Someday you're going to get married and have a wife and children."

"I remember you telling me that," my son replied. "And you said that if I worked hard and married, well, I could have a heated swimming pool."

"Well, son, you can still have the children, but by then I doubt if you can install the heated swimming pool."

"Why would I want kids if I can't have a heated swimming pool?"

"They can swim in an unheated pool. It's actually not bad when you get used to it."

"The next thing you're going to tell me is that when I grow up there won't be electric golf carts and I'll have to walk the entire eighteen holes."

"It could come to that," I admitted, "though the President didn't mention anything about electric golf carts. There is a certainty, though, that our homes will be colder in the winter and hotter in the summer. And you may have to give up electrical appliances such as can openers."

"You mean I'm going to have to open up cans manually?"

"It can be done," I assured him.

"What about my stereo set?" he demanded.

"You could be limited to four speakers."

"What kind of American dream is that when each person can have only four speakers?"

"It's not the America anyone has known in the past. But our survival depends on conservation, and whether anyone likes it or not we're going to have to give up the things we hold dearest to us— like snowmobiles and lighted tennis courts and throwaway razors. God knows I've worked and scraped so you could have everything you wanted in life. But it just wasn't meant to be. Do you think any one of us ever imagined that someday our children would have to take a bus?"

"A bus!" he yelled.

"I was saving that for last."


## AN INTERNAL AFFAIR

The "human rights" issue in the Soviet Union has the Kremlin terribly upset. The question is why? I posed this problem to my good friend Gregor, a minor functionary at the Soviet Embassy with high KGB connections.

"Gregor," I said, "why on earth are you people so excited about a few malcontents in your country? Surely you, as the first or second most powerful nation in the world, can stand a little criticism from a few dissidents who march to a different drummer."

"Is personal matter and none of your business!" Gregor said sourly.

"I'm not chiding you, Gregor, for your stand," I said. "I'm just curious why the full power of the state has come down with such force on a handful of men? Is the Communist system so fragile that it can't allow one or two people to complain about the political condition in your country?"

Gregor scowled. "Do you want détente or don't you want détente?"

"Of course, I want détente."

"Then stop asking me such stupid questions."

"Gregor, that's no way to talk to a friend who gave you an entire set of blueprints for the Edsel. I'm trying to understand what makes your leaders tick. Why do you keep arresting people for speaking out for a little more freedom?"

"There is no such thing as a little freedom," Gregor said. "There is either freedom or no freedom. America wants to destroy us with freedom."

"We do not," I protested. "We like you just the way you are. But frankly, you're very boring people. You keep saying the same thing over and over again. It's nice to hear a fresh voice from Moscow every once in a while, even if he doesn't have a following."

"How do you know he doesn't have a following?"

"I just assumed it," I said. "I can't believe, from what I read in the Soviet press, that these people are nothing more than maniacs who belong in mental institutions. Do they really have many supporters in your country?"

"We don't know and we're not going to find out," Gregor said.

"Gregor, you sound frightened. Do you really believe that a few writers and scientists would drive you into a free state?"

"Not a free state—a Capitalist state. We don't want any part of Capitalism."

"I don't blame you. It's a messy system. We have gas shortages, coffee at $3 a pound, and you can't even find a parking place when you want it. But surely Sakharov and Ginzburg, and a few others, don't have it in their power to make the Soviet Union a capitalist country."

"Maybe yes—maybe no. But that is for us to decide. Just because we buy your wheat does not give your President an excuse to write to one of our traitors."

"President Carter didn't mean any harm. He answers all his mail. It's a habit he picked up when he was selling peanuts."

Gregor hit his fist on the table. "Well, we won't stand for it. How would you like it if Brezhnev wrote to one of your dissidents, Ronald Reagan?"

"I wouldn't mind, but I don't think Reagan would like it. He might want to run for President in 1980 and a letter from Brezhnev would kill his chances."

"Why should Americans care what we do to our writers and scientists?" he shouted at me.

"That's a good question, Gregor. We shouldn't care but we do. I guess you could call it one of our weaknesses. We hate to see people anywhere locked up for their thoughts. If you were a Fascist country many of us would feel the same way."

Gregor stared at me. "This is your last warning. Stay out of our internal affairs, or else."

I refused to blink. "Don't threaten me, Gregor, or I'll get President Carter to write Sakharov another letter."


## PANAMA ARM TWISTING

There were a lot of rumors that President Carter did some old-fashioned arm twisting to get enough votes for the first part of the Panama Canal treaty vote in the Senate.

This was strongly denied not only by the White House but by senators who showed up the next day with their arms in slings.

Senator Chisholm Chippendale told me he didn't think anyone in the Carter Administration leaned on him to vote for the treaty.

"I did get a call from Rosalynn a week before," he admitted, "but she just wanted to know how my wife was."

"That was thoughtful of her," I said.

"Actually, it was kind of strange," Chippendale said, "because I'm not married."

"They're weak on research at the White House," I said. "Anything else out of the ordinary happen last week?"

"Well, I don't know if it's worth mentioning but Ham Jordan came out to the house on Monday and offered to cut my lawn. I told him it didn't seem worth cutting because of the winter, so he said he'd mulch it for me."

"All by himself?"

"No, Jody Powell came out about noon and helped him. I thought that was real nice of those two boys, what with all they've got to do."

"Ham likes to mulch lawns," I told him. "Then what happened?"

"Well, I was working in my office on Tuesday and a box with a note in this girl's handwriting arrived from the White House. It was full of chocolate-chip cookies and the note said, 'I couldn't think of anyone I'd rather make chocolate-chip cookies for than you.' At the end of the letter she said, 'I love you,' and it was signed 'Amy.' I thought that was really sweet."

"Weren't you suspicious of all the attention you were getting from the Carter people?"

"Heck, no. I just thought they were being right friendly."

"But I read somewhere they never answered your telephone calls in the past."

"That's true, but I called on Tuesday afternoon to find out what day we were going to celebrate the Fourth of July this year and guess who they put me through to?"

"Chip Carter?"

"Nope, Vice President Fritz Mondale. I was embarrassed to ask someone of his stature such a simple question, but he just laughed and said, 'That's what I'm here for.'"

"You really had a great week."

"That's not the end of it. U.S. Trade Negotiator Bob Strauss stopped by to see me that evening and invited me to go to Japan with him to talk to Japanese bankers about the yen. I'm not big on the yen, so he said I could visit a geisha house while he talked to the bankers. Heck, I never guessed Bob Strauss knew I was alive. But the best thing that happened to me was I got invited to have breakfast with the President on Thursday morning—just him and me."

"Wow! That must have been a thrill."

"Let me tell you it was. We had scrambled eggs, toast and

coffee. Every other senator I've talked to who has had breakfast with Mr. Carter says he only gives them coffee—and, if they're lucky, a piece of Danish. A full breakfast with President Carter is the equivalent of a State dinner as far as my colleagues on the Hill are concerned."

"So you voted for the treaty?"

"Sure."

"Will you vote for the second part of it next month?"

"I haven't made up my mind. You see, the senators who announced early that they would vote 'yes' didn't get a thing for their support, not even a piece of Danish pastry. But those of us who held out until the last moment not only wound up with scrambled eggs but anything we wanted as well. For example, I got a new naval base for my state and we're not even on the water."

## THE GEORGETOWN WATCHERS

You have probably all been following Jimmy Carter's transition efforts with interest. One of the headlines that keeps cropping up is "Georgetown Awaits Carter People."

There is a myth in Washington that "Georgetown" controls the country and what is said at Georgetown parties affects the lives of every man, woman and child in the United States.

The first place the Carter transition people go when they arrive in Washington is Georgetown. They stand around holding a glass of white wine in their hands hoping to find out what is happening in the nation's capital. The truth of the matter is that Georgetown over the years has lost its influence and most of the power brokers in this town have moved up to Wesley Heights and Cleveland Park.

The reason for this is quite simple. The houses in Georgetown are all bunched together, and the walls are so thin that whatever is said in one house can be heard in another. There are no secrets in Georgetown but the press people—always the last ones to get the word—still keep covering Georgetown as they did in the '60s, when the Kennedy folk used to hang out their laundry on each other's clotheslines.

It's true that there are some opinion makers who still live in Georgetown. Kay Graham, publisher of *The Washington Post*, has her home there. Joe Kraft still lives in Georgetown as does Rowland Evans, but his partner, Robert Novak, lives in Maryland. Jack Anderson is in Bethesda and Scotty Reston lives in Kalorama. Ben Bradlee, editor of *The Washington Post*, moved out of Georgetown long ago, and Woodward and Bernstein live next to "Deep Throat," wherever that is.

So what you get in Georgetown are really leftovers from the "Camelot" years.

I was at a cocktail party in Georgetown last week and the conversation went something like this.

"I hear there is talk at the agency that the Cuban exiles might land at the Bay of Pigs."

"Bobby Baker is in real trouble and may be indicted by the Grand Jury."

"Billie Sol Estes is going broke in Texas."

"Arthur Schlesinger is writing a book exposing John Foster Dulles."

"The White House is thinking of sending Vice President Johnson to Berlin."

"The CIA is tapping Dean Rusk's telephone."

"Krushchev is fighting with the Politburo and may be out any day."

"Robert McNamara is going to Vietnam to find out what the story is over there."

"Jackie Kennedy is thinking of redoing the White House."

The Carter people kept writing everything down in large black looseleaf notebooks which eventually would be turned over to the President-elect.

I tried to point out to one of them that if they wanted fresher news on Washington they should go to a cocktail party in Cleveland Park.

But the poor fellow said he didn't know where Cleveland Park was.

Besides, he said, Carter was very interested in what they were saying about him in Georgetown.

The only place in Georgetown where you can still get up-to-date news about what is going on is Doc Dalinsky's Drugstore on O Street. The reason for this is that while many of the power brokers have moved out of Georgetown, they still come to Dalinsky for their prescriptions. I suggested to one of Carter's transition men that if he really wanted the straight poop on Washington he should go to Dalinsky's coffee klatch on Sunday morning.

But the Carter man shook his head. "I was told to stay with the cocktail circuit in Georgetown. They say that's where it's all happening."

A man came by at that moment and said, "Did you hear Lynda Bird Johnson is getting married?"

The Carter man wrote it down in his big black book.

## TRANSITION PERIOD

Washington is in a terrible tizzy. Nobody has any idea who anybody is and there is nothing that upsets this town more than not knowing who is in charge.

It's gotten so bad that anyone who has anything near to a Southern accent is treated with deference and respect, just on the off chance he might be a member of the Carter transition team.

A friend of mine told me what happened in his federal building the other day. A young man wearing jeans, boots and a blue denim jacket walked into the building chewing on a piece of straw.

The alert guard at the desk immediately called upstairs. "I think it's one of 'them.' "

"How do you know?" the man on the tenth floor demanded.

"He's looking around, and he's writing names down off the list of people in the building."

"Oh, my gosh," the man on the tenth floor said. "I didn't think they'd get to us this early. I thought they would deal with State, Treasury and Defense first."

"You can't tell about that guy Carter," the guard said. "He might even show up here himself."

"Well, send the man up. Just don't let him stand in the lobby."

The guy went over to the boy in the jeans. "The man wants to see you."

"What man?"

"You mean he ain't going to be the man any more?"

"I don't know what you're talking about," the boy in the jeans said.

The guard winked at him. "I dig you, man. But I'm civil service so I got nothing to worry about. The man on the tenth floor, he's a Ford appointee, but he's hoping you'll keep him on."

"Mister, I don't have no idea what you're saying. Ah'm just looking for a job."

"That's a good cover," the guard told him. "Say you're looking for a job and people will tell you what's really going on around here. Anyhow, the man on the tenth floor wants to see you."

"Why does he want to see me? It says here 'Personnel' is on the seventh floor."

"You have to go to the tenth floor. Please, sir, follow me."

They arrived on the tenth floor and the man was waiting at the elevator with his staff. He shook the boy's hand vigorously. "Glad to have you on board, sir," the man said. "Carstairs here is my right arm. He's moved out of his office so you can use it during the transition."

"That's mighty kind of him," the boy said. "I wasn't expectin' my own office this early in the game. I was willing to start on the ground floor."

"Anything you need from the ground floor we'll bring up here to you. This is Miss Wedlock, Elfin's secretary. She's been assigned to you. Just tell her what you need and it's yours."

"Could someone get me a Coke?"

Within two minutes five people were giving the boy Cokes.

The man said, "Now I want you to know we're not making any major decisions until President Carter takes his oath of office."

"That's damned decent of you," the boy said, drinking one of his Cokes.

"We want this transition to be a smooth one. Would you like to see the budget for 1977?"

"Not particularly. I thought I'd start in the mailroom."

"I'd like to explain about the mailroom foul-up," the man said. "We put in this $400,000 mail sorter, but because GSA changed the size of our forms from an S18 to a W16 we had to change the envelopes, and then make modifications in the mail sorter of $300,000. But it wasn't our fault. Here is all the correspondence on it. You'll see the overrun was not made by our department."

The boy said, "You want me to read all this correspondence?"

"No, sir. We can get someone to read it for you."

"Good idea. What time can you go to lunch around here?"

"It's ready now, sir. Why don't we go into the executive dining room?"

## RED BADGE OF COURAGE

I had a very tough time on Election Day. The doorbell rang at seven o'clock in the morning and my neighbor Legendman was at the door.

"I have to vote today," he said, "and I'm scared."

"Everyone is frightened on Election Day," I assured him. "I wouldn't worry about it."

"I can't pull the lever for either guy," he said. "I just can't."

"Sure you can," I said soothingly. "I know it sounds impossible, but when you get inside the voting booth I'm certain you'll find the strength to do it."

"Would you go with me?" he begged. "It would be a big favor if I had somebody with me."

"Well, I hadn't planned to vote until later in the day. But if it means that much to you I will."

My wife gave Legendman a cup of coffee while I got dressed.

I found him sitting in the kitchen holding his head in his hands. "I never felt this way before," he confessed. "I used to look forward to Election Day. I had no trouble voting in past ones. Why do I have this terrible feeling in my stomach?"

"It happens to all of us sooner or later," I told him. "I'm sure all over the country people feel the way you do. But Americans have to vote. It's a privilege as well as a duty."

"But if I pull the lever for Ford we'll have four more years of the same thing. If I pull the lever for Carter nobody knows what we'll get."

"Vote your conscience," I told him.

"If I voted my conscience," he said, "I wouldn't vote. I think I'll go get a swine flu shot instead."

I stopped him at the door. "Let's go, Legendman," I said, grabbing his arm. "All you have to fear is fear itself." I bundled him into the car.

He was still distraught. "I can't pull the lever. I know I'll freeze. The TV commentators say every vote counts. I don't want my vote to count."

"This is like war, Legendman," I told him. "You think you can't pull the lever. But when it boils right down to it it's either you or them. Think of John Wayne. He would go right into that voting booth and pull the lever without thinking twice."

"I'm not John Wayne. I'm just a frightened American voter who never thought he'd have to make a choice between Gerry Ford and Jimmy Carter."

We arrived at the public school and I noticed several drivers pulling people out of their cars. They were all screaming "I can't do it! I can't do it!"

I helped Legendman out. He was shaking and perspiring. "Look, I'll come back later," he said.

"You have to do it now," I said firmly. "The sooner you get it over with the less agony will be involved."

We showed our registration cards to the lady at the table. "Booth three," she said to Legendman.

He tried to make a break for it and I tackled him.

I decided to be tough. "All right," I said, "I'm tired of mollycoddling you. You're going into booth three and you're not coming out until you pull the lever for the man you want to be the next President of the United States." I pushed him toward the booth. He opened the curtain and peeked in.

I watched him sternly.

"Inside," I ordered, "and pull the curtain."

I watched his feet under the curtain. He kept turning around. Finally, I heard a cry like a wounded animal and a click, and Legendman dashed out of the booth.

"I did it," he said. "I pulled the lever for the candidate of my choice."

"Good man," I said, pounding him on the back. "It wasn't so bad, was it?"

He looked at me with tears in his eyes. "I only hope God will forgive me."

## THE WASPS ARE RESTLESS

Whenever there is a Presidential election, reporters always go to an ethnic bar to see what the workingman is thinking. They wind up talking to Polish-Americans in Chicago, German-Americans in Milwaukee, Italian-Americans in Queens, New York and Mexican-Americans in El Paso, Texas. But no one ever bothers to get to a white American Anglo-Saxon bar to find out how the WASPs feel about the election.

In order to correct this oversight, I went to the Biltmore Bar to speak to WASPs who claim they are being ignored in the election and are getting fed up with it.

The bar was crowded with men dressed in Brooks Brothers suits. Most of them were drinking Chivas Regal scotch on the rocks and watching a discussion on Public Television between William Buckley and Norman Mailer.

At first they were very suspicious of me because I ordered a beer. Realizing my mistake, I demanded a double Beefeater Gin on the side. They relaxed a little.

"I'm from the press," I said to the man next to me.

"I'm from Westport," he replied. "We never see people like you in this bar."

"I'm very interested to find out how the WASPs are going to vote in the election."

Several of the other men in pin-stripe suits overheard me and gathered around.

"It's very puzzling," one of them said. "Both contestants have ignored the WASPs in their efforts to attract the ethnic groups, and it might cost them the election."

"Our votes are of crucial importance," another man said. "After all, WASPs make up a large segment of the population, and we have as many dreams and hopes for our children as the blue-collar working class."

"I know the ethnics look down on us," an advertising executive from Greenwich said, "because we read books and go to the theater and play golf and send our children to private schools. But where would America be without WASPs? We built this country from an agrarian society to the highest industrialized nation in the world. And we did it with private capital which our great-grandfathers invested in every conceivable project from factories to railroads. One becomes very discouraged when one hears both Mr. Ford and Mr. Carter repeating that we don't pay enough taxes."

"Frederick Campbell the Third is right," a stockbroker from New Canaan said. "WASPs seem to be the butt of all the jokes these days. We're getting fed up with it. We're as good Americans as any ethnic group in this country, and we're not dumb like everyone maintains."

"Why is it," a banker from Oyster Bay asked, "there are no situation comedies about WASPs on television? And when they use a token WASP character in an ethnic show why is he always the person who doesn't seem to know the score?"

"Well," Horace Richardson Junior, an IBM sales manager, chimed in, "the WASP image seems to have deteriorated as the ethnic image has improved."

"In what way?" I asked.

"They say we have the highest divorce rate, the heaviest drinking problems, and the largest tax shelters. We're always being accused of wife swapping because we live in the suburbs.

"These are generalizations that do not take into consideration the majority of hard-working WASPs who are happily married, have only one or two cocktails before dinner and watch the John Adams Chronicles on television."

"Very well put, Waldo," an airlines vice president said. "Every time a white-collar crime is committed, people automatically assume a WASP did it. It's true that a high percentage of WASPs commit white-collar crimes, but that is only because they are in positions of responsibility where the opportunities exist."

As the first reporter ever to visit a WASP bar I came to the following conclusion: WASPs are tired of being ignored by both Ford and Carter, and if neither candidate addresses himself to their problems they may sit out the election in November.

As one TV executive put it, "The Republicans have taken us for granted for too long. Just because we're overachievers doesn't mean we don't have feelings, too."

# VII.  She Got a Job

## POLAND IS FREE

Probably the country most affected by the Presidential debates was Poland. President Ford in his startling statement on Russian influence in Eastern Europe said, among other things, that Poland was not dominated by the Soviet Union and would remain free as long as he was President.

The Polish people received the news with joy, and a friend in Warsaw told me on the telephone it has changed their lives overnight.

As soon as I heard the news I called my friend Woljijowicz in Warsaw. (This is not his real name as I don't want to get him in trouble.) He told me, "This has been a great week for us. The day my brother-in-law Simcowitz heard the news we were free he drank half a bottle of vodka and went out in the street and told a Russian soldier to get the hell out of the country."

"That's wonderful," I said. "Let me speak with Simcowitz."

"You can't. He was hauled off to jail for insulting a foreign tourist."

"That's too bad," I said.

"It's the price you have to pay for being in a free country," Woljijowicz said. "My friend Bedicovicz wrote an editorial in the newspaper, *Red Truth*, pointing out that Simcowitz should not have been arrested because, according to Mr. Ford, Poland was an independent, autonomous nation."

"I'll bet Bedicovicz got a good reaction to the editorial."

"I don't know. I haven't seen him since. They closed up his newspaper and took him off to the Ministry of the Interior for questioning."

"I'm sorry to hear that."

"His wife hired a lawyer but the Minister of the Interior denied he had ever heard of Bedicovicz. He referred the lawyer to the Soviet Consulate for any information."

"What did the Soviet Consulate say?"

"They said the Polish lawyer should be in an insane asylum and referred him back to the Minister of the Interior."

"What did the minister say?"

"He put the lawyer in an asylum for his own good."

"That's terrible."

Woljijowicz said, "When the other lawyers in Warsaw heard about it they petitioned the chairman of the Communist Party to have their colleague released from the asylum."

"And he released him?" I asked.

"No, he tore up the petition and warned them that if they kept up their agitation the Soviets would demand that they all be sent to asylums too."

"That's terrible," I said.

"Living in a free country doesn't mean you can yell 'Soviet pig' in a crowded movie theater."

"Did anyone yell 'Soviet pig' in a movie theater?"

"A Soviet political attaché said someone did, and he warned the chairman of the Polish Communist Party that if he heard it again Moscow would have to take drastic steps to protect its friendship with the Polish people."

"I don't see why the Soviets should take umbrage since Poland is not in the Russian sphere of influence."

"That's what Aronowicz said in a poem he read in front of the Soviet War Memorial yesterday."

"I never heard of Aronowicz."

"Neither has his family since he read the poem. Listen, I have to go now. There's someone knocking on the door."

"Are you expecting anyone?"

"At three o'clock in the morning?"

## ANOTHER CARTER PROBLEM

There is always a suspicion amongst Republicans that the working press favors the Democratic candidate. This may have been the case in the past, but it is not true in this election. I am speaking now of the White House Press Corps who are not only suspicious of Jimmy Carter but live in deathly fear that he might win the election.

The White House Press Corps, as most people know, have to follow the President wherever he goes. When President Kennedy was in the White House they could look forward to going to Hyannisport in the summer and Palm Beach in the winter. When Lyndon Johnson was President they found themselves in Austin, Texas. Austin is not Palm Beach, but the University of Texas is located there and when school was in session there seemed to be enough to do to keep most of the Press Corps happy.

From the point of view of traveling, President Nixon was a dream subject to cover. When he wasn't flying to San Clemente overlooking the blue waters of the Pacific Ocean, the President went to Key Biscayne, which was an ideal place to vacation on an expense account, particularly since the President spent so much time at sea with Bebe Rebozo. Reporters could go fishing, play tennis, sit around in luxurious bars and, if they weren't married, meet very attractive bikini-clad stewardesses who lusted after members of the fourth estate.

When Gerry Ford became President the White House Press Corps traveling was cut down tremendously except for occasional trips to Vail. This took a lot of the fun out of covering a President, but it gave most of the men and women an opportunity to learn how to ski.

But the thought of Jimmy Carter as President has the White House Press scared silly. The idea of commuting between Washington and Plains, Georgia, is more than most of the reporters can bear. Mr. Carter will probably be going there a lot, if for nothing else than to check on his peanut crop, and the White House Press Corps envision themselves spending long days and longer nights holed up in Americus, Georgia, a town that hasn't seen stewardesses in 20 years.

"The only thing to do in Plains," complained a friend of mine who has been covering Presidents since Kennedy, "is play softball and kill fire ants. The idea of playing shortstop for four years is enough to make you sick."

"Maybe they'll organize square dances for you?" I said, trying to cheer him up.

"It's not funny," he said. "When we covered Nixon we could hand in expense accounts of $100 a day and no one would bat an eye. My editor checked the motel room rates in Americus, and he said if I spent more than 25 bucks a day he wouldn't sign my voucher. If Carter gets elected we'll all be broke."

"Maybe you could moonlight on his farm bagging peanuts. I hear Carter pays $3 an hour."

"This is a serious problem," he said, "and you're making light of it. An assignment to cover the President of the United States used to be the highest honor any correspondent could be given. If Carter gets elected we're all going to beg to go back to a police beat."

"I think you're being too hasty. In time you might even look forward to going to Plains, Georgia. The air is fresh, the sun is warm and the people are friendly."

"What people?" he said.

"I hear Billy Carter's gasoline station swings every night."

My friend was almost in tears.

"Then you're not going to vote for Carter?" I said.

"I'm not, but my wife is," he replied. "After all the stories she's heard about what we did in Hyannisport, Palm Beach, Austin, San Clemente, Key Biscayne and Vail, she thinks Jimmy Carter's peanut farm would make the perfect summer White House."

## DO THEY REALLY WANT IT?

My friend Rosenfeld has a wild theory that, based on what is going on in the Presidential campaign, both men are trying to throw the election.

"I don't believe either man wants the job and that's why they're trying to out-goof each other."

"That's hard to believe," I said.

"Think about it," he said.

I thought about it and came to the conclusion Rosenfeld could be right.

It probably all started when Gerry Ford first came to the White House as President and said to Mrs. Ford, "I said I wouldn't run for President in 1976, but how can I make people believe it?"

"Why don't you pardon Richard Nixon?" Mrs. Ford suggested.

"That's a good idea. If I pardon Nixon, the press will have to accept the fact that I have no intention of running for a full term."

Ford pardoned Nixon and everyone said he blew his chances to be elected in '76. But several months later the rumors started up again that Ford had aspirations to stay in the White House. "What can we do to stop the rumors?" he asked Mrs. Ford.

"Why don't I go on the 'Sixty Minutes' show and say I wouldn't be surprised if Susan had an affair before she was married? The American people would never stand for it."

"That could do it," the President said.

Mrs. Ford went on "Sixty Minutes" and the reaction to her frank remarks was more than even she had anticipated. Gerry Ford looked safe.

Then the Democrats started holding their primaries and Jimmy Carter who was just running because he had nothing else to do, found himself out in front. No one in the Carter family could believe it. Jimmy went to his mother, Miss Lillian, and said, "Ma, if I keep up the way I'm going I may win the nomination. What am I going to do?"

"You have no choice, son, but to talk about 'ethnic purity.' That should kill any chances you have of getting the nomination."

Jimmy brought up "ethnic purity" in his next speech and there was such a hullabaloo about it that Carter was certain he was out of it.

But immediately the blacks forgave him and he was still in the race.

In the meantime Gerry Ford could not avoid his party's pleas that he run for the office again. He was dispirited and Betty cheered him up. "Don't forget you have to campaign against Ronald Reagan and if you put a really bad organization together he can beat you."

Ford put his campaign organization together, started to campaign and almost lost the nomination. But Reagan goofed and Ford squeaked through. His only hope was that the Republican Party was in such a shambles after Kansas City that he wouldn't have a chance. The polls confirmed this.

Carter was terrified and went to Miss Lillian and said, "What do I do, Ma? You know I don't want to go to Washington."

His wise mother said, "You have to do three things. Announce you're going to raise taxes on people's median incomes, attack President Johnson and give an interview to *Playboy* telling them what's really in your heart. It will kill you in the polls."

As usual Miss Lillian was right and Jimmy Carter started going downhill fast.

Mr. Ford was horror-stricken and said to Mrs. Ford, "Carter is out-goofing me. What do I do now?" ·

Mrs. Ford said, "Why don't you disclose that you played golf on weekends with lobbyists. That could hurt you."

The President leaked stories about his weekends with lobbyists, but it had no impact at all, and the polls showed him neck and neck with Carter.

He was desperate and confided to Mrs. Ford, "I can't understand it. No matter what I do I still have a chance of winning."

Just then the phone rang. Mrs. Ford answered it and said to the person on the phone, "Thank you, I'll tell the President." She turned to Mr. Ford and said, "It's good news. Earl Butz just told a terrible ethnic joke on an airplane and Ron Nessen said it could ruin us."

For the first time in weeks the President smiled. "Good old Earl. He's always there when you need him."

### NOW FOR THE TEST

I warned you all that you would have to take a test after the Republican National Convention to find out if you were watching it. We will do it under the West Point honor system which means NO CHEATING. Those who fail the test will not receive their BETTY FORD'S HUSBAND FOR PRESIDENT bumper sticker.

All right, let's go.

1—The Republican Party is the party of (a) principle (b) a balanced budget (c) opportunity (d) unity (e) Abraham Lincoln, Teddy Roosevelt, Dwight Eisenhower and What's-his-name.

2—The Democratic Party is made up of (a) free spenders (b) congressmen and senators who fuel inflation and unemployment through reckless legislation that President Ford in his wisdom and courage has seen fit to veto (c) do-gooders who have made your streets unsafe to walk in (d) Wayne Hays and Elizabeth Ray.

3—In order for the United States to remain number one in the world we must (a) keep the Panama Canal (b) make our Armed Forces so strong that no nation will ever sneer at us again (c) achieve maximum value for each defense dollar spent (d) defoliate all the peanut farms in Plains, Georgia.

4—Jimmy Carter's promises would cost the country (a) $100 billion (b) $200 billion (c) $300 billion (d) $135.67 for every man, woman and child in the United States.

5—Carter wants the American people to (a) trust him (b) believe he was a good governor of Georgia (c) believe he has the experience to deal with the urgent problems that beset this nation.

6—The reason Ronald Reagan lost the nomination fight was (a) he chose his Vice President too early in the game (b) Ford could promise more things to the uncommitted delegates (c) Schweiker couldn't deliver the delegates he claimed he had in his pocket (d) Tony Orlando danced with Betty Ford just before the crucial Rules vote on 16 C.

7—Senator Richard Schweiker must now go back to Pennsylvania and explain to his constituents that (a) he was only kidding about the right-to-work law (b) Reagan had his FBI folder and blackmailed him into running on the ticket (c) he thought Reagan was offering him a role in a motion picture (d) he is a "born again" liberal.

8—Only one of these Republicans was mentioned in a speech at the convention in Kansas City: (a) Richard Nixon (b) Henry Kissinger (c) Spiro Agnew (d) Checkers.

9—Only one of these things happened in Kansas City: (a) Sammy Davis Jr. put his head on President Ford's shoulder (b) Charles Colson ran over his grandmother in front of the convention hall (c) Howard Hunt tapped Rockefeller's telephone (d) Amy Carter was interviewed on television (e) the Republicans did not wave their fists at Walter Cronkite.

10—The Republican delegates worked their tails off at their convention in Kansas City. The only time they got any sleep was during (a) Rockefeller's speech (b) Goldwater's speech (c) Howard Baker's speech (d) John Connally's speech (e) all of them.

11—Vice President Rockefeller in his speech the first night at the convention said that one of the following people played football without a helmet: (a) Knute Rockne (b) Joe Namath (c) Alexander Solzhenitsyn (d) Gerry Ford.

12—The reason that President Ford did not select Rockefeller as his running mate was because Mr. Rockefeller said Mr. Ford had (a) courage (b) the ability to pull this country through its worst political crisis since the Civil War (c) brought respect back to the office of the Presidency (d) played football without a helmet.

The final question on your exam is to write a short essay on why more people last week watched "Mary Hartman, Mary Hartman" from Fernwood than "Gerry Ford, Gerry Ford" from Kansas City.

## OPERATION BIG APPLE

New York had a love fest at the Democratic National Convention. Despite dire predictions that the city could not handle a national political convention, almost everyone agreed the people were hospitable, the cops were friendly and New Yorkers went out of their way to make the visitors feel at home.

What the hell happened? I'll tell you what happened. Mayor Abe Beame pulled off one of the neatest tricks in modern American history. The people we saw and dealt with in Manhattan last week weren't New Yorkers.

This is the true story of this remarkable week.

A month ago Mayor Beame met with his staff to deal with the problem of the convention. Beame and his aides were very nervous that the Democratic Convention could turn into a debacle. People would get raped and mugged and assaulted and, what was worse, be ignored on the streets.

One of Beame's people, a veteran of Indochina, suggested, "Why don't we do what Cambodia did in Pnom Penh?"

The mayor asked, "What was that?"

"Why don't we evacuate everyone from Manhattan for the week and drive them into the countryside."

"Where would we put them?"

"We could build relocation camps on Staten Island and ring the place with barbed wire."

The Comptroller whistled. "That's about 2 million people. How do we round up 2 million people?"

"We could make all the streets one way going south to the Battery. There will be such a traffic jam that their only escape will be over Verrezano Bridge to Staten Island. When they get there we'll make them drive directly to the camps."

"What about the people who take the subway?"

"All the trains will go directly downtown, and when the people exit from the subway, they'll find themselves on ferry boats which will take them across the harbor."

"It could work," the Commissioner of Public Transportation said. "But I'll have to pay my people overtime."

"It will be worth it if New York gets a good image," the mayor said.

"Wait. We still have the New York City policemen. What do we do with them?"

"We announce there is going to be a union meeting to discuss their pensions on Staten Island. They'll all go over without a squawk."

"But we can't leave New York entirely empty. The out-of-towners and the press will get very suspicious," a staff member said.

"I've got that figured out. We bring in friendly, smiling people from the Midwest and the South on buses and have them pretend they're New Yorkers."

"How do we pay for them to come to New York?"

"I've made a deal with movie producer Dino De Laurentiis. If he pays to bring 2 million people to replace the 2 million New Yorkers, he can use them as extras in the shooting of his film *King Kong*."

"And the cops?"

"We get them from central casting. I've hired the director of Police Woman to teach them how to smile and be friendly to everyone they come in contact with."

"What a fantastic plan!" someone said. Everyone looked at the mayor.

He finally said, "I don't like relocation camps any better than you do, but the city comes first. Put it into action!"

And so the week before the convention "Operation Big Apple" was put into effect. Two million New Yorkers were locked up on Staten Island and their places were taken by 2 million friendly faces from out of town.

All those who came to New York last week raved about their treatment from the natives. Not one of them suspected he hadn't met one real New Yorker the whole time he was there. For the 109th time Mayor Beame had saved his city from going down the drain.


## HE NEVER MET MISS RAY

I know it's hard to believe, but I met a high government official the other day who never met Elizabeth Ray. The reason it's hard is that according to Miss Ray's book, *The Washington Fringe Benefit,* she met every person of importance within a 50-mile radius of the nation's capital. In fairness to Miss Ray she didn't claim she slept with everyone she met (though the *Guinness Book of Records* has suddenly shown a great interest in her), but she does insist she knew everyone from Eugene McCarthy to Henry Kissinger.

The high government official, who asked that his name not be mentioned because he had never met Miss Ray, didn't seem to have any logical reasons to explain why their paths had never crossed.

"I'm not much of a party man," he said, "so maybe that's the reason she left me out of her book."

"But surely, sir," I said, "you could have been in a restaurant where she was dining. She said she met a lot of important people in restaurants."

"I've wracked my brain," he replied, "but I don't think I ever ran into her in a restaurant. If I had she surely would have remembered it."

"What about at the Washington Redskin games? In her book she claims she met almost everyone of importance at the Redskin games."

"I must admit that puzzled me because that would have been a place we could have met. I guess it was just chance that we didn't. My seats are behind the goal posts at the west end of the field and I understand she sat in a box on the five-yard line on the east end of the field. It's possible we could have waved to each other when the Redskins scored a touchdown. But if we did, I guess she forgot it."

"What about up on Capitol Hill in one of the orgy rooms she wrote about?"

"I never did hear about those rooms until Miss Ray started talking about them in the newspapers. I believe they were on the House side of the Capitol and I spent most of my time on the Senate side. I wish I had known about it in those days. It certainly would have been a nice place to wait while I was waiting to testify in front of a dull Senate committee."

"But didn't a congressman offer to introduce you to Miss Ray and recommend her as a dinner date?"

He said, biting his lip, "It's hard for you to believe this, but the answer is no. I don't understand why. I have a lot of power, I'm not bad looking and I like to have a good time as much as the next person. But neither Mr. Hays nor anyone else on the Hill had the courtesy to say to me, 'I'd like you to meet my secretary. She can type four words a minute.' "

"Sir, do you think the fact you weren't mentioned in Miss Ray's book could hurt your career?"

"Well, let's say it can't help it. That book is a 'Who's Who of Washington.' You're not anybody if Miss Ray didn't meet you. This town pays attention to things like that. I haven't had one call from a newspaperman or woman since my name was left out. I don't mind telling you it hurts."

"Perhaps she disguised your name because you were one of the people in the book she had an affair with," I said, trying to cheer him up.

He shook his head sadly. "No, I read about every person she gave a phony name to, and none of them fitted me. I might as well learn to live with it. I never met Miss Ray and she never met me. I think the public will have to accept the fact and decide for themselves if they still want me to serve the people."

There were tears in his eyes.

"Everyone makes mistakes, sir," I said gently. "It's a rotten deal that you never met Miss Ray, but in a few months people will forget it."

"What a fool I was," he sobbed. "If I had known she was going to tell all I could have had my Redskin seats changed to her end of the football field."


## COALS TO NEWCASTLE

A place gets an image and there isn't a darn thing you can do about it. For a while everybody thought Washington D.C. was one big Watergate. That was bad enough but now, since all the sex scandals, out-of-towners think of our town as Sodom-on-the-Potomac.

The other day I heard from Ralph, an acquaintance out of the past, who announced he was in D.C

"How's the old boy?" he chortled on the telephone.

"Fine, Ralph. How's your second—or is it third wife?"

"Third," he said. "She's not with me. I told her, 'Honey, I only get to Washington once in my life, and if I brought someone as sexy as you along, it would be like bringing coals to Newcastle.' Ha, ha, ha."

"You were always one to come up with a fresh phrase, Ralph. What did she say to that?"

"She said, 'You can take the man out of the boy, but you can't take the boy out of the man.' And she let me go. Ida's a great girl. Okay, let's forget the small talk. I have only three days. Where's the action?"

"What action?" I asked.

"Aw c'mon, get off it. The houseboats, the parties in the lobbyists' penthouse apartments, the skinny-dipping in the Georgetown pools—all the stuff I've been reading about."

"Ralph, you're not going to believe this, but I've never seen any of it. It may exist, but I'd be the last guy to know about it if it did."

"You're putting me on," Ralph said. "This town is supposed to be hotter than Havana in its heyday. I'm your buddy and I'm discreet as hell. Just give me a few numbers. I'll take it from there."

"Okay," I said. "If you go down to 14th Street there's a go-go bar and two movies that specialize in X-rated movies, and two bookstores that sell *The Story of O*. But don't use my name."

"Listen, we got more than that in Des Moines," Ralph said. "I'm talking about the secretaries who can't type and the typists who aren't allowed to be secretaries, and the runners-up of the Miss Cherry Blossom Festival. That's the kind of girls I want to meet."

"I don't know any of these girls, Ralph. Why don't you go to a singles bar in Bethesda? Maybe you'll find the girl of your dreams."

"Give me the name of someone who chairs a committee in Congress," he said. "Just give me the name of one person up there you know and I won't bother you again."

"Bella Abzug."

"Give me another name," he said.

"Ralph, the papers have been overplaying the sex scandals because they're sick and tired of writing about Jimmy Carter, Jerry Ford and Ronald Reagan. Maybe all these things happened and maybe again they didn't. But you can't just go up to the Capitol and find an orgy. In spite of what you read, it isn't like that."

"Sure," he said, "you guys are trying to keep it all to yourselves. Well, I'm a taxpayer and I got as much right to have fun as any congressman or senator in Washington. We people back home are getting sick and tired of our elected officials making hay at our expense."

"Don't get sore at me, Ralph. If I knew where the action was I'd not only tell you, I'd go with you. But a big night for most of us who live here is to go to a Safeway supermarket and see if we can get out for less than $100."

"So you're not going to help me," Ralph said. "You think I'm not good enough to meet a receptionist or a girl that can't take shorthand. Well, I won't forget this, buddy. I have other sources in Washington to call."

"I'm sorry, Ralph. I don't know how to put it, but I think you came to the wrong place for action."

"Where should I have gone?"

"Newcastle."

## IT'S IN THE BAG

You're not going to believe this but things have gotten so exciting in Washington during the transition period that people are actually arguing whether Jimmy Carter should carry his own luggage or not.

It all started when Betty Beale, a columnist for the Washington Star, attacked Mr. Carter in print for doing something so "un-Presidential" as carrying his own bags. She wrote that it gave the Presidency a bad image. Then she went on to complain about Mr. Carter refusing to wear formal attire on Inauguration Day. Betty, I must tell you, is a stickler for protocol, but Washington being Washington, she did open up a can of beans, and the town is now divided between those who believe a President should carry his own suitcase and those who believe he shouldn't.

I must admit I sided with the pro-Carter-luggage-carrier people on the theory that it shows the man who has his finger on the button is not too big to also have his hand on his own Samsonite.

Miss Beale wrote that Mr. Carter was just showing off and that he wanted to look like a man of the people by lugging his bags all around town. But I believe the President-elect is sincere when he picks up his baggage every time he makes a move.

Before Mr. Carter was elected President he had to travel on commercial airlines to every part of this land. He hardly had any staff. Until Theodore White's book, "The Making of the President 1976," comes out, we will have no idea how many times Carter lost his luggage during the campaign.

But I'm willing to bet it was more than once. After traveling on airlines a person develops a phobia about his baggage getting lost, and the more one flies the bigger the fear gets. I sincerely believe

Mr. Carter is suffering from a lost baggage phobia, which is not only natural but is justified based on the experience of most air travelers.

I prefer to believe that the first thing Mr. Carter decided was that if he became President of the United States he would never let anyone else touch a bag of his again. It was a tough decision but it was the right one. And I do not believe it demeans the Presidency to see the Commander-in-Chief walking along Pennsylvania Avenue with a two-suiter in one hand and the papers of state in the other.

The anti-Carter luggage people, and some of my best friends are in this group, maintain it is not only undignified for a Head of State to carry his own bags but is counterproductive. If Mr. Carter is sincere about putting people back to work, he is taking a job away from somebody who would ordinarily be assigned to carry his bags. It isn't just the President's luggage they're worried about, these people say, but Americans tend to follow their leaders and, if they see the President of the United States carrying his bag, they will decide it's all right for them to carry their own luggage and thousands of porters will go jobless.

They also point out that when people see a President carrying his own bag they tend to wonder what he's hiding in it, and this gets everyone very nervous.

Betty Beale says all Carter is carrying around are the blue jeans he expects to wear to the Inauguration—but we have only her word for this, and we must remember that the last person Mr. Carter would let peek into his suitcase would be Betty Beale.

So now you know what's going on in Washington this week. I know it's strong stuff just before Christmas, but I believe the people have a right to know what is going on in Washington at all times. Sorry, Walter, but that's the way it is.

### SHE GOT A JOB

"Hello, Mummy, it's Betsy. I just got a job in Washington."

"That's wonderful. What are you going to do?"

"I'm going to work for a congressman on his Oversight Committee."

"What is the Oversight Committee?"

"I'm not really sure. It's something hush hush, because the congressman said if I took the job I'd have to keep my eyes shut and my mouth closed."

"That's interesting. What exactly will you be doing for the committee?"

"He said he couldn't tell me in the office, but he'd come over to the apartment tonight and spell out my duties. He said I'd enjoy them very much."

"Did he ask you if you could take shorthand or type?"

"No, Mummy, that's the wonderful thing about the job. He said most of my work would be done outside the office."

"It sounds a little strange."

"It's a dream position, Mummy. I can go to the office when I want to and I can stay home if I wish. And it pays $14,000 a year."

"You're going to make $14,000 a year?"

"Yes, Mummy. The congressman said the Oversight Committee is one of the most important in the House of Representatives, and we have to see that nobody does anything wrong."

"I'm still not clear, Betsy, as to what you're expected to do. After all, although you're very pretty, you really aren't too well qualified to work for a congressional committee."

"Don't worry, Mummy, I didn't lie to get the job. I told the congressman the truth. I said I couldn't spell and I couldn't add and I was terrible at filing, but he just laughed and said there were enough girls on his committee to do that sort of thing. What he had in mind for me was something none of the girls could do."

"And what exactly is that?"

"He said he'd tell me tonight. He's taking me to dinner. Isn't it wonderful, Mummy? I always thought congressmen were so cold and unapproachable. But he isn't that way at all. He's so warm and friendly and he said he wanted to be my friend."

"I don't like it, Betsy. There's something fishy about all this. Why would they pay you $14,000 a year when you have absolutely no experience?"

"He explained that to me. He said that what the Oversight Committee needed was someone who wasn't too close to the problems of oversight. He felt I could see things with a fresh eye. He's so busy he said he wanted someone who could brief him on what the other people were doing. He told me he expects me to report to him two or three times a week, either at my place or his."

"Well, I guess it's a job and I shouldn't complain."

"It's a marvelous opportunity for me, Mummy. The congressman said he would introduce me to all his friends on other committees, and when I don't have enough to do for him I can do something for them."

"Who would have ever thought my little girl would be working for a congressman, and on an Oversight Committee at that?"

"I can't believe it myself."

"Do you have a title?"

"The congressman said I could be his 'Night Administrative Assistant.' His daytime Administrative Assistant finishes work at six o'clock, and then he said I could take over. He told me he does his best work in the evenings."

"Well, Betsy, make sure he doesn't attempt any hanky-panky."

"Oh, Mummy. He's a member of Congress. They don't have time for hanky-panky. He's only interested in serving the people who elected him."

"Well, I'm glad to hear you got it."

"I have to go now, Mummy. I have a date at the hairdresser. He told me one of the most important things about my job is that I had to look nice. He said it doesn't make any difference in the daytime, but at night it's very important."

# VIII. Free Medical Advice

## EVERY YEAR A DIFFERENT NAME

Every year they give it a different name. One year they call it the Hong Kong Flu, the next year they call it Virus A-1, then Texas Flu. No matter what they call it, to the person who has it, it's just plain flu.

The problem with flu is that it has no sex to it. It's not one of those glamorous diseases you can make an entire movie about. When you call someone up and say you've got the flu, they don't say, "I'll be right over." The usual response is, "I'll see you in August."

Even doctors don't want to talk to people who have the flu. Most of them leave strict instructions with their nurses. "If anyone calls and tells you they have the flu—I'm out."

I'm wise to those instructions, so when I called my doctor and the nurse asked what was wrong, I said, "Nothing really. Just tell the doctor I was sawing down a tree and I cut off my arm."

My doctor was on the phone in two minutes.

"What kind of saw was it?" he wanted to know.

"I lied," I said. "I have the flu."

"That's a terrible thing to do to a doctor," he said. "Here I am dealing with more sick people than I can handle, and you bother me with something like the flu."

"People with the flu can be sick, too," I said defensively.

"Yes," he said. "But doctors can't do anything about them. All we can prescribe is rest, liquids and aspirin."

"I knew you'd say that," I said.

"Then why did you call?" he wanted to know.

"Because I just wanted it on the record that I called you in case I really got sick."

"It's been noted," he said.

"Doctor," I said.

"Now what is it?" he said.

"I love you," I said.

I heard him shout at his secretary, "If anyone calls and says he cut his arm off while sawing down a tree, tell him I'm only taking flu calls."

With flu you go through many stages. The first is chills, aching bones, sore throat and sniffles. All you want to do is sleep. This is the best stage, because the days fly by and you really don't care about anything.

The second stage is when you still feel punk but are aware of what is going on around you. This is the most miserable period. If, for example, your wife leaves you for an hour to buy groceries, it is at that moment that the Roto-Rooter man arrives and says, "I got 200 feet of coil. You think that's enough?"

Or the man from United Parcel Service rings the bell and says, "The people next door aren't home. Mind if I leave the package with you?"

The third stage of flu is when you think you're getting well and start yelling, "I have to get out of this house or I'll go crazy." The truth is, you're not ready to go yet, but depending on the relationship you have with your wife she will either insist you stay in bed a couple more days, or encourage you to go out in the sleet and snow.

The most dangerous stage of flu is, strangely, the final one.

That's when you think you're all better, but for some reason have become hooked on the daytime soap operas and game shows, and refuse to leave the house because you're afraid you'll miss a sequence.

I guess the best way to tell when you're completely over the flu is to watch one of the game shows on TV. If Candice Bergen can't win $25,000 for some widow from Baton Rouge, and it doesn't bother you, you know it's time to go back to work.

## GOOD NEWS

"Hey, lungs. Have you heard the good news?"

"Cough, cough. What's that?"

"Congress has given the automobile companies two more years before they have to abide by the 1970 Clear Air Act."

"Oh boy. Cough cough, I was afraid of that."

"It was really touch and go because the auto companies said they'd have to close down if they didn't get the extension. They said it was unfair for the government to expect them to lower their emissions in just eight years."

"Cough, cough. What you're really saying—cough, cough—is they were buying some breathing time."

"That's well put, lungs."

"I'm not sure I can survive another two years of this gook."

"Sure, you can. You lungs have proven you can breathe in anything. What's another two years in your life compared to saving the American automobile industry? Can you imagine this country without new cars?"

"Can you imagine this country with fresh air?"

"Now don't get sarcastic. It isn't as if the automobile companies haven't been trying to develop a clean engine. But they have a lot of problems. They have to think of cost and weight and profits and retooling. Don't you have any feelings for the industry at all?"

"Well, I do have a tightness in my chest. Cough, cough. Maybe instead of passing a Clean Air Act Congress should have passed a Clean Lung Act. They could have made it a law that everyone in this country had to have stronger lungs by 1978. It would have been simpler."

"Cough and complain. That's all you ever do. You think you can have a first-class transportation system and not pay for it. If it weren't for you lungs, the automobile industry could make a first-class vehicle for $1,000 less—one that would get better gas mileage, give better performance and reap higher profits."

"Cough, cough. You're making me feel bad."

"Well, you better accept the compromise and get used to it. For the next two years you're not going to get any relief."

"I hope I can last that long. What happens in two years?"

"The automobile companies will either come up with a car that can meet the clean air standards or their lobbyists will work for another extension."

"That's nice. What happened to the clean air lobbyists?"

"They don't have the clout with Congress that the automobile lobbyists do. A lot of jobs are at stake when it comes to clean air, and you have to have trade-offs if you want to keep the economy going. When it came to making 1978 models or protecting people's lungs Congress had no choice but to go with the 1978 cars. Surely, you can understand that."

"Cough, cough. I'd like to but if you were a human lung you'd know it isn't easy. It's not just the cars, but we have to breathe factory pollutants, stuff coming out of smokestacks, the chemical dust blowing across the town. We can only take so much. Cough, cough."

"Well, if it wasn't safe, Congress would never have agreed to the compromise. Besides, they know what's better for the country. That's why the people elected them."

"I guess you're right. We lungs are always thinking of ourselves. It's just that we feel so lousy all the time we never take industry into consideration."

"The thing to do is adjust to the environment. You can't change it, so go along with it. Breathe in the emissions and enjoy them. After all, you only live once."

"Cough, cough. I'm sorry I got so upset. If you don't mind I'll lie down and rest. I don't feel so good."

"What about a game of tennis? That could make you feel better."

"No, I think I'll pass. Cough, cough. Why don't you play without me?"

## BLIZZARD OF '78

How did people cope when they were stuck in their homes during the blizzard? In order to find out I made several telephone calls to friends in New York during the snowstorm.

The first call I made was to Bob Simon who lives in Monsey.

Mrs. Simon answered the phone. "He's outside. I'll call him."

Ten minutes later, Simon got on the phone huffing and puffing.

"What are you doing?" I asked him.

"Shoveling the #@%&*#* driveway so I can get the car out."

"You're not going to drive today?"

"Got to. Got to get to the store if it kills me."

"What for?"

"My wife's out of cigarettes. She's afraid she's going to die if she doesn't get a cigarette."

"That bad, huh?"

"She's sucking on a strand of raw spaghetti now, but she says it isn't the same thing. She tried to make a cigarette out of oregano leaves, but they wouldn't stay in the newspaper."

"Suppose the store isn't open when you get there?"

"She told me to smash the windows and loot."

"But you could get prison for that."

"She says it doesn't matter. She says she'll bring the kids up every Saturday to visit me, as long as I get her the cigarettes. I've got to go. She's rifling through the garbage compactor to see if she can find a butt."

"Let her do it," I said.

"This is the third time she's gone through it. She found all the butts on the first go-round. She won't believe there aren't any left."

"Okay," I said. "And have a nice day."

The second call I made was to a friend on Long Island. His wife told me he didn't make it home and was stuck at the Waldorf Astoria. I called my friend at the Waldorf Astoria.

"Are you all right?" I asked.

"It's terrible," he said. "I tried to make the 3:45 from Penn Station but it was canceled. So I had to get a room here. I never lived through anything like this. Wait a minute, there's room service." He went off the phone and I heard him say to someone, "Honey, did you want red wine or white wine with your chicken?" Then he came on again. "So like I said, no one can move. All we can do is wait it out. I could be here for days. Hold it will you? . . . Honey, turn down the TV set, will you? . . . You're lucky you aren't here. I wouldn't wish this on anyone . . . Not too much ice, Sweetie . . . I'll never forgive the Long Island Railroad for what they did to me last night."

"Well, at least you're safe," I said.

"If you call sharing a room at the Waldorf Astoria with a salesman from Syracuse during the worst blizzard in 20 years 'being safe,' then you don't know anything about snowstorms. Listen, I have to go now . . . my turtle soup is getting cold."

The last call I made was to my sister in Kew Gardens.

"Edith, are you all right?"

"I'm fine."

"How's Harold?"

"I wouldn't know."

"Why, where is he?"

"He's right here."

"If he's right there how come you don't know?"

"We haven't been talking for two days. As long as you're on the phone tell him that dinner is ready if he wants some."

Harold came on the phone. I said, "Edith says dinner is ready."

"Tell her I'm not hungry," he replied.

Edith came on the phone. I told her, "He says he's not hungry."

She said, "Tell him that's too damn bad."

"Hey, listen, I'm calling long distance. I just wanted to find out how both of you were."

"Wonderful," she replied. "Being stuck in your apartment for two days in a snowstorm with your husband is the next best thing to having a second honeymoon."


## A MENTAL HEALTH PROBLEM

MARTHA'S VINEYARD—My good friend Professor Heinrich Applebaum has just done a sociological study on how private beaches affect the average American's vacation. He did it under a grant from the "Life Is Unfair Foundation."

Applebaum's study came to some startling conclusions.

"You would think," he told me, "that people who own their own beaches would be twice as happy as those who don't."

"That certainly figures," I said.

"Well, it's not true. My interviews indicate that those who have no rights to a private beach are three and a half times happier than those who do."

I was certainly surprised.

He said, "It appears that those who don't own beach front property believe the ocean is public and they have the right to use any beach they want to, even if it's marked 'Private.' In fact, they prefer to use a private beach more than they do a public beach because not only are private beaches nicer but it drives the owners up the wall."

"I should think so. A person with a private beach has paid through the nose for it and he doesn't want just anybody using it. There are still such things as property rights in this country."

"Public bathers don't believe this," Applebaum said. "They feel that a beach is a beach is a beach, and if they can get away with using a private beach rather than a public one, their day is made. This is particularly true of nude bathers who will walk miles across dunes, sand and rocks to camp on a piece of property that is off limits to them."

"That's terrible."

"It's worse than that. I discovered in my studies that as the summer goes by the owners of private beaches start suffering severe mental problems, including depression, paranoia and hysteria. Very few of them can cope with strangers using their beaches. At the end of the summer they are psychological wrecks."

"How so?" I asked.

"Well, they get up in the morning, and the first thing they do is go down to their beach to see if anyone is on it. The thing about private beaches is people use them not only for sunbathing in the daytime, but also at night for other things. If they find their beach has been used at night, it drives the owners crazy. 'Get off my beach!' they scream at the people wrapped in their blankets.

"Then the beachowners go back to their houses to have breakfast. After breakfast they go back to the beach to see who is on it. If no one has arrived yet, they go into town to buy the papers and shop for groceries. But they are very ill at ease because all the time they're away they keep wondering if anyone is on their sand.

"When they return from town, they immediately go back to the beach to check it out. They sit on a sand dune waiting for the invaders. Some people send their children down to stand guard, and at the first sign of an unauthorized bather the children sound the alarm and everyone goes down to the beach to drive the trespassers off. If the sunbathers refuse to move, they have to go back to the house to call the police. This can kill two or three hours."

"It doesn't sound like much fun for the beachowners," I said.

"It isn't. They can't accept lunch dates or go fishing or sailing because they believe as soon as they go someone will walk on their property."

"A person could develop a complex after a while."

"Most of them do," Applebaum said. "They have nightmares, hallucinations and crying jags. They start talking to themselves. And in some cases they even plot murder. If these people don't get treatment, they can become a danger to society."

"Then on the basis of your study you're recommending that people who own waterfront property seek psychiatric help as soon as the summer is over."

"It's essential," Applebaum said. "A person who owns a private beach at a summer resort is a walking time bomb that could go off at any moment."

## IT AIN'T A CRIME

If a neighor came into your house and started to poison your water you would immediately call the police, have the person arrested, press charges of attempted murder and do everything to see that he got sent away to the slammer for a long time.

But if a company poisons your water and also the fish and wildlife in your rivers and lakes there really isn't much you can do.

You could show up at the company office and say, "I want to see the man in charge of poisoning the lake water in this community."

"We have no such person," the receptionist will reply.

"Then I want to see the guy in charge of this factory."

If you're lucky you may get in to see the junior vice-president, in charge of cranks.

"Why are you poisoning my water and making my family sick?" you might ask.

"I'm sorry. We have no idea what you're talking about."

"Look out there. You see all that sludge pouring into the lake. Where the hell do you think it's going?"

"That's just a by-product of what we make here. We have to dispose of it some way."

"Why in the lake? Why can't you dispose of it some other way?"

"If we did it any other way we would have to charge more for the product and pass the cost on to the consumer. You wouldn't want us to do that, would you?"

"I don't care what it costs the consumer. Why should I be poisoned because you can't figure out what to do with your sludge?"

"Our laboratory technicians have measured the waste from our plant and have assured us that there is no danger to anyone's health."

"Big deal. Suppose they came in with a report that it did endanger our health."

"Our technicians would never do that. They're scientists."

"Well, I'm going to go to the government and tell them you're poisoning the water."

"I wouldn't do it if I were you. If we had to close this plant we'd put 500 people out of work. You wouldn't want to be responsible for putting 500 people out of work, would you?"

"You mean my choice is drinking poisoned water or putting people on the unemployment rolls?"

"It will be on your conscience—not mine."

Let's suppose that you did go to the government and complain.

"Do you know that the Polluted Corporation is spewing millions of gallons of water into the lake?" you ask the government official.

"We're aware of it. We have a citation against them now."

"What does that mean?"

"It means they have to show cause as to what they're doing to stop polluting the lake."

"So?"

"They've taken it to court. As a matter of fact it's been in the courts for two years. They have very good lawyers."

"Why don't you arrest them and throw the whole gang in jail?"

"We can't do that. If they plead 'No Contest' and promise to stop doing it we would accept it as a pledge of good faith. But if they fight it and then appeal, we have to let justice take its course."

"What does that mean?"

"They could be fined as much as $50,000."

"What's $50,000 to that corporation?"

"I know it's not much, but you can't send men to jail just for poisoning a lake."

"They're poisoning my family and everyone else around here. Isn't that a form of murder?"

"The courts don't consider it a crime. The only way the managers of the factory could be sent to jail is if the judge told them to stop it and they didn't. Then they could be held in contempt of court."

"And what do I do till then?"

"I would go and see the company and formally complain. It couldn't hurt."

## A DAY WITHOUT SUNSHINE

Pity the poor Florida orange growers. They are caught in a quandary since Anita Bryant's victory against homosexual rights in Dade County. The orange growers pay Miss Bryant $100,000 a year to push Florida orange juice, a job that she has done magnificently.

Anita Bryant meant orange juice and orange juice meant Anita Bryant. It is this instant celebrity identification that sponsors dream of. When you speak of Bob Hope, you're supposed to think of Texaco; mention Joe Namath and people are supposed to have a vision of pantyhose. Danny Thomas goes together with Maxwell House coffee; and, recently, when you see a picture of former Senator Sam Ervin, it is hoped your first thought is of an American Express credit card.

The problem in Florida is that when people now see Anita Bryant on television, the first thing that comes to mind is "gay," not as in breakfast but as in "homosexual."

The Florida orange juice people are not interested in selling homosexuals. That's not their business. A majority, I would guess, are sympathetic with Miss Bryant's stand on the issue, but the trouble with fighting homosexuals is that it doesn't sell orange juice.

First of all, no one knows how many homosexuals there are in this country because, despite all the publicity, many of them have still not come out of the closet.

Secondly, there are no figures on how many of them drink orange juice. But there are presumably enough of them to hurt the sale of Florida oranges. A sudden switch to California orange juice by gay people in this country could cost the Florida orange grove owners millions of dollars.

At the same time, the Florida orange juice industry is aware that if Anita Bryant is fired there could be a backlash from the heterosexuals in this country who would boycott Florida oranges in protest.

Market surveys indicate that heterosexuals are still the largest consumers of orange juice and drink it not only for its taste but also for its vitamins and the stamina it provides them. The Florida orange industry can't afford to lose the heterosexual orange juice drinkers if they expect to stay in business.

There is a solution to the problem, which I hesitate to suggest, since I don't want to get involved in the controversy. But I will because I believe the Florida orange growers need all the help they can get.

What the Florida orange industry could do is break down its TV budget. Half of it would go to Miss Bryant to continue pushing Florida orange juice to the "straight" people, and half would go to a gay spokesperson who would appeal to the homosexual drinkers. It would mean cutting Miss Bryant's fee to $50,000 a year, so the gay person would get paid the same as she does. But at the same time, Miss Bryant would only be required to make half the number of TV commercials.

It seems to me that this would satisfy everyone. The heterosexuals would be pleased to see that Miss Bryant was still selling orange juice, and the gays would be delighted to have finally broken through on big-time television. Florida orange juice consumption would have to go up because the TV commercials would appeal to everyone, regardless of race, religion or sexual preference.

Of course, the advertising agency for the Florida orange growers would have to find a gay spokesperson who could sing as well as Miss Bryant. But that shouldn't be a problem. Many of our finest performers come from the gay community and would be happy to supplement their income by doing orange juice commercials.

I would do it myself, but unfortunately I can't carry a tune.

## DEATH AND TAXES

My weatherman came on the TV screen one night and, after predicting warm and humid temperatures, he said, "As for the Air Quality Index, it's very unhealthy and should stay that way for a few days."

Then the news show went to a commercial showing two elderly people sitting in a canoe on a quiet river talking about "occasional irregularity" and what they do about it.

While the commercial was on my wife said to me, "What does it mean?"

"What does what mean?" I said.

"The business about the air quality being unhealthy."

"I guess it means that the air is not fit to breathe for the next few days."

"Then what are we supposed to do?" she wanted to know.

"That's a good question. It's probably not serious or they wouldn't have mentioned it on television. Otherwise people would panic, and if they panicked they wouldn't buy whatever they're trying to sell on TV."

"How come," my wife wanted to know, "the government bans everything that is dangerous to our health but permits the air we breathe to remain polluted?"

"Well, in the Washington area we don't have any industry so all the bad air comes from the exhausts of automobiles. You can't ban automobiles no matter how dangerous they are to your health."

"Why doesn't the government demand they make automobiles that don't pollute the air?"

"It's been trying to for some time, but every time it sets a time schedule for new clean air standards, the auto lobbyists get Congress to postpone it."

"Don't the lobbyists breathe the same air we do?"

"I imagine they do. But they have to weigh the fees they get for lobbying against their own health. Besides, it's my understanding that the automobile companies have excellent medical plans for their lobbyists, including free vacations to Arizona, in case they get sick from breathing all the gunk in the air."

"You would think congressmen would care about air quality. After all, they and their families have to breath the same air," she said.

"Congressmen are more concerned with votes than they are

with living. If you told a congressman he could get the United Auto Workers' union backing in his district if he stuck his nose in the tailpipe of a trailer truck, he'd do it."

"How bad does the air quality on TV have to get before someone will do something about it?"

"Pretty bad. I think if the weatherman keeled over as he was giving his forecast, then people might get upset. But we're so used to having him tell us how dangerous the pollution is that nobody pays any attention to him any more."

"Why doesn't the President do something about it?" my wife asked. "He and Rosalynn and Amy are all breathing the same air we are."

"They never tell the President what the pollution count is in Washington because they're afraid he'd move back to Plains, Ga. The most they do is keep him out of the Rose Garden on a bad day."

"I don't understand," she said. "This is the capital of the nation. People here have the power to do anything they want to, including blowing up the world, and no one does a thing about us poisoning each other to death."

"That's not their job," I said. "All Washington is concerned with is death and taxes—and we seem to be getting both."

My wife sighed. "I wish Anita Bryant cared as much about clean air as she does about homosexuals. I'll bet you we'd get some action then."

## THE GREAT MEDICAL BREAKTHROUGH

Professor Heinrich Applebaum called me excitedly the other day from his laboratory at the National Institute of Generic Drug Statistics. "I think I've made a breakthrough in medicine that could win me the Nobel Prize."

"What is it?" I demanded.

"You have to come out and see for yourself."

I dropped everything and took a taxi to the professor's lab.

He was waiting amongst his test-tubes.

"What did you do?" I asked.

"I've developed a stronger rat that can survive any medical experiment we perform on it."

"I don't believe it."

"Come," he said, leading me over to a cage where two white rats were sipping from a saucer of diet cola.

"I got the idea when I read the data on the saccharin dispute. Something bothered me about it. Why were some of the rats getting sick after being forced to eat enough saccharin to kill a horse? The scientists blamed the saccharin, but no one blamed the white rats. There are so many agents being fed and injected into rats that they keep keeling over. Drug companies have put millions of dollars into research, only to be told they couldn't market their product because the white rats couldn't take it.

"So I decided there was only one answer to the problem. And that was to develop a white rat who could stand up to anything we shoved down his throat.

"If I could breed a white rat immune to any kind of disease the FDA would have to give its approval for the new drug."

"Only a mind like yours would think of something like that," I said.

"The trick was to find the right breeds. In every medical experiment there are white rats who are survivors. In the Canadian tests of saccharin only 12 of the 44 rats fed the stuff developed any symptoms. The other 32 thrived on the sweetener and became saccharin junkies.

"I purchased the two healthiest specimens and mated them, and then mated their offspring, and after four generations I got what I wanted—a super white rat that could withstand any punishment medical science could inflict on it.

"These are two of them. I've fed them the equivalent of 3,000 bottles of diet drinks a day; I've had them smoke ten packs of cigarettes an hour; I've filled their cage with carbon monoxide; I've made Tris nighties for them, which they have worn for three weeks. I've even strapped them to the engine of a Concorde, and as you can see none of the experiments has had any ill effect on them."

"I've never seen two happier white rats in my life," I admitted. "I wonder why no one has ever thought of this before."

"Because they were looking for the wrong key," Applebaum

said. "When a drug didn't come up to FDA standards everyone blamed the drug and not the rat. The ordinary white rat used in laboratories is a pampered animal. It doesn't know what it is to forage for food and slink around garbage dumps. From the day it is born it is given the best of everything.

"It's no wonder it can't handle a bite of DDT or a small dose of a birth control pill."

Applebaum gave each rat a sugar cube.

"What's that?" I asked him.

"It's full of swine flu. They can't get enough of it," he replied.

"Applebaum, what does it all mean?"

"It means a bonanza for the drug and chemical industries. They will no longer have to lobby for less regulation on their products. It means that all the data we now have on what causes sickness in rats will be obsolete. It means once the orders start coming in for my white rats I'm going to be a millionaire!"

"Not to mention the Nobel Prize," I said.

"They'll have to give it to me," Applebaum agreed. "I've found the cure for every disease known to man."


### SOLVING THE EMPTY HOSPITAL BED PROBLEM

The real problem of hospital prices, the experts tell us, is not the patients but the empty beds. A hospital can keep down costs if it is absolutely full. But it starts to lose money if it doesn't have enough sick people to care for.

A recent news item said that Sunrise Hospital and Medical Center in Las Vegas is trying to solve the problem through a lottery. Sunrise seemed to be doing a good business during the week, but it was suffering from a lack of patients on weekends. So the Las Vegas hospital came up with a unique plan.

If you check in on Friday or Saturday your name goes in a hat for a lottery. Every Monday morning, a certified public accountant draws a name from the hat and the winner is given the choice of five different Mediterranean cruises worth $4,000. The winner has a year to claim the prize, and if for some reason he or she never leaves the hospital the prize goes to the patient's estate. I did not make this up.

The director of the hospital said the lottery has been an overwhelming success and weekend admissions are up by 40 percent.

While this is an innovative idea there are others that we can think of which would cut hospital costs and fill the empty rooms that are costing all of us so much money.

One idea would be for a hospital to hook up a hotline with all the doctors that are accredited to the hospital. Each doctor would have a quota to fill as to how many patients he must supply to the hospital. As soon as a bed became empty the doctor would be notified that a hospital patient was needed, and he would be obligated to find someone for the bed whether he needed it or not.

Suppose, for example, a patient came in with an ingrown toenail. As the doctor was treating it the hotline would ring and the administrator on the other end would say, "We need an in-patient for Room 211."

"Is it a private or semiprivate room?" the doctor would ask.

"Semiprivate, but Dr. Combs is sending over a patient with a tennis elbow so we just need one person."

"I've got a live one in my office now I can give you."

"Hurry," the administrator says, "we're losing money every minute."

The doctor goes back to the patient. "I don't know how to tell you this, but I don't like the look of this ingrown toenail. I could take it out, of course, but you might lose your toe."

"What's the alternative?"

"I'd like to put you in Our Lady of Deficits Hospital for observation. I think that with adequate hospital care and a nurse around the clock, we could observe which direction the nail is growing and possibly save the foot."

"How long will I be in the hospital?" the patient asks.

The doctor calls back the administrator. "How long do you need him?"

"I'll take him for a week," the administrator says. "Dr. Friedkin owes us three patients and he's promised us a pregnancy case whether the rabbit test is positive or negative."

The doctor goes back to the patient. "I'd like to keep you in the hospital for a week to avoid liver damage."

Of course, the quota system is not the only alternative to keeping hospitals full. Taking a leaf from Holiday Inns, the hospital could offer rooms for patients and put in cots for their children at no extra charge.

They could also offer "second honeymoon weekends" for couples wanting to get away for a few days with free X-rays and Epsom salt baths thrown in.

The main reason there are so many empty hospital beds has not been mentioned by anybody, and that is the poor quality of the food. After a meal or two in an average hospital most patients want to get dressed and leave.

There is a solution for this. Most independent surveys show there is 50 percent more surgery done in this country than is necessary—mainly because we have 50 percent more surgeons.

To cut down on surgery and also improve the quality of hospital food, HEW should provide retraining programs for surgeons and teach them how to cook.

Hopefully, these surgeon-chefs, once they learned their trade, could make hospital cuisine the best in the land, and patients would extend their stays in their rooms as long as their Blue Cross would let them.

## FREE MEDICAL ADVICE

If you ask Americans what bugs them the most besides death and taxes, they will usually answer, "the high cost of medical care." It has become the major domestic issue in the country, and almost everyone you talk to is furious about it.

I say almost because my friend Hopewell claims he has solved the problem. "The reason people are paying so much for medical care is that we are not making use of all the trained people in our own families who have as much experience as any doctor."

I looked perplexed.

"In my family we have specialists in every division of medicine, and they make house calls even when you don't want them to."

"I still don't understand."

"Last Sunday my Aunt Hilda and Uncle George stopped by the house on their way to visit some friends. Uncle George had a heart attack about two years ago so he considers himself in a class with Dr. De Bakey. I was complaining about slow circulation in my tennis arm. Without even examining me he said, 'I'd recommend a bypass operation.'

"Aunt Hilda said, 'Either that or open-heart surgery. My nephew by marriage had open-heart surgery last year and he's doing very well. Let them implant a pacemaker and you'll feel like a new man.'

"But Uncle George was adamant. 'Bypass is better. I wouldn't be here today if it wasn't for my bypass.'

"Maybe I should have a third consultation with a doctor?" I suggested.

" 'Go ahead,' said Uncle George, 'if you want to waste your money. But he'll only tell you the same thing.' "

I told Hopewell, "You saved yourself a $50 visit to a cardiologist."

"Exactly. My mother, on the other hand, is a regular faith healer. She calls me up on the phone and she can tell just from the sound of my voice when something is wrong. 'What is it, son?' she'll ask.

" 'I'm very depressed,' I'll tell her. 'Becky just smashed in the front of my car.'

" 'It isn't Becky who made you depressed. You're suffering from male menopause.'

" 'How do you know?' I'll ask her. 'Your father was the same age when he got depressed. The thing to do is just get through the day. I'll call you tomorrow and we'll talk about it some more.' "

"Anybody else would have had to lay out a bundle to a psychiatrist," I told him.

Hopewell agreed. "I have a brother-in-law who has back problems. He goes to a doctor. But if anybody else in the family has back problems we call him. One of my sisters-in-law specializes in sinus problems. All you have to do is hint you have a problem and she'll not only prescribe the medicine but she'll deliver it within the hour.

"My sister went to Mexico last year so she knows everything about intestinal illnesses, and I have a cousin Freddy who always watches Marcus Welby on television and can look at anybody in the family and know immediately if he or she is suffering from a vitamin deficiency.

"I had a kidney stone last summer," Hopewell said, "so if anyone is having kidney problems they call me.

"My wife knows all about high blood pressure and my aunt Phoebe deals mostly with female disorders."

"You've got a Johns Hopkins Medical School right in your own family," I told Hopewell.

"Every family does. The trick is when you go to the doctor ask a lot of questions, and then file away the information so you can help all your relatives. You can't imagine how much money you can save in medical bills. I have a brother who goes to a psychiatrist once a week. A month ago I called him up and told him about a dream I had in which I was stuck in a cave and taxis kept going by, but not one would stop for me. He told the shrink the dream as if it was his own, and then called me up the following day and said, 'You forgot to pay your telephone bill.' I saved $40 on one lousy dream. With a family like mine, who needs Medicare?"


## THE GREAT SACCHARIN CONTROVERSY

In dealing with the saccharin problem I have to confess I am not a disinterested spectator. I have a cousin who is married to Marvin Eisenstadt, one of the owners of the company which makes Sweet 'n Low, a powdered saccharin in pink packages that can be found in restaurants, grocery stores and supermarkets all over this land.

Although I do not own any stock in the company, I am very proud of Marvin and tend to brag about the relationship. You can't imagine what a bombshell I can drop at a dinner party in Georgetown when I casually say, "My cousin makes Sweet 'n Low." I can live off the reflected glory for the entire evening.

Although Marvin is a saccharin tycoon he never forgets his poor relatives, and once a year I receive a carton full of thousands of packets of Sweet 'n Low, with enough saccharin to kill every rat in Washington.

I only mention these facts because I don't want the anti-saccharin people to say that the reason I wrote an article in favor of saccharin was because of my cousin Marvin.

The truth of the matter is that whether I was related to Marvin by marriage or not I would be against the FDA ban on this artificial sweetner.

For those of us who are constantly fighting weight problems saccharin is our security blanket. It alleviates the guilt we all share when we have a large dinner with a big gooey dessert. At the end of the meal we can always put saccharin in our coffee and believe in our hearts we haven't done anything wrong.

As far as soft drinks go, there is nothing that makes a person trying to lose weight feel more noble than drinking a diet cola with a cheeseburger or a hot dog with relish, onions and mustard.

Saccharin is the cocaine of dieters, the mother's milk of weight watchers, the sweet taste of success. Without it there is nothing left for us but sugar, loaded with calories, lacking in nutrition, the biggest no-no on every dentist's list.

I do not wish to dwell on the emotional factors that make saccharin an important ingredient in the American way of life. Let's talk about the scientific reasons for keeping saccharin off the shelves of the supermarkets.

We are told that white rats were fed saccharin equal to 5 percent of their diets. This is the equivalent of consuming 800 diet drinks a day over a period of 50 years. In the first generation of rodents 8 of the 38 rodents developed bladder cancer and in the second generation 12 of 44 developed tumors. This, as far as the government scientists were concerned, was enough to ban the substance from the market.

It was, you have to admit, a fairly uneven contest. No one except a white rat would be crazy enough to consume that much saccharin in his diet, and he wouldn't do it if they offered him something else to eat. In the same labs you have white rats smoking tobacco and they're developing cancer all the time. Yet nobody in this country has dared to ban cigarettes from the marketplace. You have other rats breathing nothing but car fumes and they're dropping like flies. Yet there is no government effort to ban automobiles from the road. The only white rats they're picking on are those who were overdosed with a sugar substitute.

If the government was reasonable they would put on each package of Sweet 'n Low and on every bottle of diet cola a message similar to the ones they put on cigarettes. It could read: Surgeon

General's Warning—"A recent test showed that 12 out of 44 white rats who were fed a fifth of their diet in saccharin found it hazardous to their health."

Make no mistake, we dieters aren't going to take this lying down. If they persist in banning saccharin we'll start buying the stuff from pushers on street corners. Mexico is already geared up to smuggle the stuff across the border. If we can't get our daily fix of saccharin legitimately, we'll let the Mafia do it for us.

So it's up to the government. Do they want my cousin Marvin or the Gambino family in the Sweet 'n Low business? It better make up its mind fast.

## PLAYING WITH GENES

One of the many scientific controversies raging in the country right now has to do with genetic research. It appears possible that, in the not too distant future, geneticists will be able to join genetic material from different organisms in combinations unknown to us today.

Where the genetic research will lead no one knows. The scientists claim the unlocking of genetic secrets will benefit mankind in its fight against disease. The other school says they're messing around with something they know nothing about and could come up with the Werewolf of London (no disrespect to the English, of course).

It is a worrisome thing to contemplate and I must admit I'm rather nervous about it. At the same time, if done right, the commercial possibilities are infinite.

The year is 1985 and we're visiting the showroom of Genetic Laboratories, Inc., where the salesman in a white jacket is showing us around.

"You really have a nice selection of people," I say.

"We're wholesale," he warns us. "We don't take orders for less than a gross."

"I understand," I reply. "Could I see some of the models?"

A beautiful blonde in a low-cut gown comes out.

"Why, that looks exactly like Angie Dickinson!" I exclaim.

"It is an exact replica, including the same color eyes, hair and skin texture. It's one of our most popular models. Sears Roebuck features it in their catalogue. We're turning out 10,000 a month."

"Fantastic," I say. "There should be one in every home."

"Here is our Robert Redford model. He is also one of our best sellers. We put an advertisement in Cosmopolitan and we've had back orders for six months."

A tall man in a Green Beret uniform came out from behind the screen.

"You haven't duplicated John Wayne?" I say in astonishment.

"Down to the twang in his voice. The U.S. Army has ordered 250,000 and the U.S. Marines will take all we can make."

"What a breakthrough," I tell him. "An Army and Marine Corps made up of John Waynes is invincible."

"The government seems to think so. We're not allowed to sell any to foreign powers."

"I should hope not. Is that O.J. Simpson I see over there?"

"That's correct. Through the miracle of science every football team in the country can now have an O.J. Simpson in the backfield. We have a license with the National Football League to duplicate him, for a royalty, of course."

"And Nureyev, the ballet dancer?"

"We just came out with him. We're hoping to do a big promotion job at Christmas when every ballet company does *The Nutcracker Suite*."

"Are my eyes deceiving me," I say, "or is that Lassie sitting over there?"

The salesman replies, "They said we couldn't do it, but we can now turn out 1,000 Lassies an hour. I don't think there is a family in America that doesn't have one."

"Let me ask you something. Have you ever tried to duplicate someone and come up with a monster?"

"Off the record?" he asks.

"My lips are sealed."

"Someone in the lab once accidentally mixed the genes of Jack the Ripper with a donkey and we had a catastrophe."

"What was the result?"

"We reproduced Idi Amin."

## GLOSSARY OF TERMS

What are the key factors in the energy crisis? What are we really talking about? Here is a glossary of terms to help you understand it.

GAS—once used to explain a joke as in "that's a gas." Also used to describe someone who was long-winded as in "he is full of gas." Occasionally said to a person you wanted to hurry as in "Step on the gas."

But now it turns out that it is a colorless substance that everyone thought we'd never run out of, and was cheap, something you had nothing to do with except to open the door once a month and let the "gas man" go down into your basement and read your meter.

SNOW—once a beautiful white substance that fell two or three or six inches and gave everyone pleasure to watch from their warm living room and bedrooms which were heated by gas or oil which are now very much in short supply. People used to welcome snow; now they fear it. Now it falls in the cities and in many cases misses the ski areas altogether, which doesn't make economic sense and is another example of bad environmental planning by the government.

ICE—once used to put in drinks to make them cold. The first thing a wife said to a husband when they were giving a party was "We're out of ice." It is now found on streets, sidewalks and house steps, and what usually was palatable to mouth has now become more dangerous to foot and car. Ice usually forms under snow where you can't see it. It loves to chew up snow tires. You can spin for hours in one tiny segment of the stuff and never move an inch.

The reason your insurance rates will be going up this spring can be blamed on the ice you see this winter. The only people who like ice are people who sell safety glass or fenders or orthopedic equipment such as crutches.

SALT—once put on food, now it's supposed to be put on roads. Unfortunately, there is a shortage of salt because of the ice. The salt is supposed to melt the ice so you won't skid on it. But the salt also melts the road as well. When salt seeps through the asphalt it makes what is commonly called a pothole, which will only be repaired during an election year.

WIND CHILL FACTOR—the combination of the temperature plus the speed of the wind produces what is known as the wind chill factor. No one ever heard of the wind chill factor before television weather reports. It was either cold outside or very cold, or if you came in with a really red face it was freezing. Now you know that with the wind chill factor it is 10 below zero, 20 below zero or 40 below zero. People who would ordinarily go about their business are now so intimidated by the wind chill factor that some of them won't get out of bed for days.

SLUSH—is what gathers when it gets warm and the ice and snow melt. Its main function is to accumulate at curbs and intersections where automobiles can splash it at people waiting for a bus or to cross the street. Splashing slush on people in the streets makes people in cars feel good and sometimes makes them feel as if the long, cold winter was all worthwhile.

PRICE FREEZE—blamed by the gas people for the shortage of their product as well as their inability to deliver the stuff to the right place at the right time. Gas companies are now taking full-page advertisements telling the American people they warned them there would be a gas shortage if the government kept regulating the price of their product. The question is: If there was no price freeze on gas, would there have been enough of it to go around this winter? Or, as some people believe, was it just another snow job?

## WEATHER PARANOIA

People who talk about weather are now getting paranoid about it. They keep looking at the TV weather maps and they aren't laughing any more at the jolly men and women who are bringing them bad weather news.

I know this for a fact. I was sitting in the living room with Seltzer and the weatherman said, "Well, I guess you folks out there are wondering when it's going to warm up. Would you believe things are going to get worse before they get better?"

"I'll kill the SOB," Seltzer said, as he made a move toward the screen.

I stopped him. "It's not his fault that the news is bad."

"Why does he have to grin when he's telling it? Cronkite doesn't grin when he tells you about an Amtrak train derailing in New Jersey."

The weatherman was standing up in front of a screen.

"Let's take a look at the satellite map. This white stuff here means it is cloudy over the eastern part of the United States which means freezing temperatures, snow, sleet and icy winds. Over here in southern California, where there are no white spots, it means they're having sunny weather with temperatures in the 80s."

"He's a sadist," Seltzer says. "He gets his kicks pointing to white spots on satellite maps."

"It's his job," I said. "He doesn't like the white spots any more than you do."

The weatherman continued. "Ordinarily, we would have gotten some relief except for this cold front which is coming in from Canada."

"Aha!" Seltzer shouted. "It's Canada again. How long are we going to take that stuff from Canada? Why don't we tell 'em 'one more cold front from you people and we nuke Ottawa.' "

"It isn't really Canada's fault. The front probably originated in the Arctic and just passed through Canada."

"Why does Canada let it pass through?" Seltzer asked. "Tell me that."

"Because if she didn't let it pass through it would become a stationary front and hang over Canada. No country wants a dark cloud hanging over it day and night."

The weatherman was still talking. "Now behind this cold front is another cold front coming up from the South."

"I knew it," shouted Seltzer. "The South is sending all its bad weather north. The people down there don't care any more about us than the Canadians."

"The South is suffering, too," I said.

"Good. If they want to originate cold fronts they have it coming to them."

We turned back to the weatherman. "But what we really have to be concerned about is this low-pressure system over here of warm air meeting this high-pressure system over here of cold air which could cause precipitation of up to two feet of snow."

Seltzer threw his shoe at the screen.

The weatherman chuckled. "So be prepared to put on your long underwear and your galoshes and if you can start your car up, you'll have better luck than I did this morning."

"Let me ask you something," Seltzer said. "How come the newspapers have a little box somewhere with the weather which says 'Sunny, Cloudy, Rain or Sleet,' and television spends fifteen minutes telling you about every snowflake in North Dakota?"

"It's a good spot to sell Bayer aspirin or Anacin," I said.

The weatherman had a puppet in his hands. "Let's talk to Ezra about how cold it really is outside. 'Ezra, if the temperature is 5 below and the wind is 35 knots, and the wind chill factor is 30 below, how do you get your car started in the morning?' Ezra, the puppet, replied, 'You send your wife out in her housecoat, ha! ha! ha!' "

"I'm still going to kill him," Seltzer said.

## A PAIN IN THE NECK

It is regrettable that as the massage parlor industry grows by leaps and bounds there are fewer and fewer places that actually offer you a real massage—one that will alleviate pain and distress when you really need it.

I discovered this last Sunday when I found myself with a pinched nerve and decided that I might get some relief from the strong hands of a tough masseur or masseuse who was willing to throw me across the room, if necessary, to get the crick out of my neck.

There are 10 pages devoted to massage parlors in the Washington Yellow Pages, but very few seem to have too many massage specialists on duty on Sunday afternoon.

The listings include "Aladdin's Chest," "Bunny's Topkopi," "Bobbie Jo's Flaming Den," "Tiffany's Velvet Touch," and "Sheik Abdullah's Harem." I finally called "Lolita's Geisha House" because my fingers got tired of walking across the Yellow Pages. Lolita's ad said they made house calls.

A man answered the phone.

"I have this crick in my neck," I said. "And I was wondering if you'd send over an expert masseur."

"Of course. Do you want a blonde or a brunette?"

"I don't care about the color of his hair. I want a guy with strong hands."

"Oh you're one of *them*," he said.

"One of what?" I said.

"Well, we usually send out masseuses for men and masseurs for women."

"Look, I'm not particular as long as the person knows what he or she is doing."

"They know what they're doing, all right," he assured me. "They wouldn't be working for Lolita's Geisha House if they didn't. We can fulfill any fantasy you have in mind."

"Well, I do have this fantasy," I said, "that someone will come over to my house and take his or her strong hands and wring them around my neck and get the crick out of it."

"I see. You're into sadomasochism," he said. "Would you like her to wear an all-leather outfit?"

"I don't care what she wears. As a matter of fact, I don't care if you send over a 300-pound gorilla as long as I can get some relief."

"We've never had anyone ask for a gorilla before. You do have some strange fantasies."

"Look, I really don't want a gorilla. What I had in mind was one of those large, heavily built Swedish or Finnish women, one who is stacked like a brick federal building and has steel arms and hands that can tear a Washington Redskin linebacker in half."

"What kind of a massage parlor do you think we're running? Our girls come from some of the best families in the country. Several are graduates of Vassar and Sweetbriar, and we have one who has a master's degree from the University of Tokyo.

"We have the most beautiful girls in the Washington area, and while we try to make all our clients happy there are limits to the services we will provide. Now if you really want a gorilla you're going to have to give us a few days to find one and you'll have to pay for his trainer because we can't allow him to make house calls on his own."

"I need someone this afternoon. Don't you have a simple masseur or masseuse who just gets pleasure out of rubbing sore muscles and massaging bad backs and necks?"

"We might have," he said suspiciously. "But how do we know you're not from the vice squad?"

"I swear to you I'm not. I have an American Express credit

card, a Master Charge and a Bank Americard. Would I be able to get credit from all three if I was a member of the vice squad?"

"All right," he said. "We'll send you over Annie."

"Is she strong?"

"Strong? She'll put three lashes across your back with a horsewhip and you'll forget your neck pain in a flash."

"Thanks, but no thanks. I'll call the YMCA."

"It's up to you, but I doubt if they'll have a gorilla working on Sunday."

# IX. Whither The Dollar?

## LET'S TALK BUSINESS

My friend Russell Baker of *The New York Times* recently wrote an article suggesting that if businessmen can deduct their three-martini lunches, blue-collar workers should be able to deduct their bologna sandwiches. Mr. Baker, who claims to represent the proletariat, although he is really a closet populist, once again has missed the point. He implies that while businessmen can eat from the taxpayer's trough, blue-collar workers are forbidden to do so.

This is not so. The blue-collar worker is just as entitled to deduct his bologna sandwich as the executive is his Dover sole *providing* the worker discusses business.

The IRS is very specific about tax-deductible lunches. You can deduct the meal if you discuss business that will be beneficial to a sale, inspire a deal or endear you to a client for the rest of his life.

The trouble with blue-collar workers and other people who brown bag their midday meal is that they refuse to discuss their work while they're eating their sandwiches and drinking from their thermos bottles.

When you see two guys sitting on a girder 40 stories up munching away, you can be sure the conversation goes something like this: "What did your wife make you?"

"A meatball sandwich with green peppers and onions and Tabasco sauce and lettuce and tomatoes. She don't have any imagination. What have you got?"

"Salami, goat's cheese, scallions, sesame seeds and mustard on a rye, and a banana. How do you think the Yankees are going to do?"

"I guess it all depends if Reggie Jackson and Billy Martin talk to each other."

Now as far as the IRS is concerned this is not a business lunch. It's just two guys sitting on a girder chewing the fat, and there is nothing in the way of a deal to come out of it.

On the other hand, if one of the men said to the other, "I'll give you my pickle if you let me use your blowtorch on a number-four joint," and the other one responds, "Okay, but I want a swig of your chicken soup, and I want you to get the foreman to buy me a new pair of gloves." That would be an acceptable conversation to deduct not only the men's sandwiches but the pickle and chicken soup as well.

The same holds true for secretaries. They can deduct their tuna fish salads and iced tea if they stick to business. But most secretaries at lunch prefer to tell each other what hanky-panky X is committing with Y. The IRS is very tough about office gossip and will disallow any luncheon deductions where sex is the main topic of conversation.

By the same token if one secretary says to the other, "My boss gave me some dictation this morning and I accidentally erased 18 1/2 minutes of the tape," and the other says, "Did you have your foot on the pedal when you answered the phone?" and the first says, "Yes," and then the second one says, "That will do it every time," the secretaries have met all the qualifications for a tax-free meal.

The point that I'm making and which Russell Baker missed is that the sandwich eaters have as much right to a deductible lunch as the person who eats at 21 or the Sans Souci as long as they keep a diary of whom they ate with and what business they discussed.

Both President Carter and Mr. Baker have been demagoguing about businessmen getting a free ride at mealtime. But neither opinion maker has mentioned that, if guys on the girders talked business 40 stories up they could drink three free martinis, too.

*A CHRISTMAS CAROL*

"Uncle," said Bob Cratchit, "why not come to our house tomorrow for a three-martini Christmas dinner?"

"Bah, humbug," said Scrooge. "I don't believe in three-martini Christmas dinners."

"But Uncle, if you come we can discuss business and then the dinner will be tax-deductible and I will be able to afford to buy poor Tiny Tim a bird."

"I'm against all tax-deductible dinners *and* lunches too. I don't believe in them even when they come at Christmas time."

"Oh, Uncle, what a terrible thing to say. Where would we all be if we couldn't deduct our holiday lunches and dinners as legitimate entertainment?"

"Bah, humbug," said Scrooge as he went home to have a peanut butter sandwich.

Scrooge put on his nightcap and sat by the fire when suddenly there appeared before his eyes the apparition of his old friend Bert Lance.

Lance still had all his bank books, ledgers and deeds, and was holding in his right hand a diplomatic passport.

Scrooge said, "What do you want, Bert?"

"I came to tell you that you will be visited by three spirits. Listen to what they have to say, Scrooge. Otherwise you will be like me, doomed forever trying to unload my stock in the National Bank of Georgia."

This really frightened Scrooge, as he knew Lance was in a bad way.

The first spirit showed up exactly at midnight. "I am the martini of Christmas-past," it said. "Come." The spirit took Scrooge back to his farm. "Do you see that happy man behind the plow?"

"It's me," said Scrooge.

"Who paid for the plow and that land and the peanuts you couldn't sell?"

"The taxpayer."

The martini spirit said, "And you never said a word then about the tax laws being unfair and a disgrace."

Tears filled Scrooge's eyes. "They didn't seem unfair then. But getting farm rebates is different than having tax-deductible lunches and dinners."

"Scrooge, how are you going to keep them down on the farm if they don't serve tax-free meals in town?"

The second martini showed up an hour later.

"I am the spirit of Christmas-present, Scrooge. Come with me."

The spirit took Scrooge to a convention where a sandy-haired fellow was sitting on the stage drinking beer and talking about his kinfolks.

"Why, it's my brother Billy," Scrooge said.

"Yes, and do you realize where he'd be today if conventions weren't tax deductible?"

"Stop," begged Scrooge. "I don't want to hear any more."

The third martini showed up. "I am the spirit of Christmas-1980. Would you like to see what will happen to your tax reform bill by the time the House and Senate get through with it?"

"No more," cried Scrooge. "I have been persuaded."

"Good," said the third martini. "Then you know what to do."

Scrooge went out and bought the biggest bird he could find, for which, of course, he got a receipt. He then went to Bob Cratchit's house and presented him with it. "I'd like to talk to you about the Whitney Account over dinner," Scrooge said.

"Of course, sir. And I shall order a very good bottle of burgundy as long as we're at it. After all, a business Christmas dinner comes only once a year."

Scrooge chuckled and after stuffing himself until he thought he'd explode, he wrote in his little book, "Dinner with Bob Cratchit and Tiny Tim. Purpose—Business—to discuss new stools for Counting House Annex."

## CHECKBOOK JOURNALISM

"Louie the Louse, I am authorized to inform you of your rights. You are permitted to make one telephone call."

"Okay, I want to speak to the Heartongue Literary Agency. Hello, Heartongue? This is Louis the Louse. I think I got a good one for you this time. I heisted a Brink's truck of 20 million bucks, hijacked the Rolling Stones' private airplane and forged Cliff Robertson's name to a check for $150,000. My attorney thinks it could be a 'Literary Guild Selection of the Month.' No, I won't say anything until you get here."

A half-hour later Louie the Louse is sitting under a white electric light bulb surrounded by the district attorney and his underlings.

"Louie, who were your accomplices in the Brink's robbery?"

Louie says, "I refuse to answer on the grounds that my answer would damage the newspaper syndication rights of my story."

The district attorney says, "You told Sgt. Brophy when you were brought in that there were four of you in on the Brink's job, including an inside man. Who was the inside man?"

"Wait," says Heartongue, "*Newsweek* has just offered us $50,000 for the name of the inside man, providing it doesn't appear in *The Washington Post* first."

Louie looks straight at the district attorney. "You can burn my fingers, you can dunk my head in the bathtub, you can knock out my teeth, but I'll never rat on *Newsweek*."

"Louie, we got all the evidence we need. We have pictures of you hijacking the Rolling Stones' airplane."

"Let me see those," Heartongue says. "You have no right to these photos. I sold them exclusively to *New York* magazine."

"They're state's evidence," the district attorney says. "They're part of the public record which we hope will be used to convict Louie the Louse."

"Do you mean to say that you would use photographs that were sold to a magazine on an exclusive basis just to prove a criminal case against my client? Have you no legal ethics?"

"I'm not sure what you're driving at, Heartongue."

"The Constitution provides that every person accused of a crime is entitled to sell his story to a magazine, a newspaper, a hardcover book company and a paperback publisher. The value of his story is based on what he did *not* tell the grand jury or the FBI. If you reveal the facts in this case, the TV bidding on Louie's book could be seriously damaged."

"Maybe so," the district attorney says. "But my only concern is justice. We have a guy who stole from a Brink's truck, hijacked an airplane and forged a movie actor's name to a check. Now he has to be punished."

"He will be," Heartongue said. "But he wants to save it all for the book. Give us a break. A guy's got a right to make a buck on his own crime."

The district attorney says, "It's out of my hands. There are a hundred reporters as well as photographers and TV cameras out there. How do I explain to them that Louie's story is copyrighted and they have no rights to it?"

"That's your problem. My client has committed a perfectly valid crime which, on today's literary market, is worth anywhere up to seven figures. By making these crimes common knowledge you are depriving him of his literary and subsidiary rights under the Author's League and Dramatists Guild contracts."

The district attorney ignores him. "Okay, Louie, let's try one more. When did you forge Cliff Robertson's name on a check?"

Louie says, "I refuse to answer on the grounds that I may be getting a call from David Frost at any moment."


## SANTA SELLS OUT

Santa Claus was in his office at the North Pole when his wife came in. "There is a delegation of elves outside and they want to talk to you."

"I'll see them in a moment," Santa Claus said as he picked up the phone. "Operator, give me Tokyo . . . . Hello, Tokyo, this is Santa Claus. What happened to that shipment of dolls I ordered from you people in July? . . . . I know there was a dock strike but I have to have them right away. All right, but if I don't get them in time I'm going to start dealing with the people in Hong Kong."

Santa Claus hung up and told his wife to let the elves in.

One of the elves spoke up: "We haven't made any toys for Christmas this year and we want to know why."

"I know it's tough on you," Santa Claus replied, "but I've discovered that I can get them made cheaper in the Far East than have you people make them here."

"But we've been making toys for hundreds of years," an elf said. "It's the only thing we know how to do."

"I'm aware of the problem but costs have gone up, and it's not economically feasible for me to make my own toys any more. I can get electric trains from Taiwan for half the price that it costs you people to construct them.''

"But what are we supposed to do?'' an elf asked.

"That's a good question. When I was working for myself I could keep our factory humming. But since I sold out to a conglomerate I have to show a good earnings performance. All they're interested in at the head office is the bottom line.''

"We're the best toy makers in the world,'' an elf said. "When we made toys they lasted for years. Now they fall apart on Christmas Day.''

"Gentlemen, it's out of my hands. In the old days children used to write me and tell me they wanted a racing car, an Erector Set, a doll house or a bicycle. But now they want everything they see on television. I can't give away a toy unless a child has seen it on a TV commercial.

"Last year we got stuck with a million tons of putty because the kids didn't even know it existed. The head of the conglomerate was furious and said I had to eat it. You can't imagine how miserable they make my life when an item doesn't move.''

"Why did you sell out in the first place?'' an elf demanded.

"I needed capital,'' Santa Claus said sadly. "I was unable to compete with the major discount toy companies, and when the conglomerate came to me they made me an offer I couldn't resist. They promised me I could run my operation just as I had in the past and they would not interfere with anything I was doing.

"I believed them. Then I sent in the figures for last year and they hit the ceiling. As you know we've never been a profit-making organization. So they sent up a team of Christmas consultants who said our problem was we were making our toys without paying any attention to cost control. They recommended to the head office that we close the factory in the North Pole and build one in South Korea where elves get paid 50 cents a day.''

"So that leaves us out in the cold?'' an elf asked.

Santa Claus shrugged. "They said if I couldn't run this operation they would find someone who could. And they meant it. You know how I feel about you little fellows. I've worked with you all my life. But what can I do when the Japanese start dumping Farrah Fawcett dolls down every chimney at a quarter of the price that we can make them for up here?''

"Boy,'' said an elf, "what a Christmas this is going to be.''

"I'm sorry," Santa Claus said, "but that's the way the beach ball bounces."

Donner, one of Santa's reindeer, came charging in. "Is it true we're not going to be working this Christmas?"

Santa's face turned red. "I'm sorry you had to hear it from somebody else, Donner. The conglomerate wants me to use Amalgamated Parcel Service. They say it's cheaper and more efficient than reindeer. The real truth is the conglomerate owns the APS company."

## WHITHER THE BUSINESS LUNCH?

The "business lunch," as we Americans have known it for so many years, may be a thing of the past. President Carter, who doesn't drink, has always railed against people being able to deduct a "three-martini lunch" on their taxes.

Congressmen and senators, many of whom have been recipients of the "three-martini lunch," have offered a compromise proposal in the new tax bill, which is that only 50 percent of a business meal can be considered deductible. The other 50 percent will have to come out of the person's own pocket.

The fight against the expense account business lunch has always been a popular issue with the masses.

But let me, for the moment, be the devil's advocate and point out that the business lunch is essential to a healthy American economy. Most big deals are made at a business lunch involving not only money but orders for goods, which means jobs for millions of people.

Let us say Mr. Jay wants to sell Ms. Zee 3,000 dresses for her department store. Mr. Jay takes Ms. Zee to a beautiful French restaurant in New York and buys her a delicious meal with the finest wines. Ms. Zee feels very, very good and orders Mr. Jay's whole new line.

Mr. Jay goes back to his office and tells the factories to start humming. He deducts the paltry $80 lunch, but the government gets hundreds of thousands of dollars in return in the form of taxes from Mr. Jay's employees.

Under the new tax plan, Mr. Jay may take Ms. Zee to an inferior Chinese restaurant, order half a pot of tea and insist on splitting his sweet and sour pork with her.

Ms. Zee thinks to herself, "If this guy is so cheap at lunch, his clothes must be cheap, too. I'm not going to buy any of them." Mr. Jay calls the factory and tells them to shut down. For the lousy $40 that Mr. Jay couldn't deduct for a decent lunch, 500 good people are put out of work.

All right, if you don't like that example, what about this one?

Parsons is trying to sell the Pentagon a new anti-hand grenade. His firm has strict orders that he cannot spend more than $20 for lunch. He takes General Cain, the Pentagon procurement officer, to a five-star Italian restaurant. They order three martinis each. Parsons has blown the entire $20. General Cain says, "Let's order." Parsons says, "I didn't invite you for lunch. I invited you for drinks."

General Cain says, "Well, if that's the way you feel about it, the Army doesn't want any of your anti-hand grenades."

"Then," Parsons says angrily, "you can pay for your own dry martinis."

For a lousy filet mignon, the tax reformers could drive a breach between the military-industrial complex that could never be repaired.

Maybe you don't like that example, either. Let me try one more.

Burt Arrow, the head of one of the largest banks in Atlanta, is trying to get the account of one of the biggest paper mills in the state. He calls the chairman of the board, Billy Joe Sherman, and invites him to lunch.

"Where shall we eat?" Billy Joe says.

"How about at the University of Georgia football game at halftime? I'll fly up in the bank's private plane," Burt says.

The two men meet at the hot dog stand during the halftime show. They order two hotdogs and two bottles of cola. Burt talks to Billy Joe about moving his company's account over to Burt's bank. Billy Joe says he'll think about it.

Burt pays for the food and then writes them off his income tax, together with the plane ride. The IRS claims Burt can only write off Billy Joe's hot dog and cola.

Burt hires Clark Clifford to defend him. The ensuing publicity drives Burt's bank stock down three points, and Billy Joe decides to keep his money where it is.

It's obvious from just these three examples that doing away with 50 percent of the tax-deductible lunch is counterproductive.

Having a meal on the expense account is what the American dream is all about. Everybody should be for it and say, "Even if I can't have a complete tax-deductible lunch, some day, God willing, my children can."


## THE SOUTH IS MAD

My Southern friends are furious for what the Northern Liberal Establishment Press has done to one of their own, the Honorable Bert Lance.

Scarlett O'Hara, who lives in an old mansion in Atlanta which had been destroyed during the Civil War, called me.

"You still hate us, don't you?" Scarlett said.

"We don't hate you, Scarlett. We love the South. Didn't we elect a Southerner President?"

"Well then you hate our bankers."

"We don't hate your bankers. We think they're great. Where else would bankers let you make the overdrafts that they do in Calhoun, Ga.?"

"Bert Lance is a good ole' boy, and anything he did was just to help his friends. That's the way we do things down here."

"Of course," I said. "I only wish Northern bankers cared as much about their friends. You ask for a loan up here and the first thing they want to know is if you have any collateral. They're mean as hell when it comes to parting with a dollar. I wish I had an account at the Calhoun National Bank."

"Don't soft-soap me," Scarlett said. "You Northerners were dying to get something on one of our menfolk. When you couldn't find anything, you brought up a lot of stuff about Bert depositing his bank's money in other banks in exchange for loans and using his plane for political trips and mismanaging his own money. That's all you could get on him."

"But Scarlett," I protested, "the people have a right to know who is in charge of the U.S. budget. If Bert couldn't run his banks, how could he run the finances of the country?"

"Bert comes from one of the best families in the South, and so does his wife, La Belle. That should have been good enough for you."

"Ordinarily it would be. But when the man closest to the President is having personal financial problems, it makes some people nervous."

"That's because you don't understand anything about the South. If a man is liked down here, and Bert is loved, you don't pry into his personal affairs. It just isn't done."

"Scarlett, I know the Southern way is the best way, and I wish everyone accepted a man for what he is, and not for what he's done. But Jimmy Carter ran on a campaign against cronyism and promised high standards of morality. It just so happens that his handling of the Bert Lance affair seems to contradict his campaign rhetoric. If Bert Lance came from Massachusetts, the press would treat him the same way."

"I don't believe it. You burned down Atlanta once, and you'd like to do it again."

"I wish you wouldn't take the Bert Lance thing personally, Scarlett. I'm sure Bert is the salt of the earth. I wish he had been my banker. I wouldn't be wallowing in debt now.

"I know you're not going to believe this, but when I write out a check on the Riggs Bank in Washington, and don't have money to cover it, Mr. Riggs calls me in an hour. Bert would never do that."

"Well, now that you've got Lance, who else from the South are you going to go after?" Scarlett wanted to know.

"Nobody, Scarlett. I swear it. The Civil War is over so far as we're concerned. We Yankees are forgiving people."

"You're not going to get anyone from Georgia to believe that after what you did to Bert and La Belle."

"Will it help any, Scarlett, if I say I'm sorry?"

"Frankly," she replied, "I don't give a damn."

## GOODBYE OLD FRIEND

Like everyone else I used to have a friend at the Chase Manhattan Bank. My friend's name was Chauncey and he was like a brother to me.

When the recent Securities and Exchange Commission's report was published it turned out, according to the SEC, that Chase Manhattan was selling New York City securities to its customers at the same time it was unloading the ones it had kept for its own portfolio.

I couldn't believe it so I called Chauncey. He wasn't there.

I called him again. After four calls he finally picked up the phone and said tersely, "I told you never to call me at the office."

"Where am I supposed to call you?" I wanted to know.

"What is it? I'm very busy."

"Chauncey, is that the way to talk to a friend?"

"We stopped that advertising campaign two years ago."

"That's what I'm calling about. Remember when you were my dearest friend four years back and you called me and said you could sell me some of the finest municipal securities money could buy?"

"I don't recall the conversation."

"Well, I do. You said that New York City was on a wave of new prosperity and anyone who bought its notes would never have to worry about his financial future again."

"I said that?"

"You certainly did. You also said that because the demand was so great you were restricting sales of them to only your closest friends."

"I might have said it as a joke," Chauncey replied.

"You were dead serious, Chauncey. You didn't laugh once."

"All right, for argument's sake I might have said it. What do you want from me?"

"Well, I just read the SEC report on New York City and it claims that all the time Chase Manhattan was touting New York securities it was unloading its own notes because it knew the city was in a fiscal mess."

There was dead silence on the other end of the line.

"Chauncey, are you still there?"

"Yes, I'm here. I'm sure the SEC report is mistaken. We would never do that to our customers. We're one of the largest banks in the world."

"That's what I said when I bought $20,000 of the notes. I said if Chase Manhattan recommends them they must be good."

"They were good at the time I sold them to you," Chauncey said. "They just got bad as time went by."

"But why was Chase Manhattan getting rid of its notes when it was pushing them on its friends?"

"We felt we owed it to our customers to let them buy them. When the demand was greater than the supply we had no choice but to sell the ones we were holding for our own investment. It wasn't easy. We loved New York City securities, and it broke our hearts every time we sold one."

"Then you didn't know the city was going broke?"

"That's the most insulting question I've ever heard. I'm glad David Rockefeller didn't take this call. You would have broken his heart. I thought we were friends."

"I did too until I read the SEC report. If I had a friend I wouldn't sell him securities that I knew were going down the drain."

"Well, if you feel that way about it," said Chauncey, "maybe we shouldn't be friends any more."

"I don't know why you're getting mad at me. I'm the one stuck with the securities."

"Friendship is based on trust," Chauncey told me. "You stick by a friend not only during the good times but the bad ones as well. This call has hurt me very much. I never thought you would stoop so low as to bring up something like this. I don't think we should see each other any more."

"I'm sorry, Chauncey. I didn't mean to get you angry."

"It's too late to apologize. You've ruined a beautiful relationship. If you're so petty as to let a lousy $20,000 investment in New York City securities stand between us, then we don't have anything more to say to each other. And you can send back the toaster we gave you when you opened your account."

## SOLVING THE BUDGET

"Mr. President, Bert Lance is here to see you."

"Send him in. Hello, Bert, how's it going?"

"Well, I wanted to report to you on the budget. We may have a $60 billion deficit next year."

"Hmmn, that's serious. What do you think I ought to do?"

"First, I don't think we should call it a deficit. People get uptight about the word. Why don't we say it's a $60 billion 'overdraft.' We'll announce we just wrote out more checks than we had money in the bank."

"That's good thinking, Bert. Even I have had an overdraft at one time or another. What else should we do?"

"We ought to get a loan from a bank to tide us over."

"How do we do that?"

"Well, what we'll do is deposit a large sum of money from the Treasury in a bank. Then we'll ask the bank to make a personal loan to the country in exchange for getting our business."

"Will a bank do it?"

"They do it all the time. When I was head of the National Bank of Georgia I opened an account in Manufacturers-Hanover and the First National Bank of Chicago in the name of my bank, and they immediately made a personal loan to me of millions of dollars."

"Why?"

"Because the banks wanted the National Bank of Georgia's account. That's the way banks do things. You scratch their backs and they'll scratch yours."

"That makes sense, Bert. So we borrow $60 billion from a bank and pay off the deficit. Then what happens?"

"We have to pay the interest on the loan."

"How do we do that?"

"By borrowing money from another bank."

"How do we get the money from the second bank?"

"By opening an account with them. We deposit Treasury funds in their bank, and then we get a personal loan from them because as a client they now trust us. If we didn't have an account we obviously couldn't get the loan."

"All right, Bert, I'm still following you. We now have accounts in two banks and we borrow money from the first to pay the deficit, and we borrow money from the second bank to pay the interest on the loan from the first bank. Where do we get the money to pay the interest on the loan from the second bank?"

"By opening an account with a third bank and then making a personal loan from them."

"How long do we keep doing this, Bert?"

"I don't know. It depends on how many banks there are in the United States. As long as we can open up new accounts with them, we can borrow money from them."

"But suppose we eventually run out of banks."

"Then we go to overdrafts."

"Won't the banks get mad if we write overdrafts?"

"What choice do they have? If they complain about the overdrafts we can always threaten to close our account with them."

"Of course, why didn't I think of that?"

"You were never a banker, Mr. President."

"That's true, Bert. Let me ask a question. Suppose the banks ask collateral for their loans."

"I should hope they would never insult the President of the United States by asking for collateral. After all, you have an impeccable reputation and your signature should be enough for any loan."

"But just in case a bank does raise the question of collateral, what do we do then?"

"It's simple. We put up the U.S. Postal Service to secure the loan."

"Bert, I don't know what I'd do without you."

"Shucks, Mr. President. Any banker from Georgia could do the same thing."

## LATE PAYMENTS AND SORE LOSERS

Anyone who has had to deal with large companies is aware that they are paying their bills later and later. This is no accident. The longer they can defer paying you, the more money they can keep in their bank accruing interest. It is known as the "float."

There is an art to not paying someone when the bill is due, and it is getting more sophisticated as time goes on.

In fact, universities are now offering masters degrees in "check stalling" for students who want to be comptrollers and bookkeepers.

I attended a graduate class the other day at one of our leading business schools and watched in awe as a professor conducted a course entitled "Stalling Creditors, Contractors and Individuals 1A."

"All right," the professor opened up his lecture. "Last week we discussed what to say to an irate person who calls up your company and wants to know where his or her check is. Let's review it.

"Stevens, you're the irate caller. Joseph, you're the person in charge of the comptroller's office."

Stevens picked up the white phone on the professor's desk, and Joseph picked up the one in the back of the classroom.

Stevens spoke first. "This is David Stevens, and I want to know why I haven't received a check for the work I did for your office."

"I'll look into it," Joseph said.

"No, you dumbbell," the professor yelled. "You won't look into it. You will find someone else to look into it. You don't want to make friends with Stevens, or he'll know whom to call about the check next time."

You could see Joseph was upset. "We'll look into it, Mr. Stevens. I'm sure it's been sent out. Where can we reach you?"

Stevens gave his number and hung up.

"All right," the professor said. "It's two weeks later. Joseph hasn't called you back, so, Stevens, call him again."

"Where the hell is my check? It was due months ago," Stevens cried.

Joseph said, "I told the accounting department about it. It should have been sent the day after you spoke to me."

The professor nodded his head.

Stevens shouted, "But I didn't get it!"

"The mails are terrible these days. Let me get back to you."

"Let me speak to the comptroller."

Joseph looked blankly at the professor. "What am I supposed to do now?"

The professor said, "Give the phone to anyone, dummy. Stevens doesn't know who the comptroller is."

Joseph handed the phone to Radcliffe.

"Look," said Stevens, "I have to pay my bills, I have to pay my labor. When I'm late paying, you people charge me 8 percent interest. Why can't you pay me?"

Radcliffe said, "I've been checking the invoice, Mr. Stevens. There was a clerical error somewhere in the pipeline, and we should have it straightened out in a couple of days. You should get a check from us as soon as our treasurer, who is now in Japan, returns."

Stevens played his part to the hilt. "If I don't get my check in the mail tomorrow, I'm going to sue you people!"

"Oh," said Radcliffe, "you want the legal department. If you'll just hold on I'll transfer you."

"Excellent, Radcliffe, excellent!" the professor said. "You learned last week's lesson well. Today we will discuss how to blame the computer for late payments. After using all of the usual human excuses for nonpayment of bills, your next step is to involve the computer. It's what we call in the check-stalling business 'The Final Solution.'"

## WHERE DID ALL THE MONEY GO?

A group of us who were expecting to be included in Howard Hughes' will were sitting around in our lawyer's office the other day when the news broke that an appraisal of Hughes' wealth showed that, instead of being a billionaire, his estate was worth only $168,834,615. You can imagine the shock that went through the room.

Our lawyer spoke first. "Why that isn't even enough to pay my legal fees!"

One of the women started to cry. "I knew I should never have bought TWO cans of coffee until the estate was appraised."

It isn't easy when you discover that an estate you were told was worth between two and three billion dollars turns out to be only a paltry $168,000,000.

"Howard was living a lie," I said. "No wonder he didn't want to see anyone during all those years. He knew what he was worth but he couldn't admit it to anyone else."

"The poor guy," someone else said. "It must have finally gotten to him. He put on this multibillionaire front when in fact he was really nothing more than a multimillionaire."

One of the distant relatives was angry. "Why should we feel sorry for him? What about us? Do you realize how little there will be to cut up if the $168,000,000 figure holds up in court?"

"Don't forget my fee," the lawyer said.

"Maybe," someone said hopefully, "Howard squirreled a billion dollars away somewhere so we couldn't find it."

"That would be just like him," I said. "I'll bet you somewhere out there in the desert, between Las Vegas and Los Angeles, Howard buried the bulk of his fortune."

"Does that mean we can't get our hands on it?" asked a gas station attendant, who was slated to get one-third of the estate.

"Knowing Howard, I'm sure he'll have someone deliver a clue to the Mormon Tabernacle," I said. "He'll probably send us on a treasure hunt for years."

"I can't wait for years," the lawyer complained. "Do you realize what it costs to probate a will these days? You have to pay legal secretaries, light bills, telephone charges, not to mention what it costs to buy a notary public stamp. If I'd had any idea that the estate was only worth $168,000,000 I would have turned the whole thing over to the Legal Aid Society."

"Does that mean you're not going to handle our claim to the will any more?" I asked.

"I'm not in this business for my health," the lawyer said bitterly.

"I know it's not much," said one of Hughes' bodyguards, who was hoping to get 25 percent of the estate, "but you can't bow out now. No other lawyer will take it when he discovers there's only $168,000,000 involved."

"I could turn it over to a law student in the office," the lawyer said, "but I can't devote any more time to it."

All of us were in despair. We saw our dreams of being on easy street going up in smoke.

One of the heirs, a waiter from the Bahamas, said, "I'm sure Mr. Hughes had more money than that. Maybe he did have a billion dollars, but when he got his lawyer's bill for drawing up his will he was left with only $168,000,000."

"Of course, that's the answer," I said. "All of us are mad at Howard when it's really his lawyers we should be suing."

We all turned to our lawyer. "Do we have a case?"

"I'm afraid not," the lawyer said. "For argument's sake, let's agree that Howard had a billion dollars. If a lawyer charged him $832,000,000 to draw up his will, it would just about be in the ballpark."


## THE JOB HUNTERS

As it must happen during every change of administration in Washington, there is a great deal of job hunting going on right now. The problem for many Presidential appointees is that it's very difficult to go back to what they were doing before they got into the government. Having once tasted the power of running a billion-dollar federal bureau it's hard to return to selling insurance or working on a detergent account for J. Walter Thompson.

Unfortunately, government experience does not necessarily mean that you're qualified to handle an important job in the private sector.

Here is an example of what I mean.

"Please sit down, Mr. Maximum. Mr. Ratcliffe of the Republican National Committee spoke very highly of you. I see here you're looking for a position with our firm."

"Yes, sir. For the past eight years I was Director of the U.S. Government Inter-Office Affairs Council on Coordination and Rectification. It was one of the highest management jobs in Washington."

"What exactly did you do?"

"Our department was in charge of reviewing position papers on rectification of abuses of nonregulatory agencies involved in the areas of essential input and output, and to recommend to the White House their long-range effects on the economy."

"Could you be more specific?"

"I'm sorry, I didn't understand the question."

"What was your role in the department?"

"I was in charge of the entire operation. My staff brought me papers and I either signed them or refused to sign them. In many cases I advised that they be passed on to another bureau. In some instances I recommended hearings, and in others I turned over the matter to the Justice Department."

"Mr. Maximum, that's all very interesting, but since you are applying for a job as Executive Vice President of this corporation we're trying to find out what kind of contribution you could make here."

"I believe my strength would be in budget planning. I had 20,000 people working for me and our yearly budget was $1.5 billion. It was a great responsibility because if we didn't spend all the money in the fiscal year we had to give it back to the Treasury. I'm proud to say I always managed to spend every cent of it."

"That's very good, Mr. Maximum, when you're working for the government. But when you're working for a private company the job of an executive is to save the corporation money."

"Why would you want to do that?"

"Well, we like to show a profit at the end of the year."

"What's a profit?"

"It's the money left over, after all our costs and taxes are paid."

"That's fascinating. We never worried about profits in the government. Our job was to spend money and get the job done. I believe the best way to solve a problem is to throw money at it."

"Yes, I see what you mean. Could you tell me what you consider was your greatest accomplishment during your government service?"

"Of course. I was responsible for 'Operation Molehill.' Everyone always talks about making a mountain out of a molehill. But no one has ever actually done it. I put my research and development people on it and they came up with a pilot program which would cost $100 million.

"The Office of Management and Budget turned it down, so I went directly to the chairman of the Senate Committee on Bulldozers and told him if he could get the project off the ground, we'd build the mountain out of the molehill in his state. He immediately got the legislation passed and I got my $100 million."

"That's very good. We'll call you, Mr. Maximum, in a few days and give you our answer."

"Thank you. I'm sure I can be of great value to your company. Just give me the input and I'll give you the output, no matter what it costs."

## FOURTH OF JULY SALE

Many people have been given credit for the founding of our country, including Thomas Jefferson, John Adams, John Hancock, Thomas Paine, Benjamin Franklin and, of course, George Washington. But for some reason the history books have ignored one of the most important personalities of the time, a man who made the United States the great capitalist country it is today.

His name is Ezra Beetle, and he was the founder of the "Fourth of July Bargain Sale" that has become the biggest event in the celebration of Independence Day.

Without the spectacular Fourth of July sales in department stores, used-car lots, grocery stores and discount houses, it is doubtful that this country would have survived as a nation.

While everyone was concerned with the philosophy of the new government, Ezra devoted his efforts toward developing American commerce, because he realized that no matter what constitution the country would finally agree upon, it would not be able to exist unless merchants could move their goods.

In 1776 Ezra owned a small general store outside of Boston. When word reached him on July 2 that the Colonies had agreed on a Declaration of Independence, he recognized a golden opportunity at hand. He could get rid of all the junk that had been accumulating in his store for the previous three years.

Ezra immediately took out an advertisement in the Boston paper with a blazing headline: " BEETLE HAS GONE CRAZY—he is selling $5 horsewhips for $2.95.

"Yes, folks, in honor of the signing of the Declaration of Independence, Beetle is holding the first Fourth of July Rock Bottom

Discount Sale in American history. British flags at half price, East Indian Tea 60 percent off. Bronze replicas of the Westminster Abbey at a dollar apiece. Everyone thinks Beetle is mad, and maybe he is, but Ezra says, 'I love to lose my shirt if it makes people happy.'

"For the first 50 people who show up, Crazy Ezra will give them free a shaving mug with George III's picture on it. The next 100 customers will get ashtrays with 'GOD SAVE THE KING' inscribed in red around the rim. Has Beetle really gone crazy? Come in and see for yourself. Free parking. No mail orders or credit cards. EVERYTHING GOES FOR CASH."

Boston was flabbergasted when they saw the advertisement, and at three o'clock the next morning hundreds of patriots' wives lined up in front of Beetle's general store. It gave other merchants in the Boston area pause, and they immediately followed suit, advertising their own Fourth of July sales.

Logan's Used Horse and Carriage Lot announced spectacular buys on horse and carriages. Hancock's War Surplus Store sold muskets and powder at half price. When the South heard about it they immediately got into the act. One store in Charleston advertised two slaves for the price of one.

All over the country merchants celebrated the signing of the Declaration of Independence by holding sales that the Colonialists couldn't resist. Many people who weren't sure whether they wanted to break with the motherland or not were persuaded to join the secessionists' side when they realized it would mean that every Fourth of July they and their descendants would be able to get bargains that were unavailable the rest of the year.

In a letter to his brother, Ezra Beetle wrote,

"Long after the Declaration of Independence is forgotten, the people of America will remember the Fourth of July as an occasion when the American businessman sacrificed his merchandise in the spirit of patriotism. Two hundred years from today I can see shopping centers from one end of this country to another, flying thousands of American flags, their windows decorated in red, white and blue bunting, proclaiming bargains on goods that you and I can never dream of. We have not only started an American revolution, but a business revolution, and thanks to us, commerce as we know it will never be the same again.

"P.S. Do you know anybody in Philadelphia who would like a great buy on a Liberty Bell? It's worth $300, but I'm selling it for $19.95 because it has a crack in it."

## WHITHER THE DOLLAR?

Every time you pick up the newspapers these days you read that the Dollar is falling. Most people, except those in financial circles, are not paying any attention to this. The main reason is they don't understand it.

Perhaps I should explain it in a question and answer format.

Q—Where does the Dollar go when it falls?

A—It falls below the West German Mark, the Swiss Franc and Japanese Yen.

Q—Why is it falling?

A—Because money speculators in London, Zurich and Frankfurt are pushing it down.

Q—Is there anything worse than the Dollar falling?

A—Yes. It could be plunging or sinking.

Q—Why is the Dollar falling at the present time?

A—Because the money speculators are worried about it.

Q—Why are they worried about it?

A—Because the United States has a huge trade deficit, no energy policy, and Arthur Burns, chairman of the Federal Reserve, just lost his job.

Q—Why would Arthur Burns losing his job make the Dollar fall?

A—Because nobody knows what his replacement, G. William Miller, will do when he becomes head of the Fed.

Q—What should he do?

A—Rescue the Dollar and keep it afloat.

Q—Why can't we make a Dollar that won't fall?

A—We could, but the cost could bankrupt us.

Q—How far will the Dollar fall?

A—Until it bottoms out.

Q—Then what will happen?

A—It will start rising again, particularly if the West Germans and Japanese dredge it up.

Q—Why would they want to do that?

A—The lower the Dollar falls the harder it is for them to sell their goods in the United States, and the easier it is for the United States to sell their goods in the rest of the world. A strong currency has a lot of weaknesses.

Q—Where does the British Pound stand in all this?

A—The British Pound is rising while the Dollar is falling.

Q—How do you explain that?

A—The British have oil in the North Sea.

Q—So?

A—It's easier to float a Pound on oil than it is a Dollar on water.

Q—Can we go back to the Dollar?

A—We can, but since we've been talking it's dropped two more cents.

Q—What caused it to do that?

A—Someone in Paris just read this article and called his banker in Brussels and told him to sell the Dollar and buy Norwegian Kroner with it.

Q—How did the Norwegian Kroner get into this?

A—The West German Mark and the Japanese Yen are considered by the Belgians to be overpriced, so they're buying the Norwegian Kroner instead. They may not keep Kroner for long.

Q—What will they do with them?

A—Probably buy gold in Amsterdam as a hedge.

Q—What can I do to keep the Dollar from falling?

A—The first thing is to let it slide, then prop it up and finally pump some life in it.

Q—How do I do that?

A—You have to get through to the gnomes in Switzerland.

Q—Gnomes in Switzerland? What do they have to do with all this?

Q—They're behind the whole thing. When you see the Dollar fall you can bet there's a gnome in Switzerland dropping a rock on George Washington's head.

## GOOD AND BAD LAWYERS

Chief Justice Warren Burger has enraged lawyers by saying that 50 percent of them are not competent to practice in a courtroom. The American Bar Association, reacting angrily, said only 20 percent of the lawyers now involved in courtroom litigation are unqualified for such service.

The Chief Justice, who has been complaining about court loads in the past several years, is trying to figure out ways of resolving the traffic jam. While I am in sympathy with him on the issue, I'm not sure what he wants to do about it. If his figure is correct, and most of us are willing to take it on face value, the next question is, "Should we prevent from taking trial cases those lawyers who are incompetent and leave the courtrooms open to those who know what they're doing?" I would assume that is what Mr. Burger is driving at.

If it is, then I'm afraid he's wrong. It isn't the bad lawyers who are screwing up the justice system in this country—it's the good lawyers. The competent trial lawyers know how to postpone a case and string it out twice as long as necessary. They know how to file every conceivable motion, and eventually make every known or unknown appeal. A competent first-class lawyer can tie a case up in knots, not only for the jury but for the judge as well. If you have two competent lawyers on opposite sides, a trial that should take three days could easily last six months, and there isn't a thing anyone can do about it.

I know many competent lawyers and, while all of them hope justice will prevail, their idea of justice is to win the case no matter how much it costs the client or the state. It is they who are jamming up the courts and making it difficult to hold a fair and speedy trial.

On the other hand, an incompetent lawyer is a friend of the court. In many cases he will present his case so badly that it is no problem for the judge to throw it out on the first day.

A trial lawyer who doesn't know what he's doing has no idea how to stall. He knows none of the fine points of the law that would force a judge to recess for 48 hours to study them. He is incapable of questioning a witness for any length of time and, because he does not know how to cross-examine a witness, he usually says, "I have no questions, your honor," thus speeding up the wheels of justice.

A bad lawyer is actually a boon to society. His fees are usually lower because he doesn't know how to sustain a trial to keep the clock running. A judge has no compunction to shut him off when he presents irrelevant evidence. A good lawyer can usually prove irrelevant evidence is relevant, and in doing so make a fool out of the judge.

Judges love incompetent lawyers because they have no fear of being overruled by a higher court since the case probably won't be appealed.

But when a competent lawyer is litigating, the judge is doubly careful on every ruling he makes so he won't look like a dummy when the good lawyer goes over his head to appeal.

So, while Mr. Burger's heart is in the right place, he is making a big mistake by advocating that incompetent trial lawyers be kept out of the courts.

It is the able lawyers who should not be permitted in the courtroom since they are the ones who are doing all the damage.

It was William Shakespeare who wrote in "Henry VI": "The first thing we do, let's kill all the lawyers." In the interest of speeding up justice I think this should be amended to apply only to competent trial lawyers. I believe the bad ones should be allowed to live and multiply.

# X. Decisions! Decisions!

## A LETTER TO SANTA

To: Mr. Santa Claus, North Pole

From: Occupational Safety and Health Administration, Washington, D.C.

Subject: Violations of OSHA Codes

Dear Sir,

1—Our inspectors have just completed a study of working conditions at your toy factory at the North Pole and find you in violation of Section C, Paragraph B of Regulation 1098, Article Seven, Division Four of Safety Factor 3-H and Rule 105, Registration No. 90087, Appendix Three of Safety and Health Regulations (See Items 54, 56, 69 in OSHA Code Book 361), in regard to manufacture of toys and other harmful objects.

2—To be more specific, our inspectors have discovered that your wife, who helps you make toys, does not have her own bathroom facilities. Under Section Five of Code 345: "A male and female bathroom must be provided on the ground floor of a house engaged in the production of stuffed animals. The bathrooms must each have their own sinks, hot water as well as shower, and must be 43 feet apart from each other with signs clearly marking what they are being used for."

3—Our inspectors have also discovered that you were opening mail with a scissors. OSHA Regulation 763 specifically says that all business mail must be opened by a mail opener nine inches long and no more than an inch and a half wide. You can get a waiver of this rule by filling out Form 987 A, but since it must be made at least 90 days before inspection it would not apply in your case, and you must pay a fine of $100 per 50 letters not opened in the manner as described in Code Book 19 B.

4—I also regret to inform you that we have received a very negative report from Inspector X in regard to the space allotted to your reindeer. Under Section C of Article Four each reindeer must be tethered in his own stall of ten feet by eight feet covered with 1.6 feet of hay. In the case of Donner and Blitzen their stalls were only nine feet long and our Inspector measured 1.4 inches of hay in Donner's stall and 1.3 inches in Blitzen's stall in contravention of Reindeer Regulation 43.

You can appeal this charge by filling out OSHA Form 2356 in triplicate and posting it to our branch office in Anchorage. A hearing will be held at which time you will be given an opportunity to explain the shortage of hay in the stall. If the board finds you in error you can further appeal to our office in Seattle, but you may not have the use of Donner and Blitzen until a ruling in writing is handed down from the Seattle office and signed by our Chief Inspector in Los Angeles.

5—It has been brought to our attention that on the evening of December 24th you intend to deliver the toys manufactured in your plant by reindeer sled, climbing on roofs and houses and sliding down chimneys. Our safety co-ordinator advises me that if you indeed go ahead with this form of delivery you will commit several infractions that would subject you to fine and possible imprisonment. The first is that if you arrive on any roof with a clatter you will be violating our regulation regarding noise. Any clatter over 1.9 decibels cannot be permitted. (See Index Three, Page 14)

6—The manner of entering and leaving a house by chimney is of utmost concern to us. You may descend a chimney providing you are not carrying any type of bag with you, and providing the inside of the chimney has steps one foot apart with a safety railing along the side. Once in the house you may not leave any packages that could be tripped over or broken. The packages must be neatly piled with 1.9 feet between them. Filling of stockings is permitted providing they have the strength to hang from the chimney of four pounds per stockings, or twice the weight of the articles to be deposited.

Our inspectors will be out on the night of December 24th and any infractions of the rules will be dealt with severely.

We hope you accept this letter in the spirit it was written, and let me take this opportunity to wish you and Mrs. Claus a very Merry Christmas.

Sincerely yours,

E. SCROOGE

Director, Xmas OSHA

When replying please refer to Letter No. 135 A O-190 Z.

## THE WORK ETHIC

One of the big issues of the last Presidential campaign was unemployment. We've had so many different figures on who is out of work and who isn't, that nobody knows what to believe any more. One of the reasons we can't get hard figures on unemployment is that there is a certain segment of the population that isn't sure whether it wants to work or not.

Sometimes this segment is included in the figures and sometimes it isn't.

I discovered this the other day when I was having a drink with my friend Clancy.

Clancy has a 21-year-old son who is unemployed. As Clancy explained it to me, his son Robert is screwing up the unemployment statistics because some days he wants to work and other days he doesn't.

"This morning I went into Robert's room," Clancy said, "and he was sacked out after arriving home at four in the morning. I shook him and asked him if he was going to look for work today. He said he might in the afternoon. I told him most jobs advertised in the newspapers were taken by afternoon, and that if he was serious about wanting a job he had to get up early in the morning to find one. Was I being unreasonable?"

I told Clancy I didn't think so.

My friend said, "The problem seems to be that Robert isn't certain he wants a job. He claims that most of the jobs being offered are not very interesting and require you to do things you weren't trained to do."

"What is Robert trained to do?"

"Nothing," Clancy said. "He has three years of college and majored in psychology. There are very few jobs open for someone who has three years of psychology. It's not enough psychology for some personnel managers, and it's too much psychology for others."

"Did he say what he would like to do?"

"He isn't sure. He told me he would like to make a lot of money so I wouldn't bug him all the time about getting a job. I think he would like to start off as an executive vice president of a large corporation where he could get stock options and bonuses at the end of the year and have the use of the company airplane on weekends."

"Well, you have to admit he has set his sights high."

"In one way he has, but in another way he says while he wants to make a lot of money, he doesn't want to be corrupted by the system. He told me he's not going to 'sell out.' "

"That's admirable," I said. "I admire someone who wants to make a lot of money and doesn't want to 'sell out.' He hasn't told you how he plans to do this, has he?"

"He says in our system it can't be done, so why should he look for a job?"

"That three years of psychology must have had a big impact on him."

"I feel terrible about it," Clancy said, "because I know Robert is being carried on the labor statistics as being one of the seven million eight hundred thousand unemployed. It's correct that he isn't working, but if he isn't looking for a job I'm not certain that he isn't flying under false colors. There are so many sincere people trying to find jobs that it seems unfair to have someone like Robert lumped in with them. I guess there are thousands of kids like him who want to start at the top, so it's impossible for the Labor Department to know how many jobs they have to provide to make the economy strong again."

"Maybe Congress could pass a special bill for people like Robert. They could set aside 300 or 400 executive vice presidential positions that kids who dropped out of school could apply for," I suggested.

"It would be a solution," Clancy admitted, "providing the government was willing to interview them after two o'clock in the afternoon. You can't expect kids like Robert, with their educational backgrounds and upbringing, to start looking for work in the morning."

## SOLVING THE COAL STRIKE

We saw an awful lot of miners on television of late. Without taking sides in the dispute, the one thing that comes across is that they're a tough breed and very free spirits. They don't like to be pushed around by anybody, including the government, the courts, the President of the United States or their own union leaders. If anyone orders them to do anything, they have no hesitation in telling them to "Stuff it."

It is for this reason that I do not believe invoking the Taft-Hartley Act makes any sense in getting the coal miners working again. It was written to give everyone a cooling-off period in a major labor dispute. But in the case of the coal miners it's made them hotter than ever, and more determined to hold out against the mine operators.

I believe President Carter would be much further ahead of the game right now if he had gone on television last Thursday and announced that during the Taft-Hartley period no miners would be permitted to go back to work. He should have said that, as President of the United States, he would see to it that not one ton of coal left any shaft of a union-operated mine, even if he had to use troops.

He also might have said that if the miners attempted to go to work without a contract, he would fine the unions $10,000 a day and ask the courts to hold them in contempt.

Can you just see what would have happened if Mr. Carter had said that?

The miners would have been in high dudgeon.

They would have met in their union halls where their leaders would have broken the news to them.

"Carter says we can't mine coal unless we have a contract."

"Down with Carter."

"He says he's going to use the Taft-Hartley Act to keep us out of the mines instead of going down into them."

"No President of the United States is going to tell us when we can or cannot mine coal. If we want to mine it, we'll mine."

"He says he'll use troops and federal marshals to keep us out."

"Let him try it. We'll break their heads with our pick axes if they won't let us down in the shafts."

"We're sick and tired of the government telling us what's good for us. If they don't want us to mine, we'll dig out so much coal they'll choke on it."

"They'll have to build 50 new railroads to haul it all away."

"We'll dump 300 tons on the White House lawn."

"Suppose our union president, Arnold Miller, says we can't go into the mines?"

"Then we'll dump him on the White House lawn with the coal."

"All right then, are we agreed that if the court upholds the President and says we can't mine coal, we all go back to the pits?"

"We're ready now, even before the court acts. Let's go into the mines and show them who is really running this country."

"Any guy who refuses to mine coal gets his tires blown out."

"Are we going back into the mines?"

"YESSSSSSSSSSSSSS!"

"When?"

"NOWWWWWWWWWWWWWWW!"

"Shout it so they can hear in the Oval Office!"

"NOWWWWWWWWWWWWWWW!"

That's what President Carter should have done. But his problem is he doesn't watch enough television.

## PLUMBERS STICK TOGETHER

Investigators claim that $1.5 billion were wasted building the Alaska pipeline. You are probably asking, "Where did the money go?"

To find out, I spoke to Stanton Carruthers, my plumber.

Stanton wasn't surprised at the overrun since he's had similar ones fixing the pipes in our house. Although he didn't work on the pipeline himself, he has some good ideas why the Alaska pipeline cost so much to install.

"I figure a billion of the overrun went for labor," Stanton said. "It's not easy to get a plumber to make a house call in Alaska. Then there was the pipe. The cost of pipe is going up every day, and probably the people who bid on the job didn't take this into consideration at the time. Then, of course, there were the washers. You have to have a lot of washers on a pipe 800 miles long."

"It sounds like one of your jobs," I said.

"Well, there's not much difference in building a pipeline and installing plumbing in someone's house. You have to expect an overrun or the plumber wouldn't make a profit. The guy who got the Alaska contract also forgot to include the joints in the pipe. Joints really add up, particularly if you have to thread them before you join them."

"I guess you do have to have joints in an 800-mile pipeline. You would have thought the plumber would know he needed joints."

"You only find this out after you start the job. Remember that sink I installed for you?"

"The one you said would cost $200 and wound up costing me $500?"

"That's the one. Well, what happened was after we installed the sink and the pipe we forgot to hook it up to the main water line."

"I remember that," I said. "I had to shave without water for a week. I cut up my face pretty bad."

"That can happen. So what we did was tear out the installation, drill a hole in your wall and hook up the pipe with the water. That's why we had to charge you $300 more than we figured the job would cost."

"And something like that might have happened on the Alaska pipeline?"

"I'm sure of it. They probably got the whole thing built and then discovered it wasn't hooked up to the oil. Then they had to tear it up and begin all over again."

"They said a lot of the welding was of poor quality and the X-rays and records were forged."

"That's possible," Stanton said. "When you're working with pipe, you can do a lot of sloppy work. It's like that shower head I installed for you and it leaked all over the bathroom, and we had to come back and put in a whole new faucet system. That was faulty welding."

"Why did you charge me for it if it was faulty?"

"Who was I going to charge—the guy next door? Everyone thinks plumbers are infallible. We're human, too. We make mistakes."

"That's for sure," I said. "But the one in Alaska was a lulu."

"You can say that because you didn't do the work. But if you were a plumber, you'd think differently. Look, the pipeline was supposed to cost $1 billion. Instead it cost $8 billion. Most of that probably went for overtime. The $1.5 billion that went down the drain was ordinary spillage that anyone has on a job. I'd say for a billion-dollar original bid, bringing in a pipeline for $8 billion is just about right."

"Then you don't see anything wrong with how they constructed the Alaska pipeline?"

"Even if I did, I wouldn't say so. In our profession, it's unethical to criticize another plumber's work."


## THE LOBBYIST AGAINST IMPORTS

Randolph Habermeyer, chief lobbyist for the American Hot and Cold Steel Company, was awakened by his Swiss-made Computer Alarm Clock. He got up and turned on his Sony television set to hear the news.

Then he showered and shaved with the new electric razor his wife had bought which said Made in Germany.

He then started dressing. Since he was going to testify in front of a congressional committee he selected his suit carefully, deciding on an imported Pierre Cardin pin stripe. He also chose a conservative silk tie that came from Thailand. Finally he put on his Italian-made Gucci shoes. He filled his Paris-made Hermes briefcase with all the papers he would need for his testimony.

It was raining out so he grabbed his trench coat. It was his favorite coat, and he was amazed that the Spanish, of all people, could manufacture trench coats at a third the price of the American ones.

Habermeyer kissed his wife goodbye and got into his Mercedes-Benz to drive from Potomac to the Capitol. In the Mercedes he had a phone, which had been made in Taiwan, and he called his office to dictate several messages to his secretary on a German-made Grundig machine.

He also had a pocket-size Dutch-made Philips recorder in the car to remind him of things he wanted to do the next day.

Suddenly he looked at his gas gauge and realized he was short of gas.

He stopped at a BP (British Petroleum) station and filled up the tank.

Habermeyer was listening to his radio as he drove along. They were advertising a new "Star Wars" rocket ship from Hong Kong. He made a note to buy one for his son for Christmas.

The next commercial had to do with a French Cuisinart blender. Habermeyer decided to get one for his wife because she had said they were still the best on the market.

As he was driving along he realized he had time to buy some cigars. Since Cuban ones were still not on the market, he favored the ones made in the Canary Islands.

The clerk was pushing a new cigar that had been manufactured in the Philippines, but Habermeyer said he'd stick with his Flamencos.

He also bought a throwaway lighter Made in South Korea.

Then he got back into his Mercedes and drove up to the Hill.

Before going to the committee room to testify, he dropped off to see a congressman friend and gave him a box of Swiss chocolates that one of the people from the company had brought back on a recent trip. The lobbyist knew the congressman had a sweet tooth, and he couldn't think of a better gift to give him.

Finally Habermeyer went to the committee room to testify. He was the second witness. He sat at the table, took out his prepared statement and began to read.

"On behalf of the American Hot and Cold Steel Company, as well as all American steel companies, I am raising my voice in angry protest over the flagrant dumping of foreign steel in this country. Mr. Chairman, this committee must decide whether we will permit the importation of foreign steel at the price of sacrificing American jobs and doing mortal damage to the American economy.

"The time has come for us to say, 'Enough is enough.' We cannot survive when we have to compete with the labor costs of other nations. It is your patriotic duty to see that the United States is protected from the flooding of foreign imports which I, as an American citizen, find despicable . . . "

Habermeyer took 30 minutes to read his statement and then looked at his Japanese Seiko watch and realized his time was up.


## THE GREAT COFFEE SHORTAGE

The first inkling that the price of coffee had gotten out of hand was in early 1977 when the IRS announced you could deduct the price of the first cup of coffee, when discussing business, but you could not deduct the second cup. Also, you could no longer buy your wife a cup of coffee unless you could prove it was necessary for her to be there when the business conversation was held.

In a few months coffee had become a luxury item and was only served in the finest restaurants. At $20 a cup, some eating places offered to give you a free meal if you bought a cup of coffee to go with it (cream and sugar was extra).

But soon the idea of serving coffee after a meal was reserved for special occasions such as weddings, anniversaries, Bar Mitzvahs and New Year's Eve. It wasn't enough to just serve the coffee. People began to toast each other with their cups, and waiters showed the can the coffee came from, before they poured it from a pot wrapped in a white napkin.

The coffeemakers started to put vintage years on the cans and connoisseurs emerged who could comment on the quality of each brand. They would say such things as "It's an unassuming little Maxwell House, but I think you'll be amused by its presumption" or "This Chock Full o' Nuts has a nobility to it that you rarely find in any of the domestic brands. I would put it up against a 1975 Chase & Sanborn anytime."

The hostess or host would say rather proudly, "My grocer recommended this 'Instant Brand' over Nescafe. But it has to be drunk young when it's at its peak."

People started keeping "Coffee Cellars" which they showed off to their friends. There, gathering dust, lying on their sides, could be found Medaglio 1974, Wilkins 1976, Safeway All-Purpose Grind 1970 and A&P's Perculator Ground which came from beans picked from a special plantation outside of Rio de Janiero.

It became such a luxury that voters accused their congressmen and senators of only being interested in "coffee, women and song."

Lockheed lobbyists gave away cases of coffee instead of money, and Arab middlemen insisted on being paid off in Italian espresso instead of Swiss francs.

Dictators and generals opened secret numbered coffee accounts in Geneva and Zurich, where multinationals deposited bags of coffee beans in vaults. The Soviet Union sold gold to buy coffee.

The Shah of Iran canceled his order for F-16 jets from the United States and ordered six shiploads of Yuban instead.

Brazil took the F-16s to defend its coffee plantations from Ecuador.

But the worst thing that happened is that employees all over the country could no longer have a "coffee" break. Instead they were given "wine breaks," which were much cheaper but caused a tremendous amount of accidents and mistakes in productivity.

Things became so desperate that President Carter asked James Schlesinger to drop his energy projects, and find a way of making coffee out of coal.

Just as World War III looked as if it would erupt over the coffee shortage, Brazil, Colombia, Kenya and Angola had bumper coffee crops, and the price dropped back to one dollar a pound.

Once again signs started to appear in diners which read SECOND CUP OF COFFEE FREE. People turned their coffee cellars into air raid shelters, and the coffee break in offices all over America was restored.

When Joe DiMaggio was called out of retirement to sell "Mr. Coffee" machines again, he called it "The greatest day of my life."

## MOVING THE ECONOMY

President Carter says his two major priorities are jobs and getting the economy moving again. It isn't as easy as it sounds.

Let me explain what I mean.

Rootin' Motors is visited by a salesman from Glutton Machinery. The salesman explains to Rootin' that Glutton can now provide machinery that will do the jobs of 1,000 men at a saving of $5 million a year. The president of Rootin' is impressed and decides to install the machinery. A year later the pink slips go out and 1,000 men, including Laidlaw, get one.

The president of Rootin' makes a speech to the departing men and women telling them he is sorry about the layoffs but there was no way Rootin' could stay in business if it did not install the new equipment.

While the new machinery helps Rootin' make 200 more Dolphins a day, sales are way off. The president calls in his dealers. "Why aren't the Dolphins moving?"

"Because Laidlaw is still looking for a job," one of the dealers says.

"Who is Laidlaw?" the president asks.

"He's one of the men you fired when you installed new machinery so you could be in a competitive position in the economy."

"All right," says the president. "Let's forget Laidlaw. Aren't there other customers out there for our Dolphins?"

"Streeter was, but he bugged out."

"Who is Streeter?"

"He's a bricklayer who was laid off when Laidlaw decided not to build a new house because he didn't have a job. When Streeter was laid off after Laidlaw was fired, Feldman canceled his Dolphin."

"Feldman?"

"The furniture man who was going to sell Mrs. Laidlaw a new dining room and living room set. Not only did Feldman cancel his Dolphin, but he told his brother-in-law not to buy one either, because they were laying off men at the Rootin' plant which was a sure sign of a recession."

"Just when we can make Dolphins at a price people can afford," the president of Rootin' moans, "no one can afford them any more."

"Wait a minute. What about all the people at Glutton Machinery," a dealer says. "They're all working."

"Of course," the president replies. "Why didn't we think of them?"

The president of Rootin' calls the president at Glutton and says: "How many people do you have making the machinery you sold us so we could lay off 1,000 men?"

"We had 5,000," the Glutton president says, "but then the Robot Tool Co. installed a new plant for us and now we have four. Why do you ask?"

"We're trying to get someone to buy our Dolphins."

"I wouldn't call Robot. They recently developed a new assembly line which requires the services of just one man, and they're waiting for him to reitre in six months so they can replace him with a computer."

The president turns to his dealers. "Okay, we have the best factory in the United States but no customers for our cars. What do we do?"

"Why don't you hire back Laidlaw?" somone suggests.

"We can't afford him," the president shouts.

"Maybe instead of hiring Laidlaw back we can give him a tax cut. Then he'll want to buy a car again."

"Laidlaw doesn't pay taxes," the president says. "He's on unemployment. We've got to find a job for Laidlaw."

"How?" a dealer asks.

The president says, "That's Carter's problem, not ours."

### DECISIONS! DECISIONS!

When President Carter was running for office he criticized Henry Kissinger's policy of closed-door diplomacy, and he vowed that, if elected, he would keep the American people informed on everything the government decides when it comes to foreign policy, including our "options, commitments, progress and even failures."

It sounded great at the time, but now that it is being put into practice it's getting the American people rather unhinged.

Markay, with whom I was having lunch, was drinking rather heavily and I asked him what was bothering him.

"I don't know what to do now that the SALT talks are in such disarray," he said.

"I don't see why that has you upset," I told him. "After all, you're in the handbag business."

"Yeh, but Carter wants every one of us to get involved in foreign policy. He does not want any more secret diplomacy. He says every American should know what's going on."

"So?"

"What do I say to Gromyko now?"

"I don't think the President expects you to answer Gromyko personally. All Carter wants to know from you is what *he* should say to Gromyko."

"I'm telling you it's too much for me. I used to only have to worry if Gimbels or J.C. Penney was going to buy handbags. Now I have to worry if we can afford to give up the Cruise missile without the Soviets giving up the Backfire bomber. I'm in leather, not disarmament."

"I know it's tough for you, but Mr. Carter does not want to make any foreign policy decisions without informing the American public. If he has to make a large expenditure for arms he wants you to be in on it."

"That's just great," said Markay. "I'm supposed to decide whether we build nuclear aircraft carriers or B-1 bombers. I don't even know what kind of buckle to put on my fall line of evening bags. How the hell am I supposed to decide what new weapons the country needs?"

"You'll have to read up on it. For too long we've been operating in the dark. If the American people are not brought into the decision-making process of government, mistakes could be made which we'll all have to pay for."

"Look, we give the President, the Secretary of State and Congress very good salaries. I don't ask them what I should do about putting a shoulder strap on a handbag for Macy's. Why should they bug me about what we should do with Zaire?

"I'll tell you something," he continued, "I liked the way Kissinger operated—in the dark, with no one knowing what he was up to. When the Middle East was falling apart it was Kissinger's problem. He only gave us the good news. The bad news he kept to himself. Under Kissinger I could devote all my energies to my business. With Carter and Vance I have to spend half the day figuring out what I want to do about Castro."

"But President Carter believes the American people should know the bad news as well as the good news. After all, under our system it is the people who must finally decide what has to be done."

"I don't want my brp9o4.ing in the field of foreign policy. If it was up to him we'd MIRV Moscow tomorrow," Markay said. "He almost lost the Neiman-Marcus handbag account for us when he said Texas was cheating on its gas reserves."

"Nevertheless," I said, "President Carter will not proceed with SALT until he knows what you want, what I want and what your brother-in-law wants him to do. We've got until May to come up with some good ideas."

"Okay, but if I work on SALT, Carter and Vance better come up with some new designs for our straw tote bags or we're not going to make our payroll this summer."

## ARE WE READY FOR REFORM?

President Carter's long-awaited civil service reforms have finally been unveiled and, like most of Mr. Carter's plans, they sound swell on paper. The President wants to get the government on a more businesslike footing by rewarding those who do a good job with merit raises and by punishing those who do a bad job with dismissal. He would also protect whistle blowers who, by going public, embarrass their bosses and find themselves booted out in the street.

All well and good. So what's the problem? The problem is that no one, including the President, Congress and the Supreme Court, has ever defined exactly what a government employee should do. There are job descriptions in the civil service regulations, but since the government is not a profit-making organization it is almost impossible to accurately measure a civil servant's productivity.

For example, I work in a building on Pennsylvania Avenue in which six of the thirteen floors are rented to a government agency. Since I am located on the thirteenth floor I come into contact with government employees every day. Some are going from the sixth floor to the seventh. Others from the second to the tenth and still others from the fifth to the ninth. They are always carrying official-looking papers in their hands so I have to assume they are doing something very important.

The question is, are government employees who move up and down in the elevator and whiz to and fro more productive than those who sit in their offices reading *The Washington Post* funnies?

The elevator rider, you may say, is giving us a bigger bang for our buck. He or she is engaged in the nation's business of writing new regulations, interpreting old ones, sending out memoranda, stamping classified material, setting up committees, turning out reports and doing all the things expected from a servant of the people.

So surely he or she should be given a raise and a promotion.

Perhaps. But the elevator rider is also the person making the government more unwieldy and impossible to control. By going from the second floor to the tenth he or she may be responsible for a new regulation putting 10,000 people out of work, making a national park into a coal mine or giving the go-ahead on a new missile that will never fly.

A short trip from the fifth to the sixth floor by an innocent-looking chap with a pipe clamped in his mouth could cost every man, woman and child in this country $165.

After traveling up and down the capital's elevators for 16 years, I have come to the sad conclusion that those government employees doing the most work in Washington are also doing the most damage.

Therefore, before I go along with Carter's reform package he's going to have to spell out exactly what he expects government employees to do for their salaries. My fear is that, by instituting a merit system and causing government employees to compete against each other, the President will not reduce but add to all the red tape he said he was going to eliminate when he became President.

If employee Brown submits a 10-page regulation on the amount of whipped cream permitted in an Amaretto liqueur, will employee Guggenheim write a 20-page regulation to outdo him?

Compared to other countries, the bureaucrats in the United States have been like a sleeping giant. But if you threaten them with demotion and dangle financial incentives in front of them, they could become an aroused beast, prepared to regulate anything that gets in their way.

Before it approves the Carter Administration's reform package I believe Congress should ask itself the following questions:

1—Is a government employee who puts in an honest day's work making any worthwhile contribution to society?

2—By taking an elevator from one floor to another is a bureaucrat saving us money or merely wasting the country's energy?

3—If you fire all the drones in the government and keep only the overachievers, who will be left to blame when a giant federal program fails and goes down the tube?

# XI.  Lies—All Lies

## IS THERE ANYBODY THERE?

A recent nationwide survey has just revealed that there were 789,345,678 unreturned telephone calls made in 1977, an increase of 10 percent over 1977. Phone experts believe that at the present rate the figure of one billion could be reached by 1980.

Mark Stampel is the head of a nonprofit organization named The Unreturned Telephone Call Institute, whose main function is to investigate all unreturned telephone calls and decide on the basis of this information whether there is life on earth.

He told me at the UTC Institute's plush estate in Middleburg, Va., that the fact someone does not return a telephone call doesn't mean that the person called does not exist. "It only means that the person who made the call doesn't exist for the person who didn't call back."

It took me a few minutes to digest this.

Stampel tried to spell it out in layman terms. "Let us assume Pleeder calls Arragant to get a job. Arragant's secretary says that Arragant is in a meeting and will get back to Pleeder as soon as possible.

"Arragant has no intention of calling back Pleeder. Pleeder waits by the phone—one hour, 24 hours, a week. No word from Arragant. He calls back again. This time Pleeder can't get through the switchboard to even speak to Arragant's secretary."

"Arragant's a cruel man," I said.

"Aha," said Stampel. "You would think so. But the reason Arragant has not called back Pleeder is that he is waiting for a call from Byer. Arragant is trying to sell Byer a shipload of railroad ties. Arragant keeps asking his secretary if Byer has called."

"Byer hasn't?" I asked.

"Of course not. He doesn't want Arragant's railroad ties."

"Why doesn't Byer call and tell him so?"

"Because he doesn't want to tie up the phone. He's waiting to hear from his girlfriend who hasn't returned his call for three days."

"Why?"

"Because Byer won't get a divorce from Mrs. Byer, and the girlfriend has decided that she has had it with him."

"That's reasonable."

"After the girlfriend made the decision to give up on Byer she calls Altman, whom she met at a party, and leaves word she's available for dinner. Now she's waiting by her phone for Altman to call back."

"Why doesn't Altman call her back?"

"He can't remember what the girl looked like and he's afraid to take a chance that she may be a dog."

"Altman sounds like a male chauvinist."

"He is, except that he's afraid of his mother. He's particularly frightened because she hasn't answered his call."

"Why not?" I wanted to know.

"Because Altman didn't call her the week before, and his mother is going to make him pay for it. Besides she's waiting to hear from the Board of Health to complain because the furnace in her apartment house is on the fritz."

"And of course they don't call back."

"You have to be kidding. The heating inspector for the Board of Health is sitting by his phone waiting to hear from the mayor's deputy assistant on whether he can hire more people to handle telephone complaints."

"The mayor's deputy doesn't call back?"

"No, because he's waiting for a call from Washington, which will never come, telling him whether the city can have the funds it needs, not only for the health inspector but for Pleeder, who still doesn't have a job because Arragant never answered his call."

"On the basis of what you just told me," I said to Stampel, "does your institute really believe there is life on earth?"

"Well, there's *something* out there." Stampel said. "And I have to believe they're trying to communicate with us even if they refuse to do it by telephone."

## THE SON OF HUEY

The call came in at seven o'clock.

The dispatcher ran over to his chief, "Someone's hijacked the President's energy bill and is holding it as hostage until we give them $40 billion."

"Get the SWAT squad and surround the Capitol," the chief ordered.

When everyone was in place the White House representative said over his loudspeaker, "This is the Carter Administration. We know you're in there. Come out with your hands up."

"This is the Son of Huey," a voice shouted from a window, "and if you people make so much as a move we'll kill your energy bill once and for all."

"Hold it!" the White House man called. "We're willing to talk. Don't hurt the bill. Who else do you have in there with you?"

"We have some stubborn congressmen from the House, a few bleeding heart senators from the East, whom we have tied up, and we're going to stay here until hell or the country freezes over."

"We don't care what you do to the congressmen or the senators. Just release the energy bill."

The Son of Huey laughed. "You'll get your energy bill, but you won't recognize it."

The White House representative shouted, "How do we know you have the energy bill at all?"

The Son of Huey held up the bill to the window. It was battered and torn almost beyond recognition.

"Here it is. But we're not finished with it yet. Now are you going to meet our demands?"

The White House man got on the radio to the President. "They have your energy bill all right. It's still alive, but just barely. What should I do?"

"Find out what the ransom is for getting it out."

The White House man got on the loudspeaker. "Listen, Son of Huey, we're ready to bargain. What do you want?"

"Now you're talking sense. We want an increase of gas prices to $2.03 as opposed to $1.75 per thousand cubic feet."

"We can live with that," the White House man said.

"We also want the revenues from the new crude oil tax to go back to the oil companies as incentives for drilling new wells."

"But that money was supposed to go to consumers who couldn't afford the high fuel rates."

The Son of Huey held up the energy bill. He had a knife and was about to slash it.

"Wait," the White House man pleaded, "I've got to talk to headquarters."

The White House man reported the demands back to the President. Mr. Carter thought about it for a moment. "He's cutting the heart out of my bill, but maybe we can live with it."

The White House man shouted, "You can have the incentives for the oil companies! Now can we have the bill?"

"Are we talking about new oil or old oil?" the Son of Huey yelled.

"Which one do you want to talk about?" the White House man asked.

"Both. We should get rebates on old oil as well as new oil."

"Okay, you have it. Is there anything else?"

"I want a private plane to take me to Louisiana for Christmas."

The White House man got on the radio to the President one more time.

"He says he'll release our energy bill providing we give him a private plane to take him home for Christmas."

"It's blackmail," the President sighed, "but when the country's only energy bill's life is at stake, what choice do we have?"

## DISNEYLAND IS NOT ENOUGH

Hardly a week goes by when some head of state doesn't visit Washington. In the old days if they saw Disneyland while they were in the United States they went home happy.

But things have changed. Most heads of state now come to Washington to see how much military aid they can get out of the United States.

Several weeks ago the President of Zemululu arrived in Washington for a State visit. The Zemululan ambassador to the United States met him at the plane, as did the American Secretary of State and an honor guard from the U.S. Army, U.S. Marines and U.S. Air Force.

The Zemululan ambassador whispered to the President, "The first thing you must do is review the honor guard."

The President said, "Those are nice rifles they're carrying. Can I have them?"

"No," said the ambassador, "not yet. First we have to take a helicopter to the White House where President Carter will greet you."

After reviewing the troops the President of Zemululu got into the helicopter. "Should I ask the Secretary of State for 34 of these?"

"It's too early in your visit. We have to go through formalities."

The President looked very disappointed.

The helicopter landed on the White House Lawn where President and Mrs. Carter were waiting to meet the party. President Carter made his opening remarks calling Zemululu one of the great countries of the world and a friend the United States could not do without.

The Zemululan ambassador said out of the side of his mouth, "It is now your turn to respond."

"Good, I'll ask him for two squadrons of F-15s and three squadrons of F-16s."

"Wait. It's not the time. You never ask for military equipment in the Rose Garden. It's against protocol."

"What should I say?"

"Just say the ties between Zemululu and the United States are stronger than they have ever been, and the admiration for America as the preserver of peace is something every Zemululan cherishes."

"All right, but I think we're wasting a lot of time. I have only two days here."

The Zemululan President made his remarks which were followed by a 21-gun salute.

The Zemululan President took out a notebook. "I almost forgot the cannons. How many 105-mm cannons should I ask for?"

The ambassador replied, "I think they said they'd give us five."

"Five? My generals told me to come back with no less than 50."

"We'll talk about it later. We have to go in to lunch."

The Zemululan President said, "When can we go to the Pentagon and see the stuff?"

"We have to lunch with the President and Mrs. Carter first. After that we have to place a wreath at the Lincoln Memorial."

"That will blow the whole afternoon," the Zemululan President complained.

"The Pentagon is just over the bridge from the memorial, Mr. President. We can go there after the wreath-laying."

"How late do they stay open?"

"Five o'clock."

"Five o'clock? I won't even have time to pick any gunboats for our navy."

"We'll go back the next morning."

"Suppose all the F-15s are gone by then?"

"The Pentagon always keeps a dozen in the stockroom for its special friends. Oh, by the way, there is a State dinner tonight and Beverly Sills is going to sing."

"That's nice. Maybe I can talk President Carter out of some Cruise missiles during *Madame Butterfly*."

## FOGGY BOTTOM

The U.S. State Department is in a snit because it is not being consulted on every move that President Sadat and Prime Minister Begin are making.

Every time you pick up the newspapers the headline reads something like this: STATE DEPARTMENT SURPRISED BY LATEST SADAT INVITATION or STATE DEPARTMENT ADMITS IT WASN'T CONSULTED ON ISRAELI TALKS IN JERUSALEM.

I don't know if this has anything to do with President Carter's policy of candor, but I, like millions of Americans, have been brought up to believe that the State Department knows EVERYTHING and that it is never SURPRISED.

Maybe it's not true, but it gives you a warm feeling to think it is.

I ran into an old State Department hand the other day who was terribly depressed about how little people over at Foggy Bottom know about what is going on.

"I see where Sadat postponed his conference in Cairo," I said.

"Where did you hear that?" he asked excitedly.

"I saw it on the Cronkite show," I replied.

"He never told us," my man said bitterly.

"Sadat doesn't have to tell you before he tells the American people," I said.

"He makes us look stupid."

"I think that's very unfair," I told him. "If Sadat feels more comfortable talking to Walter Cronkite than he does the U.S. Secretary of State you should be grateful."

"What else did Walter say?" the State Department man whispered.

"You don't have to whisper," I said. "Everyone in America who watches Cronkite heard it."

"I hope Walter realizes that he violated State Department security," he said.

"You know Begin has turned down Kurt Waldheim's invitation to go to the U.N. for a pre-Geneva summit meeting," I told him.

"I don't believe you. If he had we would have been informed."

"Well, he told Barbara Walters on ABC News that he wasn't coming, and Barbara never lies."

"You saw it on the ABC News? How come the CIA didn't tell us about it?" he said.

"They're cutting back in personnel. They can't cover everything," I explained. "Did you hear that the rest of the Arab world is sore as hell at Sadat for going to Jerusalem?"

"We know that," he said, "but who told you?"

"John Chancellor and David Brinkley."

"They promised us they wouldn't tell anyone. It could mess up our whole policy in the Middle East."

"What policy?" I inquired.

"Who said we don't have one?" the State Department man asked.

"I believe it was Tom Brokaw on the 'Today' show. Either him or Johnny Carson. I don't remember.

"You know of course about the meeting in Tripoli, Libya, last week where the hard-line Arabs vowed to fix Sadat's wagon," I said.

"Sure, we knew about it."

"It could blow the Geneva Conference," I remarked.

"We didn't know that. Where did you hear about it?"

"I believe Mike Wallace mentioned it on '60 Minutes.' Don't you people at the State Department ever watch television?"

"We don't have time," he replied. "We're always in meetings trying to figure out what's going on in the Middle East."


## WAITING FOR JIMMY

A few weeks ago President Carter called two Washington correspondents, Hedrick Smith of *The New York Times* and Jack Nelson of *The Los Angeles Times,* and spent a long time on the phone explaining how close he was to Vice President Walter Mondale and also how hard he, Mr. Carter, was working in the White House.

When the President of the United States calls a newspaperman to explain what he's doing it makes you a big man in this town.

Since then every newspaperperson has a fantasy that he or she will get the next call from the President.

I have to confess that I, too, have been dreaming about it. In my fantasy Jody Powell goes into Mr. Carter's office and says, "You better call Buchwald. He's got it all wrong concerning your position on the three-martini lunch."

The fantasy has become so real that things have become pretty rough around my house.

The first night I said to my wife, "Any telephone calls for me?"

"The Volvo service people called and said it would cost $321 to fix your car."

"I don't mean that kind of call. Have there been any from a high government official?"

"Why would a high government official want to call you?"

"Well, if you must know I'm expecting to hear from the President of the United States."

She started to laugh.

"It's not a joke," I said angrily. "He's starting to call newspapermen in this town and he might be doing it alphabetically."

"If he does call," she said, still giggling, "should I say you're here?"

"Of course, you can tell him I'm here. You don't tell the President of the United States your husband isn't home when he is. And don't tie up the phone for the next two weeks talking to your sister."

The next night I found my son on the phone speaking to a girlfriend.

"How long has he been talking?" I asked my wife.

"About an hour."

"That's just great," I said. "The President of the United States is probably trying to call me and all he can get is a busy signal."

"I'm sure if the President was trying to get you the White House would interrupt the call."

"Well, tell him to get off."

My wife said to my son, "Finish the call. Your father is expecting to get one from the President."

My son said to his girl, "I have to hang up now. My Dad is waiting to hear from President Carter. . . . I'm not trying to get you off the line. That's what he says. Yeh, he has been acting a little funny lately. As a matter of fact, he hasn't been the same since Watergate."

"All right," I said, "everyone can make fun of me, but when the call comes through you'll be laughing out of the other side of your mouths. And because of your attitude I'm not going to let any of you listen in."

Since then, every time someone calls my wife says, "I can't talk. Art's expecting a call from President Carter."

"Big mouth. Do you have to tell everyone?"

"I think it's kind of impressive. If he doesn't call by next week, why don't you call him? It might relieve the suspense."

"No way. You don't get the Pulitzer Prize if you call the President. The only way they'll give it to you is if he calls you."


## THE CIA AND THE PRESS

Carl Bernstein's revelation that 400 members of the press were also working, in some way, for the CIA overseas in the 1950s and 1960s has made every newspaperman who was stationed abroad suspect.

I worked in Paris for fourteen years for the International Edition of the *Herald Tribune* and, ever since the story broke, even I have been asked if I was involved in any overt or covert operations concerning our most famous secret service.

The answer is, "Not to my knowledge." I'm fairly sure of it because the salary the Paris *Herald Tribune* gave me was way below the prevailing CIA rates for reporters, and I have to believe the chintzy *Herald Tribune* management was paying me out of its own pocket.

I should have had some suspicions, even in those days, that several of my colleagues were working for somebody besides the papers they pretended to be accredited to.

One American friend was living in an eighteen-room villa in Vienna, with three servants and a chauffeur. I never could understand it, because the only paper he was working for, at the time, was a weekly magazine published in Terre Haute, Ind.

I once asked him about his elegant lifestyle, and he replied, "The Terre Haute publisher believes its overseas bureau chiefs should live well."

I should have smelled something fishy when he once asked to take an article he had written back to Paris and hide it in a tree near the American Embassy.

"Is that how you file your stories?" I asked.

"Yes," he replied. "It's much faster than sending them over the teletype."

"But the article is on microfilm," I said.

He got angry. "Look, you file your stories the way you want to, but don't tell me how to file mine."

Possibly one of the reasons the CIA never sought to recruit me is that they may have thought I would not make a very good agent.

I recall going to Carlsbad in Czechoslovakia for a film festival in the 1950s. When I returned, I had a visit in my office from two very well-dressed men who said they were from the Dulles Broadcasting Company in Waco, Texas. They told me they were unable to attend the film festival and asked if I would brief them on it.

I said, "Certainly, what do you want to know?"

"How many anti-aircraft guns did you see around the festival hall?"

"None that I can remember," I said. "There were searchlights at the film festival, but there always are."

"Were there any land mines near your hotel?" the other one asked.

"Beats me," I said. "I didn't see anyone step on one."

"How many Soviet divisions did you see?"

"You mean in the films?"

"No, you dummy. Real Soviet divisions with armor."

"Hey, what's that got to do with a film festival?" I asked.

"It's hopeless, Joe," one of them said as he got up.

The other one got up, too. "I told the Company we'd be wasting our time." And they stomped out.

Had it occurred to me I was being tested, I certainly would have been more co-operative. But in those days I really believed there was a Dulles Broadcasting Company in Waco, Texas. Heaven knows I could have used the extra CIA money.

I don't know which of my fellow correspondents worked for the CIA and which didn't. But in the late '40s and '50s I played a lot of poker with them. And I now suspect several of them were more than they said they were. How do I know? Well, some of them used to stay in the hand to the very end, with a pair of twos. It dawned on me just the other day that only a guy on a CIA payroll could afford to do that.

## YOU CAN'T CUT PAPERWORK

President Carter is pledged to cut down paperwork in Washington. Abernathy, a government bureaucrat, says he can't do it.

"It's a question of communication," he said. "There are two ways of communicating in the government—orally and in print. I could communicate verbally with somebody, but no one would be aware that I was doing my job."

"The person you communicated with would know," I said.

"That's not enough," he said. "In government it is essential that as many people as possible are aware that you are working. The only way they can know this is if you send them copies of memoranda that you have originated. The more people there are on your 'need to know' list the more important your job with the agency will seem."

"It makes sense," I said, "but surely even these communications could be cut down to achieve Carter's goal."

"They could," said Abernathy, "except that a memo does not have value unless the one who sends it demands a response. What good is a memorandum on an issue until you can get ten people to comment on it in writing?"

"They probably welcome the opportunity to do it," I said.

"Of course, and this is where the President is up against a wall. Since I originate the memorandum there is a certain amount of jealousy because it is now known as the 'Abernathy Memo.' The only way the other bureaucrats can get back at me is to respond with a report on the memo which they can then put their names on. For example, Freedman would title his the 'Freedman Report in Answer to the Abernathy Memorandum.' To play catch-up, he would be obligated to circulate this to twice as many people as I did."

"Now you're really getting into paper," I said.

"That's only the beginning. Altshuler would have to top Freedman by calling a meeting, at which he would give an audio-visual presentation of his opinions with copies to all those present as well as those who couldn't attend. He would include graphs, statistics and research in various colors. It would be called the 'Altshuler Response to the Freedman Answer on the Abernathy Memorandum.' "

"But suppose you cut the distribution list for memos in half. Wouldn't that cut down the paperwork?"

"It might if status didn't play such an important part in government communications. Suppose you sent a memo to Crosby but left Schuster off the list. Schuster would consider that you were trying to push him out of the picture and retaliate by cutting you off *his* list. It could get very rough because it doesn't pay to have Schuster as an enemy, particularly when he could sabotage you in the dining room by saying he saw your memo to Crosby and it made no sense at all."

"I can see where that wouldn't work," I said.

"You have another problem," Abernathy said. "It's dangerous to send out a memorandum in the government because by doing so you're sticking your neck out. But if you can comment on *somebody else's* memo, you're in a safe position because you weren't the originator of the idea.

"If you cut people off your list and they start cutting you off their distribution list, you will be forced to write more *original* memos which eventually will get you in trouble. Harper, who used to work in the next office, did this. He only sent his memos to two people. He got so few memos back in return that they decided he didn't have enough to do and they fired him."

Abernathy said, "The only way you can measure productivity in the government is by how much paperwork a person is producing. If he has nothing in his files, there is no way the President knows he's doing his job."

"Is Mr. Carter aware of this?"

"Yes, I just sent him a long memorandum on it this morning."


## AN EX-UNIMPEACHABLE SOURCE

The worst thing for anyone to be in Washington right now is an "unimpeachable source" from the Ford Administration. No one will take you to lunch, no one will answer your telephone calls, and your chances of getting invited to a decent cocktail party or dinner are nil.

I am one of the few people in town who will still speak to an "unimpeachable source" from the previous Administration. I don't like doing it. But at the same time I don't just drop a guy because he's absolutely useless when it comes to leaking the government's business.

Just the other day I took a call from a fellow who supplied me with some of the best information I ever had during the Nixon and Ford years. I'll call him "Deep Laryngitis."

"I think I have something hot for you," he said hopefully.

"Look, Deep," I told him, "I'm awfully busy."

"Don't hang up on me," he begged. "Everyone's been hanging up on me all week."

"What have you got?"

"William Morris is trying to work out a deal to get Gerry Ford to do the American Express card commercial—where the guy says, 'I know you don't know my name, but I used to be President of the United States.' "

"I'm sorry, Deep," I said, trying to be kind, "but it's not a big story."

"Well, how about this? Secretary William Simon got caught trying to smuggle a machine gun under his raincoat out of the Internal Revenue Service Building on the day before he left office."

"It won't fly. No one cares any more. Do you have anything on Billy Carter?" I said.

"No, I don't have anything on Billy Carter. Do you know where Jack Ford spent the last weekend?"

"I don't know and I don't care. You've got to realize we're in a new era. You can't live in the past."

"I was very good to you for eight years," he said. "I gave you the story on the 18½ minute gap on the tapes. I told you about how the Committee to Re-elect the President laundered its money in Mexico. I tipped you off on Earl Butz' joke on the airplane. Doesn't that count for something?"

"Look, Deep," I said, "as an unimpeachable source you were one of the greatest, and I'll always be grateful for all those calls you made to me at midnight. But it's over for you now. Even Sonny Jurgeson knew when it was time to retire. Why don't you go away somewhere and start a new life?"

"Rockefeller? What do you want to know about Rockefeller? I've got stuff that would make your ears burn."

"It's no good, Deep. I can't quote you as an unimpeachable source any more."

"Why not?"

"Because you're an *impeachable* source. Do you think it's easy for me? I have to cultivate a whole new team of sources—guys who talk with Southern accents and don't know a good government leak even when they're standing under it."

He just wouldn't give up. "I went through Henry Kissinger's garbage last night."

I started to lose my patience. "Don't you understand? Kissinger's garbage is not a story now. It's just garbage."

"Look," he said, pleading. "Even if you can't use any of my stuff, would you just be seen with me at the Sans Souci, so it doesn't look as if I'm all washed up?"

"It's out of the question. If I'm seen with you, the Carter people will know about it in minutes. They don't forgive easily. I'll tell you what. Maybe we could meet under the arch at McDonald's in Annapolis. No one knows either of us there, and it will be fun to see you again for old times' sake."

His voice broke. "You're all heart."

He got me choked up. "What are friends for?"

## NEW BOOKS FOR THE FALL

I went out to San Francisco recently to the American Bookseller's Convention to flog a new book I have coming out in the fall. (Modesty prevents me from telling the title.) At least 15,000 book buyers, bookstore owners, publishers, editors and promotion people were there, and I would estimate at least 10,000 new titles were being pushed.

I can't remember all of the titles, but as I went from booth to booth I got some idea of what awaits the book reader this fall.

The first booth I stopped at, the salesman said:

"Here is a free copy of the book of the year, *How to Perform Your Own Heart Transplant Operation.* You save $3,000 by cutting out the middleman."

"You mean the doctor?"

"Doctor, heart surgeon—whatever you call him. The book tells you everything from where to find a donor to how to deal with vascular rejection."

I went to the next booth and was handed a book entitled, *How to Make a Million Dollars in Real Estate and Have Sex at the Same Time.*

"This is a racy title," I said.

"It's a self-help book. Many real estate agents make a lot of money, but they're very shy about sex.

"This book helps them overcome their inhibitions, particularly when they're showing an unfurnished house. As you notice it's chock-full of illustrations. The author feels real estate people have to come out of the closet."

A few booths down a man was autographing books. He was apparently a psychologist because the title of his work was *Releasing Inner Energy by Biting Your Fingernails.* When he saw I was a reporter he explained his theory. "All lifegiving energy starts in the fingernails. Most people have pent-up energy, really electric charges, that has to be released before they explode. By biting your fingernails you make it possible for the energy to escape out through your hands, which relaxes the joints in your knuckles and gets you through the day." He gave me an autographed copy, which I read on the plane— and much to my amazement it worked.

Two aisles down I found a publisher's rep pushing a book entitled *The Joy of Oil Spills*, which tells people how to have fun when a tanker goes aground off their beach. It shows you how to build tar castles out of oil and sand, how to swim through an oil spill and still breathe and how to organize a fish fry from all the fish that have rolled up on the beach.

A few booths down I found *The Idi Amin Book of Etiquette, Confessions of an Oral Surgeon, The Last Chance Food Stamp Diet Book, Dating Jackie Onassis on $5 a Day* and *Is There an IRS After Death?*

Christmas shoppers can expect many supernatural books this fall. One that caught my eye was entitled *Anita's Baby.* The plot concerned a child who drank nothing but Florida orange juice and found himself wanting to be a woman. He has a transsexual operation and winds up winning the women's tennis singles at Wimbledon.

The success of *Roots* has forced many publishers to come out with their own versions. One was entitled *Leaves* and told of a

WASP's search for his roots over a period of twelve years. He remembered his grandmother sitting on the porch in Southampton repeating a story about her great-grandfather who founded the Standard Oil Company of New Jersey. Taking a $50,000 advance from his publisher, he went to New Jersey, and there in a small village called South Orange he found the very place his great-great-great-grandfather had come from. The people of South Orange were so happy to meet one of their own that they made him a member of their country club for life.

The author is now suing his publisher for $5 million because he couldn't find *Leaves* in any New Jersey bookstore.

## "THAT'S SHOW BIZ"

There was a time when being President of the United States was the highest office that any American could aspire to. But in recent years the Presidency is only a steppingstone to fame and fortune in show biz. A recent article in *The New York Times* revealed that the William Morris Agency has made deals for President Ford, Mrs. Ford, Jack Ford, Susan Ford and Steve Ford. The former President and his wife have contracts for two books with Harper & Row and Reader's Digest worth a million dollars. Ford will also work for NBC for the next five years doing documentaries, for which he will get a million dollars.

Mrs. Ford has a contract with NBC for the next two years to do documentaries and also appear on the "Today" show. She will be paid $500,000 for her services. Jack Ford has been signed as an assistant to the publisher of Rolling Stone; Steve Ford will act in a television series in Hollywood, and Susan Ford has just sold her photographs to "Good Housekeeping."

Even President Nixon, who was driven out of office in disgrace, stands to make two or three million dollars from his book and TV appearances.

With this kind of money being thrown around no one has any idea what President Carter's worth will be. But several big-name agents are already working on Mr. Carter's future as soon as he leaves office. I spoke to one of them.

He was very excited. "We'll get more money for the Carters than for any family that has ever lived in the White House. We're talking mega-bucks when we're talking about the Carters."

"But isn't it kind of early to start packaging the Carter family?" I asked. "He's only been President for a couple of months."

"We have to move fast. Carter's hot right now. In four years the bidding could go way down. I can get more money for Amy's memoirs now than for Ford's and Nixon's combined."

"I hope she's keeping a diary," I said.

"Guess what I've cooked up for Miss Lillian?"

"I have no idea."

"I've been talking to CBS about her being co-anchorwoman with Walter Cronkite on the evening news."

"Does Walter know about this?"

"It's not *his* decision," the agent said. "ABC sports wants Rosalynn Carter to do Monday Night Football with Howard Cosell."

"I didn't know Rosalynn knew anything about football."

"It doesn't matter. Rosalynn is interested in mental health and what better place to talk about it than with Howard during a pro football game."

"Billy Carter's tied up with another agent now so I guess you can't use him," I said.

"It doesn't matter. By the time the President is out of office Billy will be overexposed."

"What have you lined up for President Carter?"

"I have a firm $3 million offer for his book. NBC is offering $2 million for a documentary on how he brought peace to the Middle East and another $2 million to host the "Saturday Night" show, as well as to fill in for Johnny Carson when Carson goes to Las Vegas."

"You've really been working."

"You know Carter's sister," he said.

"You mean Ruth Stapleton, the faith healer?" I replied.

"No, dummy, Gloria Carter Spaan, the one who rides a motorcycle."

"Of course."

"I got an offer from the Dallas State Fair. They want her to fly over fifteen Greyhound buses on her bike in tandem with Evel Knievel."

"What about the President's sons, Chip, Jack and Jeff?"

"*Playboy* wants all three of them."

"Gosh, I didn't know there was that much money in being President of the United States?"

"Are you kidding? Any agent who can't get a minimum of $10 million for a former President and his family shouldn't be in show business."


## FLAUNT—IF YOU HAVE THE COURREGES

There is something going on in the clothing industry of which you may or may not be aware. Designers and manufacturers are now putting labels on the outside of their clothes instead of on the inside. It started a few years ago when Pierre Cardin, Courreges, Christian Dior, Gucci and others discovered that since women had paid so much for their outfits, they wanted everyone to know where they bought them.

The practice soon spread like wildfire and the saying "You are what you eat" has been replaced by "You are what you wear."

I was at a party the other evening and I noticed a lady with a large "CD" on the back of her fur coat.

"What a beautiful Christian Dior coat," I said.

"How did you know it was a Dior?" she said in amazement.

"I just guessed from the cut of it," I replied. I helped her off with the coat and she gave me her silk scarf. It had "Givenchy" printed all over it.

"What a beautiful Givenchy scarf," I said.

"Oh, is that what it is? I just grabbed one out of a drawer."

"I'd know a Givenchy scarf anywhere. Say, is that a Pucci blouse you have on?"

"Yes, it is. How did you know?"

"It says 'Pucci' on the collar, the sleeves and the cuffs."

"You are observant. You're the first person who ever guessed this blouse came from Pucci."

I blushed modestly and then said, "It goes beautifully with your Diane von Furstenberg skirt."

"Don't tell me your wife has one just like it."

"No, she doesn't. I just noticed the 'DVF' embroidered along the entire hem—on the outside."

She looked down. "Why, of course. I never noticed that before."

"Would you be insulted if I told you I've never seen anyone look better in Pierre Cardin black silk stockings?"

"Now how on earth did you know they were Cardin stockings?"

I was looking at your Gucci shoes with the big 'G' on each toe and my eye naturally traveled up to the 'C' which is stitched every inch along the seams of your stockings."

"You are the wicked one," she laughed.

"The Courreges leather belt is smashing with your Hermes handbag," I said.

"You have very good eyes," she said.

"I once read a Calvin Klein logo on a woman's sweater 200 feet away," I bragged.

"You're putting me on."

"I am not. This may come as a surprise to you, but I know you're wearing an Oleg Cassini slip."

Her eyes widened in surprise. "How do you know that?"

"I can read his name on the lace through your Pucci blouse."

"You devil you," she parried.

"Don't be embarrassed," I said. "I have Sears Roebuck stamped all over my boxer shorts."

"Well," she said, "I guess there is nothing you don't know about me."

"Yes, there is," I said. "I don't know your name. What is it?"

She gasped, "It—it's, oh my God, I forgot my own name."

## CLOSE ENCOUNTERS

A group of us were jogging in Rock Creek Park the other morning when a flying saucer from outer space hovered over us and then made a perfect three-point landing. Out of it stepped a dozen little green people.

One of them, who wore four stars on his shoulders, seemed to be in charge.

"Take us to your leader," he said.

We all looked at each other perplexed.

"What did you say?" Sullivan asked.

"I said take us to your leader. Don't you understand English?"

"We don't really have a leader," my friend Guggenheim said. "But we have a President."

"Maybe," said Lindstrom, "we should take him to Senator Robert Byrd. He has more clout than the President."

"I'm not sure," Redfern said. "Senator Russell Long is the real power in this country. Nothing gets through without Long's approval."

"What about Tip O'Neill? He's really calling the shots on the Hill," I said.

The four-star green person was getting impatient.

"We don't have all day. Will you make up your minds? We heard Henry Kissinger was your leader."

"That was a year ago. Everything is changed now. Kissinger is only a professor at Georgetown University."

"Look, we came a long way," the green person said, "and we're tired. Are you going to take us to your leader or aren't you?"

"We'd like to," said Guggenheim apologetically, "but at the moment nobody is really in charge."

"How do you get things done if no one is in charge?" the green leader asked.

"We don't get much done," I told him. "We just seem to go along with everyone doing his own thing. The President says he wants to do one thing, Congress says it wants to do another, and finally a compromise is made which doesn't satisfy anyone. Would you like to meet Arthur Burns?"

"Is he your leader?"

"No, but he's in charge of our money supply and he's giving President Carter fits."

The green person thought we were putting him on.

"Every country has to have a leader," he said, menacing us with what looked like a laser pistol.

"Please," begged Redfern, "we're trying to be helpful. But no one has ever asked us to take him to our leader before. Carter promised to be our leader but he's still trying to get the hang of it. It isn't easy to be a leader in the United States. If you had landed in the Soviet Union you would have been taken to the Kremlin right away."

The green person said something to the other green persons that we didn't understand. They all started chattering at the same time.

Then the green leader turned to us.

"Since you don't have one, they want to know if you would like me to be your leader."

"I wouldn't mind," Guggenheim said.

"Suits me," Redfern agreed.

"It's up for grabs if you want it," Lindstrom told him. "But as a matter of courtesy you ought to clear it with Fritz Mondale in the White House."

"Who's he?"

"He's in charge of all Administration appointments for outer space."


## LIES—ALL LIES

While the mini-series "Behind Closed Doors" was very entertaining, I'm afraid it's going to give people a wrong impression of Washington. Since it was meant purely for entertainment, the producers took liberties with the way things work at the White House and in the rest of the town. This could damage the cause of clean honest government which the people in the country expect of Washington and fortunately get.

The idea of the film is as farfetched as anything ever seen on the TV screen. It is unthinkable that a President of the United States (in this case Jason Robards) would use his power and that of the CIA and the FBI as well as unsavory people in the White House to do harm to his political enemies. While this makes good theater, it obviously could never happen. If anyone suggested such a thing, the President would fire him immediately.

In "Behind Closed Doors," the characters, supposedly based on such real people as Bob Haldeman, John Ehrlichman, John Dean, John Mitchell, Howard Hunt and many others, were portrayed as schemers and sinister hatchet men, ready to protect the President at any cost, even if it meant violating the law of the land.

This, of course, makes a good story, but it could never have happened. The men who have worked in the White House always came from the best families, were educated in the best schools and raised in the American tradition of fair play and patriotism. They never would have resorted to any illegal act to further the re-election of the President. It just wasn't in them, and even if a President had suggested it, which no President would, they would have immediately resigned rather than carry out his orders.

The television drama also gave another very unreal picture of Washington. It showed a businessman trying to buy an ambassadorship for his wife with a large political campaign contribution. Now this is where the writers have gone too far.

In the history of American diplomacy, no ambassadorship has ever been given in exchange for a political campaign contribution. If this were true, we would have ambassadors all over the world who didn't know what they were doing, and we would have some of the most unqualified people in the country reporting back to Washington on the affairs of state.

For those of us who live in Washington, the most unfair incidents in "Behind Closed Doors" concerned the women of this town. The TV series showed them going to bed with men in power to whom they weren't married. The CIA director in the plot even left his wife for a widow, and a young college girl had an affair with a White House aide in hopes of getting a job.

The implication was that the morals in Washington are "loose," and that people go to bed with each other whether they're married to them or not. This is a terribly unfair picture to show because it gives the wrong impression of what Washington is all about. As long as I've lived here, I've never known sex to play any part in government.

Washington women think too much of their reputations to bed down with a man just because he is in power. And a man in power would never take advantage of his position to seduce a woman he was not married to. For one thing, it would compromise the high ideals the constituents expect of their politicians and high government officials. For another, it would be a sin.

When it comes to politics, power and sex, Washington is above reproach. Even the newspapermen who cover this town would never do anything to sully their reputations, such as lie, cheat or go to bed with someone just to get a story.

The reason this city has never been touched by scandal is that everyone from the President down to the most humble South Korean businessman has a sense of morality and ethics which, unfortunately, cannot be found in the rest of the country.

"Behind Closed Doors" has done a great disservice to the political system by presenting Washington and the people who work here in a terrible light. It is a fairy tale and should be seen as such. If there was even a smattering of truth to it, G. Gordon Liddy would *not* be our President today.

## JIMMY'S BEST FRIEND

"Hi, my name is Bert Lance."

"And I'm the Sheik of Araby."

"You're just the man I want to talk to. How would you like to loan me $5 million?"

"What on earth for?"

"Well, you see I owe the First National Bank of Chicago a bundle of money, and this bank in Tennessee, and I have to unload my stock in the National Bank of Georgia. If you let me have the loan, I'll be able to take over Financial General Bank in Washington, D.C."

"It sounds good to me. Say, are you the same Bert Lance who is considered the President's best friend?"

"Heck, I hardly know Jimmy. We've howdied a few times, but we ain't shook."

"Didn't I read where you go in the back door of the White House once or twice a day?"

"That's just to pick up my mail and have my hair cut. I would never use my connections with the President to put over a bank deal."

"Of course not. But didn't the President give you a diplomatic passport?"

"Yeh, but he gives everyone from Georgia one. Some Presidents give out tie clasps, other Presidents, cufflinks. Jimmy likes to give people diplomatic passports. I gave mine back."

"Why?"

"I didn't want anyone saying I was using my White House connections to buy up banks with Arabs."

"Well, my people are always interested in loaning $5 million to Americans, but at the same time it would be nice if I could say you know the President."

"I couldn't take the loan under those conditions. A man in my position has to stand on his record in the banking business, and not on who he knows in Washington."

"I respect you for that, Mr. Lance. Most people who come to us for money try to impress us with their connections. But you're the first one I've met who refuses to cash in on your former high position in the government."

"LaBelle chides me for that all the time. She says, 'Bert, everybody pretends to know the President intimately for private gain. Why don't you?' And you know what I tell her? I'm just a poor boy from Georgia, but if I can't put a bank deal together without using Jimmy's name, I'd rather pick peanuts."

"Since this deal you're talking about involves a great deal of money, my fellow sheiks would want some assurance that the U.S. government won't step in and stop it before it gets off the ground."

"Trust me. Check me out. Look what I did in Calhoun. Where would the National Bank of Georgia be right now if it weren't for me? Do you think I don't know how to take over a bank without getting into trouble with the SEC?"

"This bank that you're planning to take over, where is it?"

"Just a hop, skip and a jump from the Oval Office."

"That close?"

"It's in walking distance of the Treasury Department, but since I became a private citizen I never walk there."

"Then we can assume that if we get involved, we won't be embarrassed because everyone thinks you're the President's best friend?"

"Trust me."

## A COSMOS INVESTIGATION

It didn't take the Soviets long to start their own investigation as to why their nuclear satellite Cosmos 954 fell down after being sent into orbit.

Don't ask me how I found out, but this is how the hearings have been progressing.

"Comrade Master Scientist Mickelov, you were in charge of sending up Cosmos 954?"

"Yes, Comrades."

"And you are aware it fell down?"

"I heard it on the 'Voice of America,' but as you know as loyal member of the party I do not believe anything I hear on American radio."

"Unhappily, it is true, Comrade Mickelov. Cosmos 954 is no longer a happy satellite in the sky."

"I'm sorry to hear that, Comrades."

"We're glad to hear you're sorry, Mickelov. We're sorry too. What we want to know is why 954 is no longer in orbit."

"Maybe Americans have way of shooting down our satellites without us knowing it."

"Maybe. Or maybe the person who sent up the satellite in the first place made dumb, stupid error!"

"But, Comrades, I sent up 953 satellites and I never made mistake before."

"We know that, Mickelov. So our question is what happened to the 954th?"

"Let me see. The rocket was supposed to go into orbit 150 miles up in the air. It was launched on September 18, 1977, and was 46 feet long and weighed 8,000 pounds, of which 100 was enriched uranium which, if it worked correctly, would stay in space for 600 to 1,000 years. Now if you multiply $x$ by $3$ and then add $y$ you should have $z$."

"Aha," said one of the investigators, "$x$ *times* 3 added to $y$ doesn't equal $z$."

"It doesn't?"

"Where did you put the decimal point, Mickelov?"

"Here, where I always put it."

"The decimal point belongs over here."

"But nobody told me to put the decimal point there."

"Ignorance is no excuse. Mickelov, do you realize that because of your equation Cosmos 954 would have to crash into earth within five months of its launch?"

"Everyone is so picky, picky, picky. So I put decimal point in the wrong place. Do we have to make a people's federal case out of it?"

"That decimal point cost us 500 million rubles, not to mention the fact that parts of the satellite are strewn over all of Northern Canada. When Americans find the pieces they will know exactly what we put in satellite to make it fly. Our spy system will be destroyed."

"Nobody's perfect."

"You know what's going to happen to you, Mickelov?"

"I can only guess."

"You are getting the Order of Lenin for Scientific Achievement With Three Red Sickles."

"I am?"

"We have no choice. If we punish you we will be admitting we did something wrong. If we give you award, it backs up our story that we always intended Cosmos 954 to fall down in Canada after staying in orbit for only four months."

"Thank you, Comrades. I knew you would have faith in me. When I get my award do you know what I'll say? 'Cosmos 954 was one small step for man, and one giant step for mankind.' "

"That's very good, Mickelov. You may not know where to put a decimal point, but you certainly have a way with words."


### GOODBYE TO ALL THAT

I'm going to wax nostalgic today. *The International Herald Tribune*, still known to everyone around the world as the Paris *Herald Tribune*, is moving from its grubby offices on the Rue de Berri, where it has been printed since December 10, 1931, to a snooty new home in Neuilly.

As someone who worked there from 1949 to 1962, I was deeply

sorry to hear of the move. It always seemed to me that the Paris *Herald Tribune* (I refuse to call it the International Edition) was in the perfect location for an American newspaper abroad. It was within walking distance of many tourist hotels and the Champs Elysees. From the outside the building looked fairly new compared to the ones around it. But inside it was another story. The original paint was still on the walls, the elevator creaked in pain when it went up. The stairs were crooked. The city room was straight out of the '30s.

Through the years management would never replace a chair until someone sat in it and it broke under his own weight. The reporters' desks were from the Clemenceau period, and the lighting had been designed by Thomas Edison. In France nothing is ever thrown away and the typewriters we used were bought at garage sales of Gertrude Stein, Ernest Hemingway and Marcel Proust.

It was in this atmosphere that a handful of people put out a newspaper that went to nineteen countries every morning—a paper that many people still consider one of the best in the world.

The men who printed the paper in the cavernous basement of 21 Rue de Berri, all belonged to the French Communist printer's union. They used to sing Communist songs as they prepared the edition, but they never let their ideology interfere with their work. There were far less mistakes in the Paris *Herald*'s first edition than any newspaper put out by American printers in the United States.

What made the Rue de Berri offices so interesting was that they were so conveniently located near the Champs Élysées where most major political demonstrations were held. All a reporter had to do was stroll a block to the Champs, watch the demonstrators throw café chairs and tables at the police, and report on how many rioters were clubbed over the head by the gendarmes.

One time a colleague, Robert Yoakum, came back from a left-wing demonstration with his head bloodied. He said he had been whacked by a policeman for just standing on the sidewalk.

"Why didn't you show your press card?" Eric Hawkins, the managing editor, asked.

"I did," said Yoakum, "that's when he hit me."

The first edition came out at eleven thirty in the evening, and a small crowd of Americans used to gather in front of the building waiting for it to come off the press. They were all thirsting for the New York Stock Market results, and there were times when, after reading them, they attempted to throw themselves in front of our delivery trucks.

Because of its location, we had a constant flow of visitors in the city room. One of them was a deported American gangster who offered to blow the whistle on all his pals in Naples. After I wrote a column about him he returned and said he wanted to kill me. I was off at a film festival so he said he would kill the general manager, Sylvan Barnet, instead. Mr. Barnet told him it would be better to wait until I returned.

Fortunately, by the time I got back the French had decided to deport him. I was forbidden by Mr. Barnet to write about deported gangsters for six months.

The 21 Rue de Berri building of the Paris *Herald* survived everything from bombing threats to a second world war to attempted coup d'états, and heaven knows how many French governments.

I may be prejudiced, but I believe most Frenchmen had more faith in it than they did the American Embassy Building at the Place de la Concorde.

There was some talk that the present owners were seriously thinking of moving the paper out of France when they closed down the Rue de Berri offices. Fortunately, cooler heads prevailed. No matter how many countries the paper is sent to, the soul of the *Herald Tribune* belongs in Paris.

The Paris *Herald Tribune* is still alive and well in Neuilly. For those of us who worked in the vineyards of the Rue de Berri it is a painful thought. How can you put out a paper in the French suburbs, after you've seen Paree?